I0816897

# Carlo Scarpa
# Layers

Anne-Catrin Schultz

# Carlo Scarpa
# Layers

Edition Axel Menges

ISBN 978-3-930698-14-1

Third, revised edition



Printing and binding: Graspo CZ, a. s., Zlín, Czech Republic

Editorial work: Nora Krehl-von Mühlendahl
Translation into English: Ilze Klavina
Design: Axel Menges
Layout: Helga Danz

**Contents**

## Preface

1. Diagram of influences.

2. Portrait of Carlo Scarpa.

»The experience and memory of humankind are laid down in layers in the physical environment, concretely and graphically. Every new part exploits ancient forms, materials and ways of making. Building is, at base, a sign of hope, a sign of society's belief in future, a gesture forward in time.«[1]

This book is intended as a contribution towards giving Carlo Scarpa's work an adequate place in the context of 20th century architecture. It does not seek to define him stylistically; rather, it is an endeavor to uncover his multiple connections with his contemporaries and with historical models. I am using Scarpa's architecture to examine the principle of stratification in architecture and its complexity while producing a definition that could be applied to other architectures as well.

Essays about the different fields of interests that influenced Scarpa in the first chapters will be complemented by a diary of photographs and analytical drawings about three of his projects. Stratification describes the arrangement of elements but is also a cultural attitude of parallel existence. Stratification is a constantly recurring theme in 20th century architecture criticism and architecture theory. My own observations in this book are a result of my Ph.D studies done as a second generation scholar. Having not met Carlo Scarpa personally, all my conclusions were derived from his work and related publications. Guido Pietropoli who has worked with Carlo Scarpa extensively throughout his career, will enrich the content of this book by sharing more personal information and also by addressing Scarpa's way of drawing as well.

In most buildings, the principle of stratification may be regarded as something that is part of the nature of building. Functional conditions call for planes, elements, or »layers« to provide the supporting structure, and others to protect from rain, cold, or the heat of the sun. Here, stratification is a method of assigning a particular façade element to each individual function through technical specification. Design-related wishes in connection with a building may lead to additional decorative layers, unless they can be combined with the elements of the technological requirements. These concepts have long been accepted when it comes to looking at a façade from a technical point of view and are commonly referred to as layered façades. However, architectonic layering goes beyond merely fulfilling technical requirements – the principle of layering may be used as a formative method that allows elements of different origins to be combined into a non-hierarchical whole. Layering exists in a realm of complexity and implies a capacity of being interpreted that goes beyond itself and creates references to the world at large instead of narcistically contemplating itself alone. A building becomes a cumulative composition made up of elements of varying materials and provenance. In contrast to the architectural monolith,[2] which demonstrates a sheer three-dimensional volume made from one material and negates the »hollowness« of architecture that is implied by its function, layered architecture celebrates the parts and the process of its genesis. Instead of the compositional unity of a monolith, layering features a compositional balance of elements.

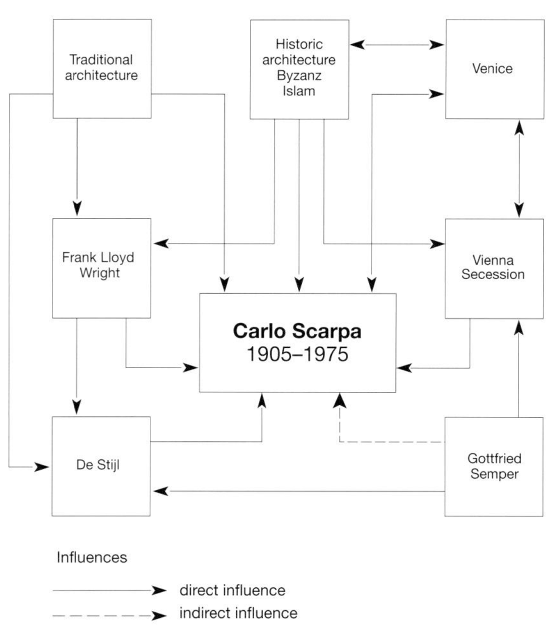

Scarpa's work in northern Italy is an embodiment of multidimensional stratification and is at the same time a focal point for architectural movements of his time that have stratification as their theme. I chose three projects to illustrate the physical and intangible appearance of layering: Castelvecchio in Verona, the Fondazione Querini Stampalia in Venice and Banca Popolare in Verona. The Castelvecchio Museum in Verona is an illustration of the stratified updating and reinterpretation of a historic and existing structure. The Fondazione Querini Stampalia in Venice represents an interpretative and thematic renovation within the historic city of Venice. The Banca Popolare in Verona shows how Carlo Scarpa builds anew layers he »finds« among the historical components, and supplements them with his own elements. Formal and narrative layers are illustrated analytically, while digressions into relevant subject areas provide information about Scarpa's background and inspiration. Layering is a nonhierarchical principle that appears in various forms and has not only a physical but also a substantive component.

In recent decades, Scarpa's relevance has been steadily on the rise. At a time when architects have to use existing city and building structures as a point of departure for their work, his œuvre is a source of inspiration. Buildings such as the Castelvecchio in Verona show us that architecture is capable of communicating its own history, has meaning, and develops a contemporary dynamic of its own. Fragments serve as building blocks for complex systems, functioning as additions, interacting and communicating with each other. They become essential elements of the creative process that is architecture. Scarpa's layered architecture makes visible the process of becoming and the time-related sedimentation of material and meanings. It is especially at points of transition and interface that layering becomes a narrative element that elucidates the tectonic qualities of the building. Overlaying includes leaving a record of how an object came into being – either by means of the sediments of its history or through the intervention of the architect.

Carlo Scarpa saw himself as part of the cultural context of Venice and of the Veneto, whose motifs and construction methods form the basis for the way his own architectural idiom developed. Initially profoundly shaped by the civilization of his region, Carlo Scarpa based his work on an extensive knowledge of the history of art, architecture, and culture. His lectures[3] and his library[4] tell us about architectures and trends that have influenced his work.

Scarpa's architectural sources represent a cross section of 20th century architectural trends. Movements such as De Stijl contribute in various ways to Scarpa's method of working with stratification and are part of overlapping design systems that are present in his work. Scarpa was influenced by the Vienna School, Byzantine, Japanese, and Islamic architecture, as well as by the American architect Frank Lloyd Wright. His work owes its much-quoted poetic charm to the integration of historic and cultural knowledge in didactic endeavors that create a far-reaching and complex narrative architectural idiom – and beauty. An understanding of the history of style that forms the background of his work is helpful not only in formulating a new position in architecture criticism, but also in developing formally independent mechanisms that enable one to learn from Scarpa instead of quoting him. Stratification is a system which, by means of two-dimensional, add-on elements, conveys a multilayered complexity that allows narrative (memorative) or formal subject matter to become operative simultaneously. This principle of layering informs the aesthetics of many 20th and 21st century architectures.

Layering is part of our day-to-day perception, based on the simultaneous existence of objects of different age and provenance. Added to this, there are the traditions, connections, and memories that give our daily existence an historical dimension. History, personal roots, and thought patterns are overlaid with new impressions and learning processes that are constantly expanding what is already there. In the same way, built configurations provide the framework for new construction. Interventions in the existing context are integrated as additional layers leaving the visible sign of their time and referring to the conceptual essence of their cultural belonging.

My interest in Scarpa's work and the phenomenon of layering is deeply connected to my search for concrete reasons for design decisions. It is essential to me to work with a composition system that is able to accommodate flexible aesthetic expressions while being strongly connected to the building's place and function. I am hoping that this reseach will contribute to my own capability of leaving a conscious architectural testimony of my time while preserving, celebrating and often altering the existing literal and phenomenal context as Carlo Scarpa was able to do.

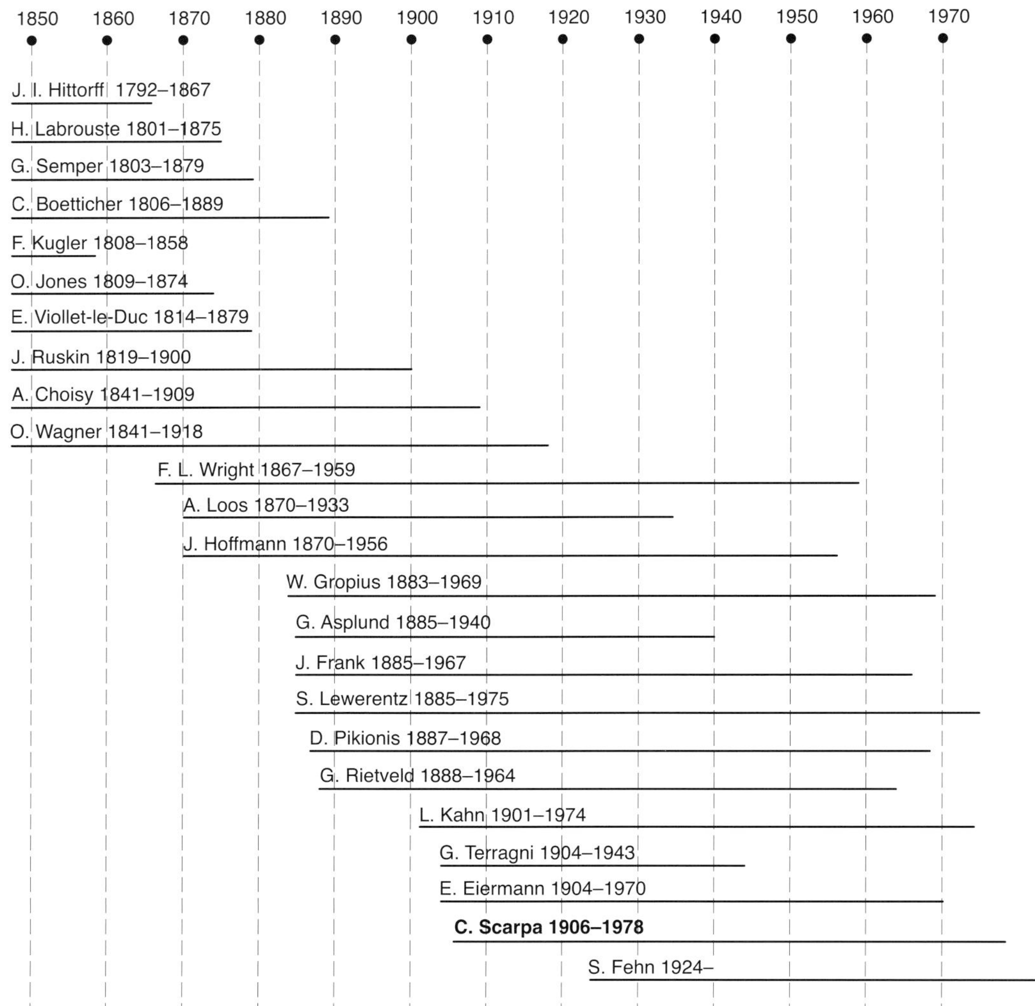


3. Time table.

4. Archaeological site exposing layers of the city, Verona downtown.
5. Diagram of volume created by the elements floor, wall and ceiling.
6. Cross section through the Alps.

## 1. The principle of layering: precedents

### 1.1. Layering and stratification in architecture

The term for layering, »stratification«, is etymologically derived from the Latin words »stratum« (cover) and »ficere« (make).[1] In the figurative sense, a layer needs a frame, a base material, or an additional layer in order to carry out the function of »cover«. Stratification involves the plurality of individual elements and the relations between them.

The concept of stratification in political science refers to the »vertical structuring of the members of a society on the basis of socially relevant characteristics that influence the behavior of people toward each other«.[2] Geology uses the term stratification for the purpose of interpreting how material is arranged.[3] »The type of stratification establishes the relative age of the rock strata. When the strata occur in a normal sequence, the understratum is older, while the roof is younger than the stratum.«[4] The order and composition of the stratification contains information about the development of the geological formation. The chronological component of the succession of sedimentary deposits and the process of a mechanical change of this stratification is an essential component of the definition. In archeology, too, the position of individual strata contains information about where they fit chronologically. The study of archeological finds involves the analysis of largely horizontal strata created as cultures, peoples, or settlements declined and as human settlements were reorganized. In psychology there are various theories that are concerned with the stratification of the human personality and its repercussions. According to Ruttkowski, the existence of each layer is made possible by the layer that lies under it.[5] Writing about an »aesthetic of strata«, he also discusses connections with art, particularly painting: »It is the nature of art, after all, that it is layered, and that it appears to us layer by layer.«[6]

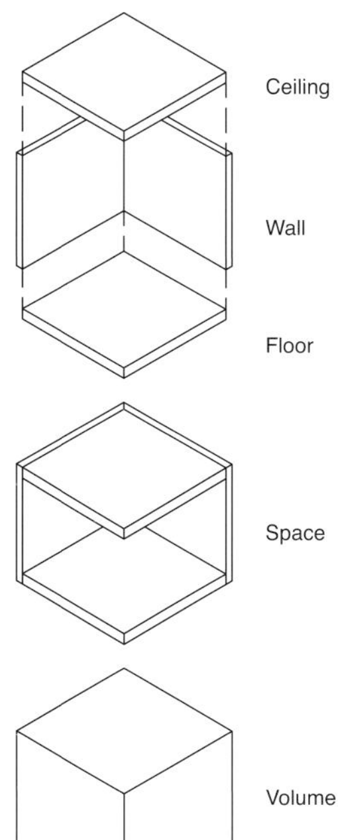


### Stratification in architectural discussion

»Long before the human spirit was moved to build, a movement to create structures existed in the universe, and thus layers and joints were formed. And so it has remained to this day. Just as we erect our walls, the earth, since time immemorial, has been creating layer by layer from the precipitation of the air and the sediments of the water.«[7]

Applied to the objectlike components of architecture, stratification means the superposition and apposition of layers of material. Just as the position and order of geological strata says something about their age and their origin, the position and formulation of an architectural stratum may contain information about its function and provenance. The aesthetic effect of stratification is expressed in the details of how it is joined together and in the visualized superpositioning, which demonstrate the processlike nature and changeability of architecture. A purely sedimentative analysis of strata includes such nonphysical components as memory, metaphors, and references to other places or buildings. Architectonic volumes consist of elements that formulate a floor, wall, and ceiling, or combinations thereof. The joining of these individual elements into a whole may take place as a series of sediments and create strata that react to the various requirements of a building.

In European architectural theory there have been many different attempts to define »strata« or »layers« in architecture, and these were consulted particularly in a definition of modern architecture. In his book *Die Tektonik der Hellenen* Carl Gottlieb Boetticher describes an attempt to separate architecture into the core form as the »mechanically necessary»[8] structure and the art

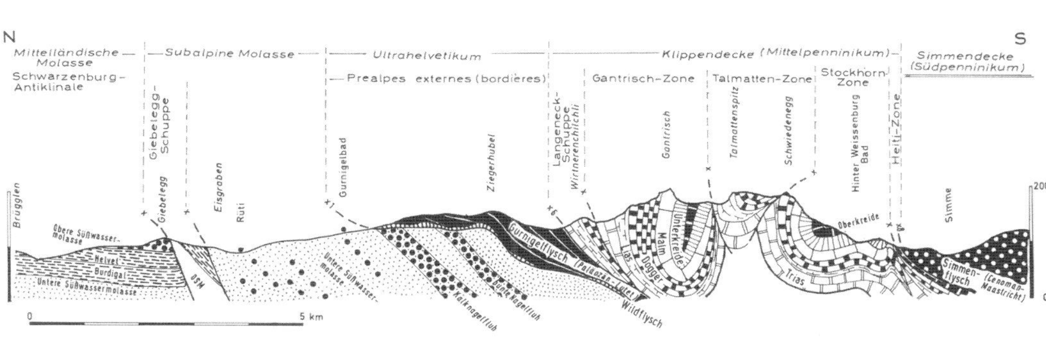

form as the »explanatory characterization»;[9] his main emphasis is on the core form – it is merely supplemented and clarified by the art form. Gottfried Semper develops the principle of cladding, based on the components of textiles as the origin of all architecture. Looking at buildings as something formed of an ornamental shell and a core[10] refers not only to the duality of the load-bearing structure and façade but also to the essence and function of a building in relation to its decorative appearance. (I shall refer to this in greater detail in the course of this book.)

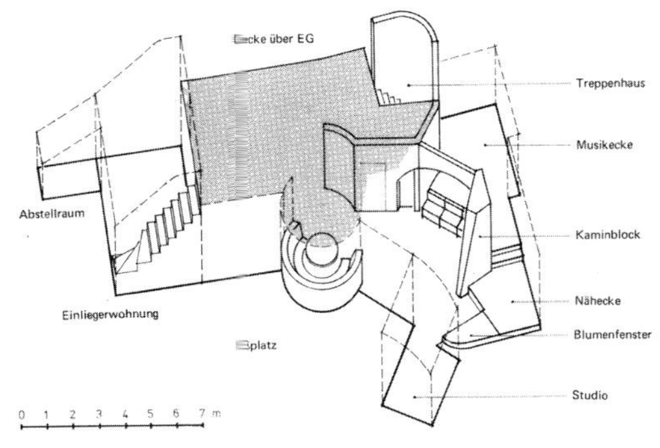

## Spatial stratification, material stratification, and cladding

In analyzing space, the term stratification is used to describe the succession of planes or spatial sequences. Let me give a few illustrations. Here is how Eckehard Janofske describes Hans Scharoun's Mohrmann House in Berlin-Lichtenrade (1939): »A sequence of layers is noticeable when we look through from the dining room in the direction of the window for flowers and houseplants. Apart from the doorlike opening of the room in the direction of the dining area, the buttress between the semicircular dining area and the straight wall of windows in the living-sitting area represents the first layer; the fireplace block is the second. The window behind it, or rather the flower window, is the third and last layer before our eyes are arrested by the landscaping in the garden. It is basically because of this sequence of layers that we have an impression of spatial complexity and distance. As a result of components such as the fireplace block, the surface arch over the sofa, or the masonry pillars between the two spaces that move into our field of vision, the borders of this space are not immediately recognizable, as is the case in a room with four walls.«[11]

Franco Fonatti applies the term layering not so much to the spatial disposition of a building, but rather to the façade. Separating the functions of construction, shell, openings, and shading elements, and shifting them horizontally means that construction is separate from weather protection and causes them to appear »layered« because of their additive arrangement. In his analysis of the Giuliani-Frigerio House by Giuseppe Terragni, Fonatti separates the façade into four layers. The metal frames of the balustrades form the first; the projecting parts, such as the balconies, the second; and perforated façade the third layer. The fourth, innermost layer is formed by interior parts such as windows and shutters. Fonatti analyzes the agglomeration of the elements, but without ascribing a function to them. The façade creates a transition between inside and outside that gains depth through vertical differentiation.[12]

Pierre von Meiss associates the term with suggesting spatial depth, particularly in painting. He interprets the use of spatial layers as a phenomenon whose function, together with perspective, is to produce the effect of depth. What is of fundamental importance is that the layers overlap, »since we recognize that an object which partially conceals another is located in front of the latter.«.[13] »From the Renaissance until well into the 19th century, painters do not conceal their preference for perspective and spatial depth. Medieval painters and those who paint in a different way, such as Gris, Braque, Le Corbusier, and later Slutzky, are masters of shallow-depth space, in which superposed planes appear crowded and close together. The architects, too, have tried to structure their buildings and spaces by these means. Some, in their work, use the parallel planes, with minimal and undefined intervals between them, not only shallow-depth space, but also the phenomenon of transparency created by fragmentary disappearance and reappearance of one plane behind the other. This is the principle of several shallow-depth spatial layers superposed, particularly in the area of the façade, favored by Terragni in the Frigerio House in Como, Le Corbusier in the Villa Stein in Garches, or Carlo Scarpa in the articulation of the walls and windows of the Museo di Castelvecchio in Verona.«[14]

Material stratification, the gapless layering of material planes, corresponds with the geological meaning of the term explained above. Unlike spatial layering, which is defined by the space between layers, material layering consists of material planes that lie immediately on top of each other and together form an element. Increasing functional demands made of components such as façades have led to the separation of the individual functions that are expressed in a multilayered façade. »Resolution of the construction into individual layers, which was carried out intentionally, divided a particular building component – for instance, a ›two‹-withe masonry wall – into different elements for different functions. Only the totality of the layers makes the wall physically adaptable to divergent climatic conditions.«[15] Technical factors lead to a formal expression that influences the form of the architecture. This type of »variability through layering»[16] helps to optimize the implementation of technical requirements. Modern standards for façades demand that

7. Hans Scharoun, Mohrmann House, Berlin, 1939. Axonometric diagram of the interior spaces.
8, 9. Hans Scharoun, Mohrmann House, Berlin, 1939. View of spatial stratification showing a sequence of interior spaces.

10–16. Giuseppe Terragni, Casa Giuliani-Frigerio, Como, 1939/40. Façade photograph, analysis of elements: elevations and axonometric view.
17. Diagram illustrating material stratification. Plan and axonometric view.
18. Diagram illustrating spatial stratification. Plan and axonometric view.

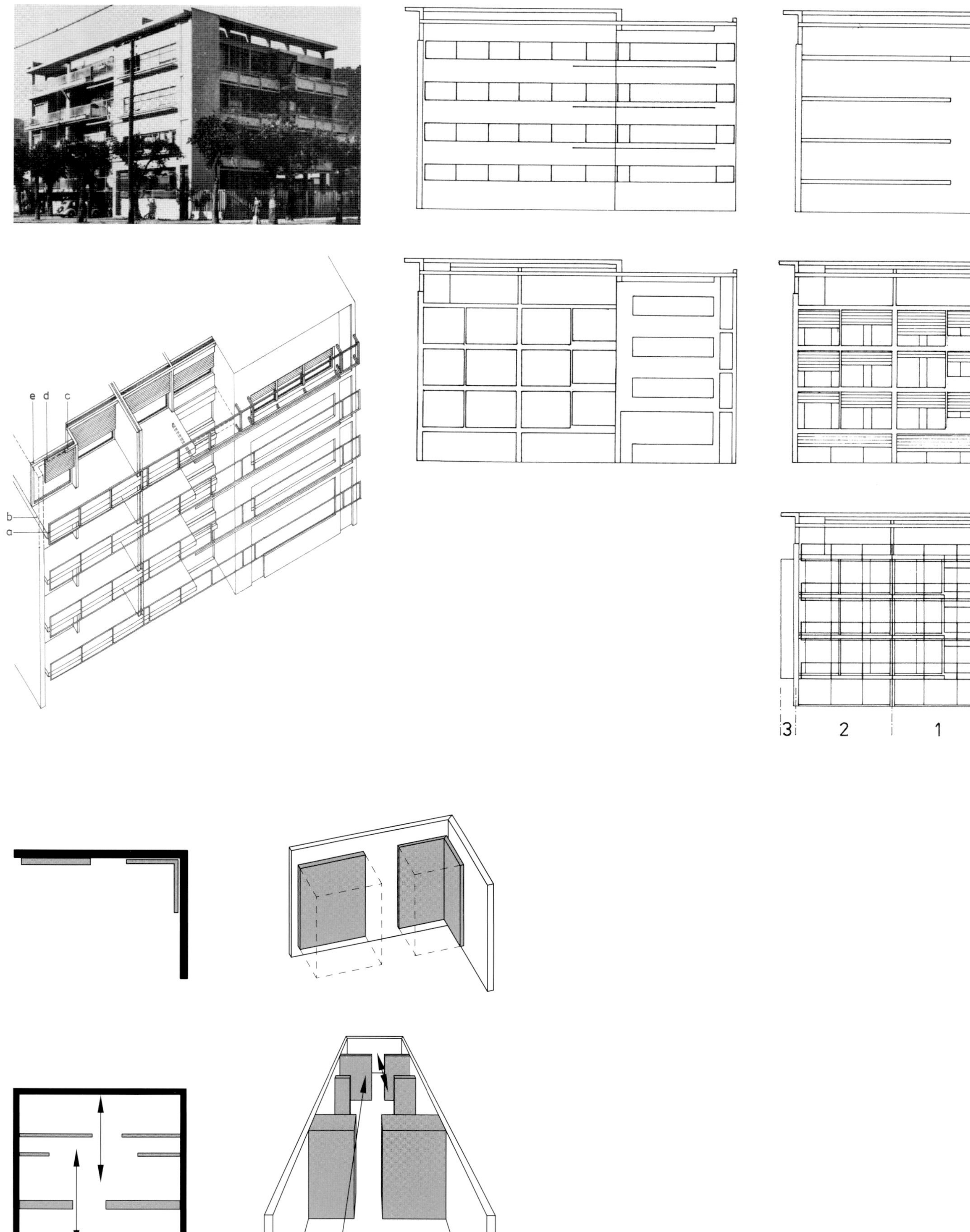

e
d
c
b
a
3
2
1
2
3

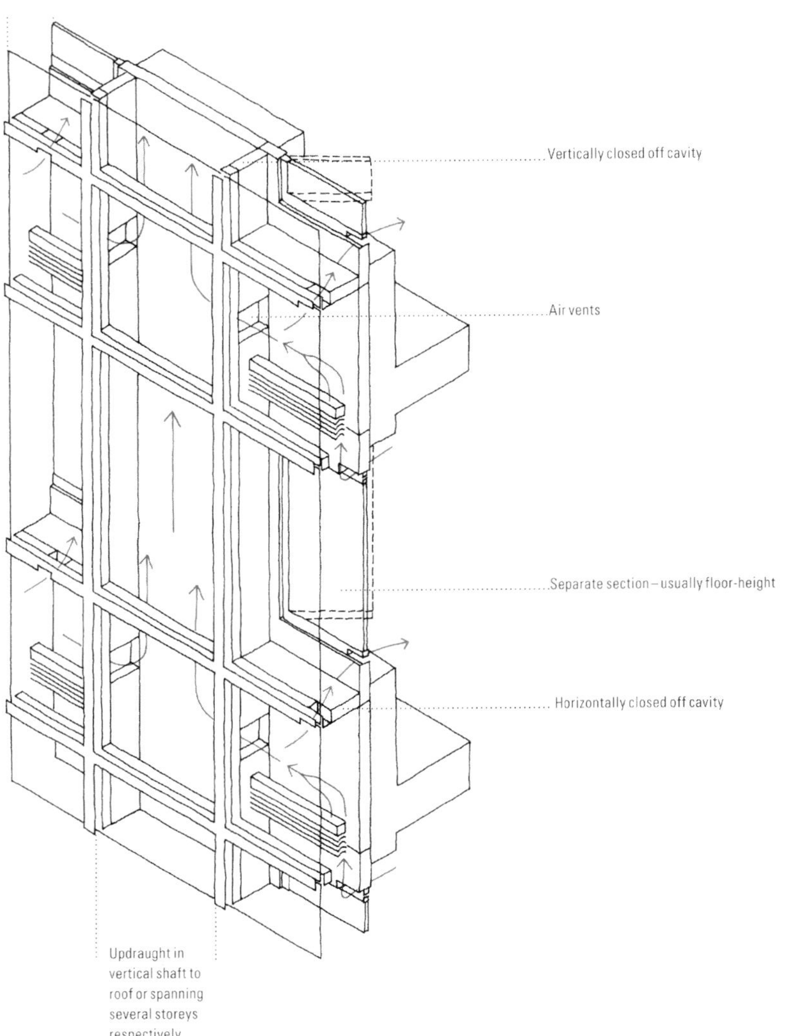


19. Klaus Daniels. Alko Twinface façade. Diagram of functional principles.
20. Andrea Compagno, intelligent glass façade. Diagram of polivalent wall.
21. Diagram of joints between material layers.

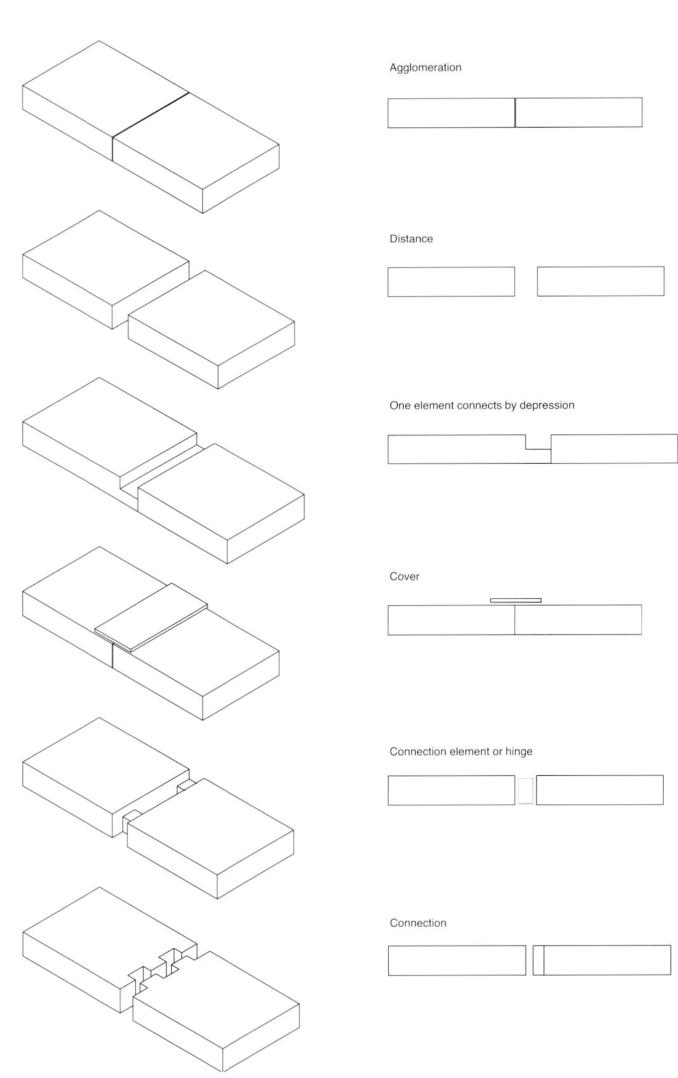

Gotttfried Semper's architectonic principle of cladding be developed further in order to meet current requirements.[17] Double façades fulfill present-day technical challenges with new aesthetic effects.[18] Technical development does not stop with the separation of building elements according to their function: the goal is the automatic variability of building components that spontaneously adapt to changing conditions. The focal point of this architecture is the variable outer wall that adapts to indoor and outdoor climate, takes into account specific user demands, and at the same time permanently resists physical stress factors, such as weather conditions. The term outer wall, in this context, does not appear to be appropriate for describing such building elements. It actually consists of multilayered, thin strata or skins, sensitive and capable of lightning-speed reaction while their appearance changes continually.[19]

Mike Davies developed the element of the polyvalent wall, which once more unites the separation of functions described above into a single element that consists of several micro-thin layers. These individual skins fulfill a number of different requirements and are capable of reacting to changing outdoor conditions. He developed the intelligent façade, which adapts to prevailing circumstances.[20]

The genesis of layering mechanics lays in the aesthetic realm of architectonic cladding. This may be defined as a layer applied to the structure. Independence from constructive factors offers the designer free play in terms of choice of material and implementation. Two different forms of clothing may be defined. One completely clothes the space provided by the structure, follows its contours and forms a type of »outer or inner lining«, it shows this aspect of clothing space only in parts. The other type of clothing is independent of existing conditions, forms its own spatial configurations – slabs and panels – and is visible in joints and side views, demonstrating its stratified character. Depending on the material, there are a number of different forms of clothing, which can take the shape of a coat of paint or plaster, and paneling or wainscoting.[21] Paint or plaster as a »coating« is the thinnest form of clothing. Mark Wigley writes about the use and significance of white paint in the classic modern period: »What has to be concealed is the fact that the white is a layer. After all, the stripping off of old clothes, advertised by the original promoters of modern architecture and its contemporary dealers, is not simply a stripping of all clothing.«[22]

## Aesthetic »overlapping«: the concept of transparency

The position of layers and their placement in relation to each other determine their effect. When planes overlap congruently, their material qualities become visible only at edges or cross sections. When examining stratification, it is primarily the spaces between layers that are relevant. In overlapping we get common or touching surfaces, which thus fuse into one system. The overlapping of elements makes it possible to experience and see what lies underneath. Gyorgy Kepes investigated the simultaneity of overlapping forms and the resulting spatial effect: »If one spatial form obstructs our view of another form, we do not assume that the second ceases to exist because it is hidden. We recognize, as we look at such overlapping figures, that the first or uppermost has two spatial meanings – itself and beneath itself. The figure which intercepts the visible surface of another figure is perceived as nearer. We experience spatial differences of depth. Representation of overlapping indicates depth. It creates a sense of space. Each figure appears parallel with the picture-plane and tends to establish a receding spatial relationship.« He goes on to write about transparency and superposition: »Transparency, interpenetration: If one sees two ore more figures partly overlapping one another, and each of them claims for itself the common overlapped part, then one is confronted with a contradiction of spatial dimensions. To resolve this contradiction, one must assume the presence of a new optical quality. The figures are endowed with transparency; that is, they are able to interpenetrate without an optical destruction of each other. Transparency however implies more than an optical characteristic; it implies a broader spatial order. Transparency means a simultaneous perception of different spatial locations. Space not only recedes but fluctuates in a continuous activity. The position of the transparent figures has equivocal meaning as one sees each figure now as the closer, now as the further one.«[23]

Kepes speaks of spatial information that is defined by the situation and visible parts of layers. The perceptual psychologist Rudolf Arnheim describes that overlapping occurs when one part partially conceals another. The resulting overlap intensifies the relations between forms, simultaneously comprising the complete form and the fusion. It detracts from the completeness of at least one of the forms involved, and generally all of them. The outcome is not only a »correlation« – that is, an exchange of energies between independent, completely intact entities. The en-

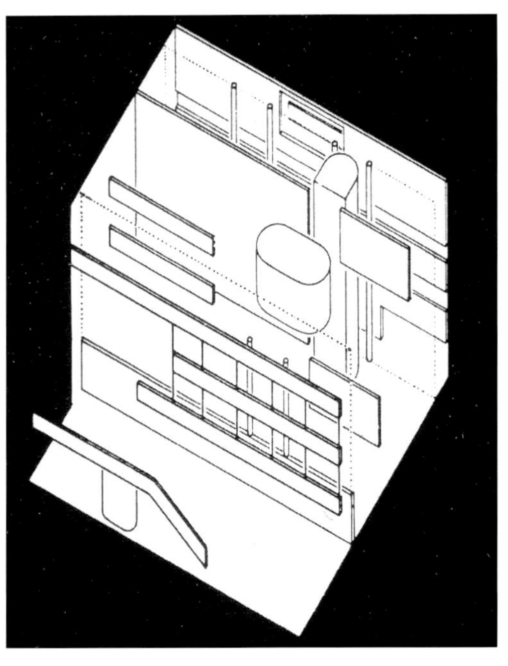

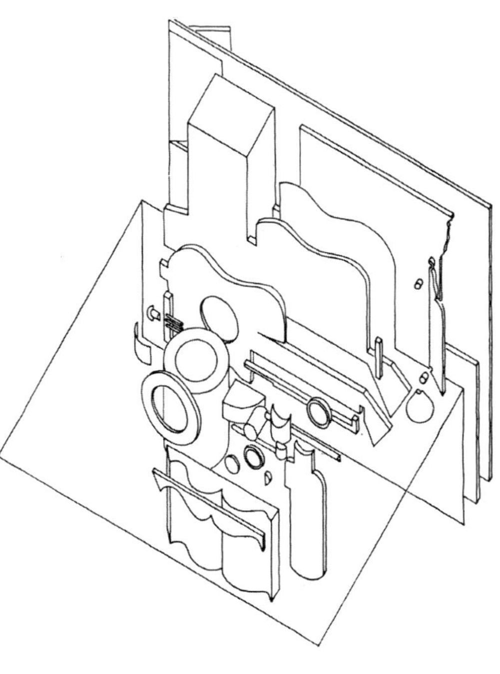

22. Colin Rowe, Robert Slutzky, transparency analysis of Le Corbusier's Villa Garches, interior.
23. Rudolf Arnheim, illustration of superposed perception.
24. Colin Rowe, Robert Slutzky, transparency analysis. Spatial layering in a painting by Le Corbusier.
25. Clifford Eitel (student of Gyorgy Kepes), study of transparency.

26. Carlo Scarpa, Olivetti showroom, Venice, 1957 to 1958. Wall panel detached from ceiling, almond shaped window overlooking St. Mark's square with sliding wood shutters.

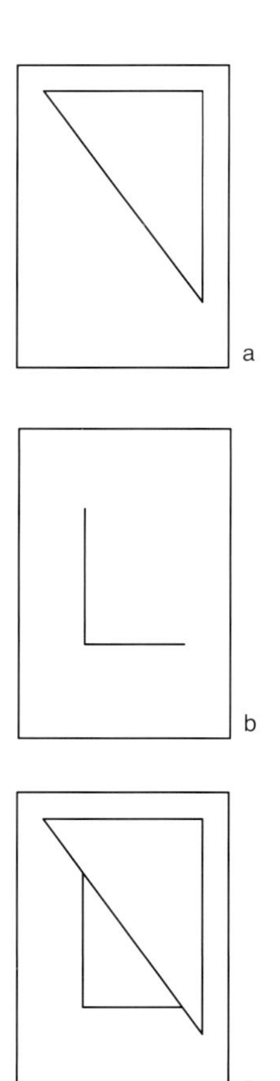

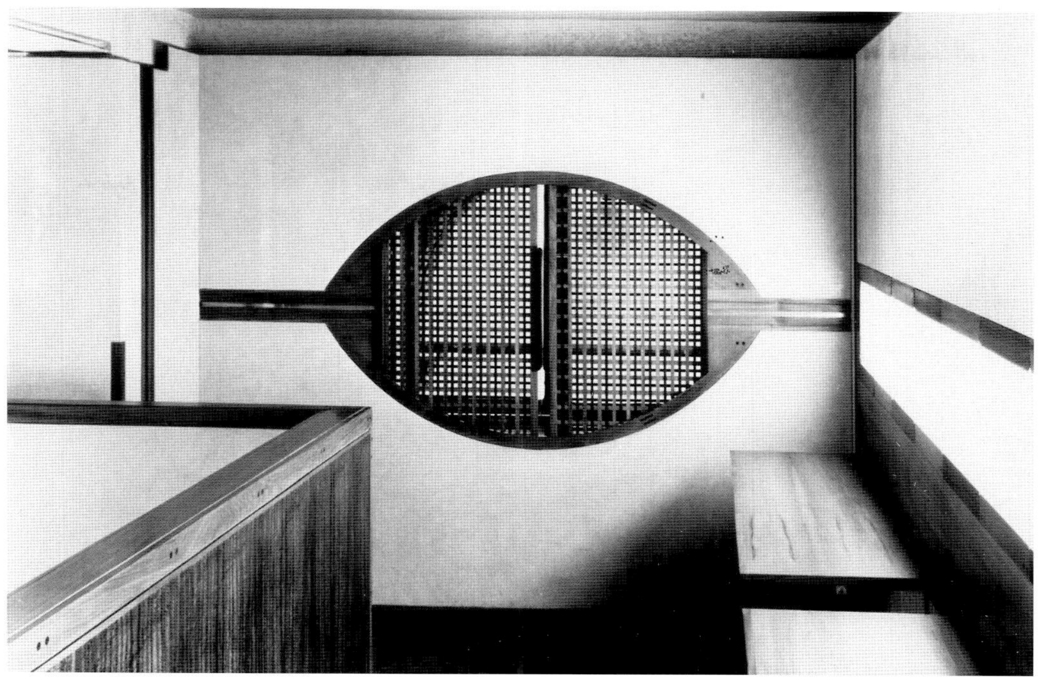

tities go together, there is a bond because they reciprocally modify each other.«[24] In order to make the layers perceptible, there need to be places of transition that function simultaneously as a link and separation. The frames and edges cause the form and material to stand out against surfaces that are meant to be differentiated. The process of layering separates individual planes, which are thus able to have their own meaning as an element and simultaneous part of a total complex.

Colin Rowe continues the examination of the concept of transparency with reference to Kepes. He uses the term layering in the context of a spatial analysis of Le Corbusier's Palace of the League of Nations.[25] By way of analyzing the »system of spatial stratification«,[26] he shows a relationship between Le Corbusier's façade of the Villa Garches and one of his paintings. The façade consists of fragmentary planes, it is put together »with these parallel planes as a connected whole«, »and the effect of all of them is a vertical stratification of the building's interior.«[27] In the Bauhaus complex, too, he observes spatial layering »presented as a composition of slab-like buildings whose forms suggest the possibility of construing space in layers.«[28]

Transparency »can be a characteristic inherent in the material, as in a glass curtain wall, or transparency may imply an organizational priority. Consequently it is possible to distinguish between real or literal transparency and apparent transparency or transparency in the literal sense.«[29] An examination of the texts of Kepes, Rowe, and Slutzky reveals the complexity of a definition that in this case is taken from the analysis of paintings and, applied to the Villa in Garches, is transformed into the concept of spatial stratification. »Stratification« as they see it may be used as the »tool of contemplation«[30] that reveals the spatial interrelations of an architecture. Spatial layering in Le Corbusier is applied to spatial segments and is dependent on the use of architectonic elements that are homogeneous in form and have no direct narrative bearing on references or traditions. The examples that are examined in this book are to be understood in terms of a concept of layering that consists of material distinctions and nonphysical associative components.

### 1.2. Carlo Scarpa – layered spaces

Carlo Scarpa's career began in the glassworks of Murano, where he acquired his aesthetic and cultural knowledge. His work as a consultant for the Biennale (1948–72) gave him the opportunity for the international exchange of information about art and architecture and direct contact with international artists and architects from all over the world.[1] In 1933 Scarpa began teaching architecture as a lecturer in decoration at the Istituto Universitario di Architettura di Venezia. In 1951 he became a freelance lecturer in interior design. His architectonic works include, among other things, apartments and houses, exhibitions and museums, stores and designs for public spaces, located with few exceptions in the northern Italian region of Veneto. In most of his projects, he works with architectonic strata that complete an existing context.

»Spatial thinking for Carlo Scarpa is so precise that he clearly separates things that are either chronologically or materially different – sometimes as sharply as though they had been severed with a knife, although they are one. He removes stratum by stratum from the structure, exposes, gives back its meaning to each part as though it was not worthwhile to fuse it with the whole. He uses the following process: separation, excision, and contrast. In the service of a poetic idea he uses the separated strata as overlapping and transition, joining together adjacent segments and parts of buildings.«[2]

Stratification denotes both – isolating and identifying individual elements and at the same time combining them in a stratified configuration. Scarpa's details speak of intensifying and didactically exposing architectonic detail on the most varying scales. The fitting together of elements begins with abstracting the individual parts; at the end of the process a system of references is created that is not only limited to material and form, but communicates as an inseparable whole and may include reminiscences of artistic or architectural themes.

Scarpa himself writes: »To achieve anything, we have to invent relationships.«[3] Using a passageway in Castelvecchio as an illustration, Karljosef Schattner points out how Scarpa avoids »intermixture«,[4] so that each part is assigned its own identity. Spatial stratification or stratification of material serve not only to create space but also to formulate a certain atmosphere that links tradition and the past with the present. Scarpa's use of forms has »symbolic depth«,[5] whose interpretation is tied to a knowledge of his cultural sphere and range of interests. »Like the physical, psychic, and intellectual reality of a human being, the artistic reality of architecture, too, has symbolic dimensions.«[6] The concept of stratification is given an added dimension by an immaterial component. Otto Friedrich Bollnow distinguishes mathematical space from »lived-space«,[7] which flexibly reacts to lived relationships and meanings. This is what Scarpa adds to his »strata« by elevating them from a simple arrangement of materials and filling them with communicative significance.

In order for the architect to be able to form volumes by means of the principles described above, these volumes must be understood as compositions consisting of planes. The basis of the language of a stratified architecture is the fact that the architectonic elements are organized as floor, wall, and ceiling.

In creating space, Scarpa's use of spatial strata serves to form individual zones or to provide a transition from one area to the next. His strata of material serve to define space and transport narrative components involving the locale, history, or material. In his building modifications, his intervention is one stage among many in the sedimentative process by which the building was created. He uses the mechanics of stratification to make visible levels that chronologically follow each other, and formal givens. At the same time, the design process does not stop with implementation and continues to be a reaction to existing conditions. What was there earlier remains in existence like a kind of palimpsest and begins a communication with the newly added elements. The way layers applied at different periods of time are made visible illustrates the development of the buildings. Different epochs and different ways of using forms can exist side by side with their content legible.

Hermann Czech speaks of the »historical multilayering«[8] and of the »overlapping of different ideas of space that coincide (or else are simulated)«,[9] or the »ambiguity of colors that on the one hand play an abstract role in the color wheel and on the other hand have a concrete role in certain associations»[10] and thus alludes to both components of stratification, the combined effect of different concepts of space and the transport of associations. The process of overlapping planes makes possible the simultaneity of forms whose nonvisible parts can be supplied by the perceiver. In the case of individual elements, not only the mechanics of how they are installed but of their manufacture as well are made visible. Traces of how they were tooled and used become an additional component of the design. Scarpa refers to the thickness of the material by creating a visible cross section. The placement of material has didactic components, it makes reference to the material, its context, its processing, and its surroundings. Form and choice of material can carry memories of contexts that create mental connections between buildings and cultures.

### Working method

If we extend the investigation of Scarpa's architecture to include his working method and manner of representation, we find that his procedure is also characterized by the overlapping of various

27. Carlo Scarpa, Olivetti showroom, Venice, 1957 to 1958. Staircase with treads assembled as if they were floating.
28. Carlo Scarpa, Olivetti showroom, Venice, 1957 to 1958. Joint of floor and wall assembly, stucco paneling exposing a concrete wall where it joins the concrete floor.

From left to right

29. Carlo Scarpa, Castelvecchio, Verona, 1958 to 1964. Concrete wall layer added to plastered exterior wall.
30. Carlo Scarpa, Olivetti store, Venice, 1957 to 1958. Double door with internal wooden door leaf and an external door leaf matching the stone cladding of the façade.
31. Carlo Scarpa, Correr Museum, Venice, 1960. Wall paneling as part of the interior exhibition design.
32. Carlo Scarpa, entrance to the Istituto Universitario di Architettura, Tolentini, Venice, 1966. Multiple layers of concrete wall elements and a sliding door out of a stone.
33. Carlo Scarpa, Fondazione Querini Stampalia, Venice, 1961 to 1963. Stair to canal with stone layer applied to concrete steps. Cuts into stone emphasize thickness and craftsmanship.

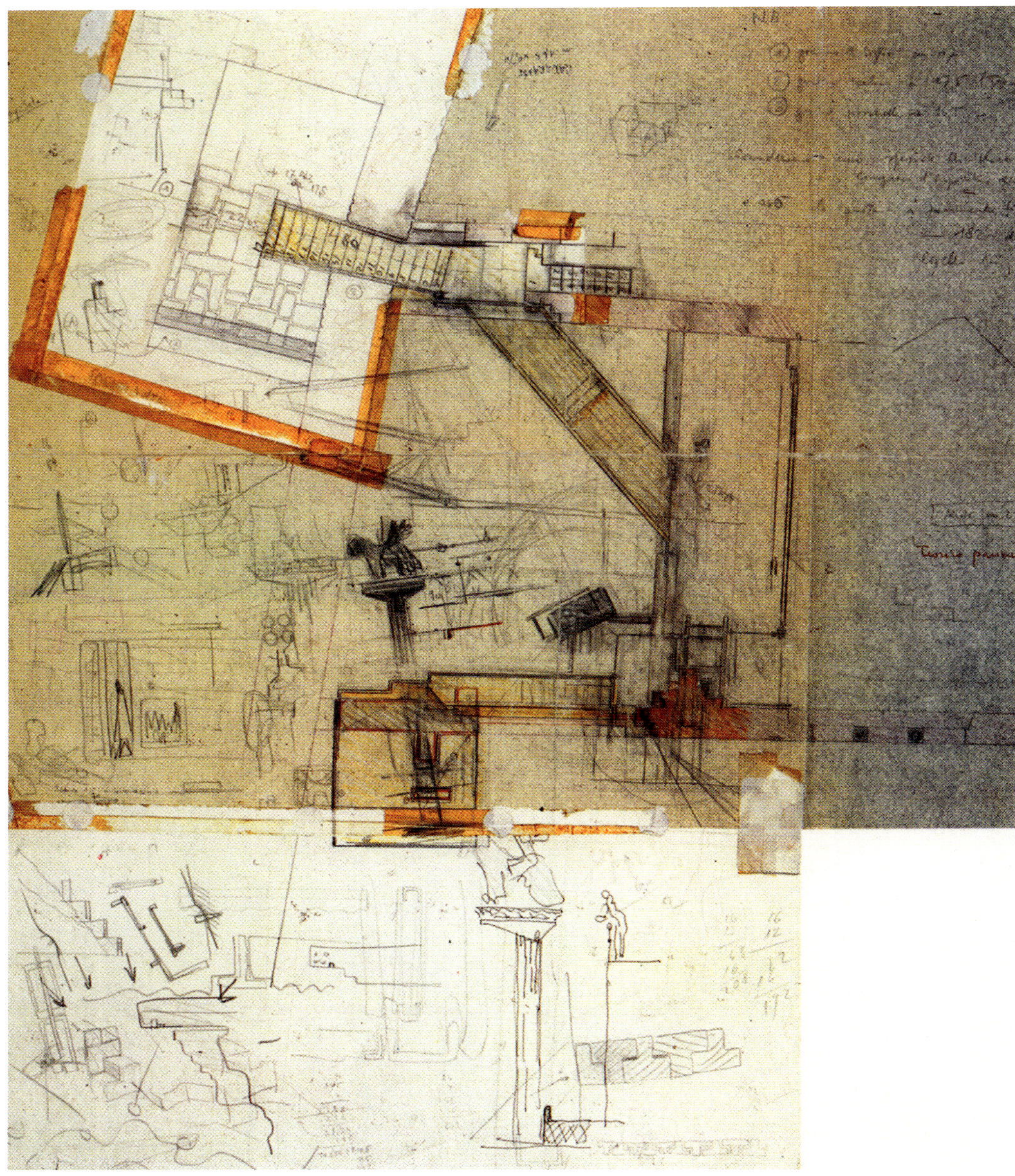

34. Carlo Scarpa, Castelvecchio, Verona, 1958 to 1964. Drawing of ground plan of area with Cangrade statue, palimpsest-like sketches illustrating the thought process.

35. Diagrams showing space generated by additional layers added to an existing room – dedicated for the positioning of sculptures. Key: 1 layer added to the floor, 2 layers added to the walls, 3 layer added to the ceiling, 4 layer added to wall and ceiling.

physical and narrative planes. Often ground plans, cross sections, and elevations are found on a plan sketched above and inside each other. The complexity of the drawings is emphasized by the use of different-colored pencils. As though on a palimpsest, erased, earlier versions often exist one on top of the other, making it possible to see the formative process. Scarpa's capability did not exclusively consist in the ingenious composition of intensively elaborated details, but rather in making them part of an overall concept. The integration of all aspects also takes place in drawing by way of stratification.

Marco Frascari writes as follows about Scarpa's drawings: »Scarpa's designs are drawn on heavy drawing card stretched on a board – his favorite support for the formulation of his architectural thought, where architecture is the result of successive ›strata‹ of meditation. On the precious surface of a heavy card are set and superimposed the nervous marks of charcoal and pastel, the deeply incised marks of the hard pencil – memories that remain, despite erasures. Finally there are the definite signs of the India ink, diluted so as not to be antagonistic to the pencil. Next to heavy paper is white or yellow tracing paper, the translucent support of a quick dialogue, for superimposing onto ideas already recorded on the opaque card. Beyond these desk drawings are pen sketches traced with the quick, masterly gesture on the backs of cigarette boxes of his favorite Oriental tobacco. These drawings record an architectural thought, and became his lifeline.«[11]

Scarpa himself describes his working method as follows: »I want to see things in front of me, and this is the only thing I trust. I put them here in front of me on the paper so I can see them. I want to see, and that is why I draw. I can only see a thing if I show it.«[12]

His method of working can be linked with the principles of composition expressed in his architectural œuvre. Layer by layer, the plans are brought up to date, photos, ideas, and new insights are incorporated in a collagelike process.

### The practical implementation of the process of stratification in Carlo Scarpa's work

In an interview, speaking of how he creates space, Carlo Scarpa explains in reference to the Castelvecchio:

Carlo Scarpa: »The floor is one of the key surfaces in defining the geometry of space. The square geometry of the rooms provides the information for the model. It was necessary to resolve the problem of the seam between the wall, which had a vertical luminous surface, and the floor, which had a darker, horizontal surface.«

Martín Domínguez: »Like water.«

Carlo Scarpa: »Exactly, exactly. I thought of the water surrounding the wall of the castle. That gave me the idea of making a negative seam. The floors of each room were individualized, as if they were a series of platforms. I changed the material of the edge, from slate to a clearer stone in order to better define the square. In this way, the movement was modulated.«[13]

The wall element functions as a vertical element of spatial demarcation and directs the movement of users through the space. Additional wall strata are used for zoning within a space; they, too, can join together and structure different spaces. In Scarpa's work additive layers appear within spaces in the form of panels that reference the objects contained in the space, e. g., a sculpture, and form a kind of architectural aura within the interior. A virtually created space surrounds the work of art and removes it from the arbitrariness of the context. It is thus closely linked with the space.

Richard Murphy writes about the structuring of the walls in the Castelvecchio: »Of primary importance is the idea of the material – the solidity of the building – which at the borders reveals itself as a series of planes or strata: what is involved is the progressive accumulation of thin layers, or deposits, as on sedimentary rock. Beyond doubt this idea is confirmed by the treatment Scarpa reserves for the façade of the Napoleonic barracks, where he decides to create thin planes, which, while layered side by side, are irregularly arranged. That is, the idea is particularly evident at the furthest end, where the substance of the fortress wall is emphasized by means of a cut made by Scarpa. Here it is clearly visible at what point the stratifications that occur terminate, each clearly different from the others.«[14]

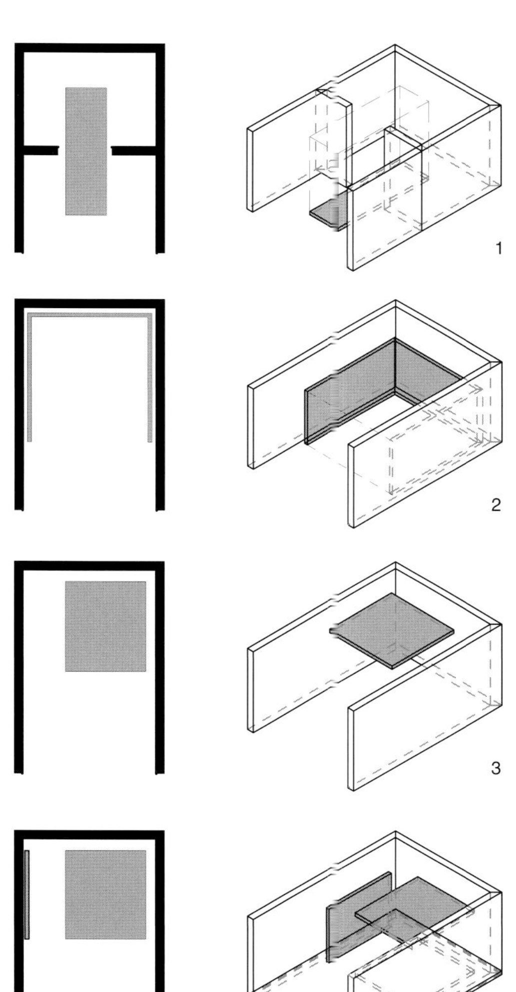


The creation of special places for individual works of art forms a web of spaces that provides a background or an underspace for the exhibits by means of an additional layer of color or material. In his voluminous library[15] Scarpa owned works on 19th-century architecture theory such as *Histoire de l'architecture* by Auguste Choisy, and *L'art de bâtir chez les Romains* by the same author and the *Entretiens sur l'architecture* by Viollet-le-Duc.[16] Also among his books were standard works of 20th century architecture theory. When Scarpa is classified in Italian history of architecture he himself is mostly referred to as an »isolated master«.[17] His reception as a sensitive restorer of historic buildings constitutes a very emotional evaluation of his life's work and disregards important other aspects. Bruno Zevi classes him as a representative of organic architecture and refers to the ornamental nature of pure materials: »The taste for ornamentation that prefers to play with the overlapping of different materials (for example, stucco walls near walls made of wood, concrete juxtaposed with natural stone and glass), the new sense of color, a new inspiration of joy following in the wake of the stern coldness of functionalistic theory, are determined by deeper psychological scrutiny.«[18]

Scarpa's development was not linear. Many of his architectural motifs already appear in early works and are later refined and developed further. Carlo Scarpa was born in Venice in 1906 and spent a large part of his life in that city. After technical school he studied at the Academy of Fine Art, which he left in 1926. While at the Academy he worked on the Vienna Secession, particularly the works of Josef Hoffmann and his influence on Guido Sullam,[19] and the Art Nouveau style of someone like Henry van de Velde. During this period he worked on various projects in the studio of Vicenzo Rinaldo and received his diploma in 1926 in architectural drawing. He then became the assistant of Prof. Guido Cirilli at the newly founded Istituto Universitario di Architettura of Venice.

Early blueprints of the Licelli airport or a draft for the Villa Bianca show the influence of the Razionalismo with clear unornamented lines. In 1927 Scarpa established contact with the crafts after his application to be placed on the professional register was rejected. He finally became artistic consultant for Cappellin & Co in Murano. »From now on Scarpa preferred to move in the direction of skilled crafts, doing patient work as he contemplated the hard human work in the glassworks.«[20] From 1933 to 1947 he designed art glass for Venini. During these years he carried out »aesthetic investigations«[21] and furthered his cultural education.

Ada Francesca Marcianò describes the time with Venini as follows: »In the lamps and murrhine vases, and in the ancient ritual of hands and mouths and fire Scarpa learned the inexplicable intermeshing that links beauty to chance, making both necessary and binding: being clearly aware at the same time that any project is nonrealizable.«[22] Manlio Brusatin mentions the emotional consequences of Scarpa's work: »In the seclusion and peace of the workshop Scarpa rediscovered his true calling, expressing the secrets of craftsmanship as a moral conviction: knowledge of the craft, patience, the means to define and the passion to touch things; pleasure and artisanal motivation are born from the conviction that one knows how to do a few things well.«[23]

In the early projects of the Angelo Velo House in Fontaniva (1926) and the Aldo Martinati House (1926), both created in collaboration with F. Pizzuto, we have a classic horizontal articulation of the façade. Both houses are divided by ledges into a base, a middle part, and a roof zone. In 1927 Scarpa designs a project for a teatro sociale that already heralds motifs of a much later project, the Brion cemetery. The roof zone is separated by a corbelled parapet, and the texture of the

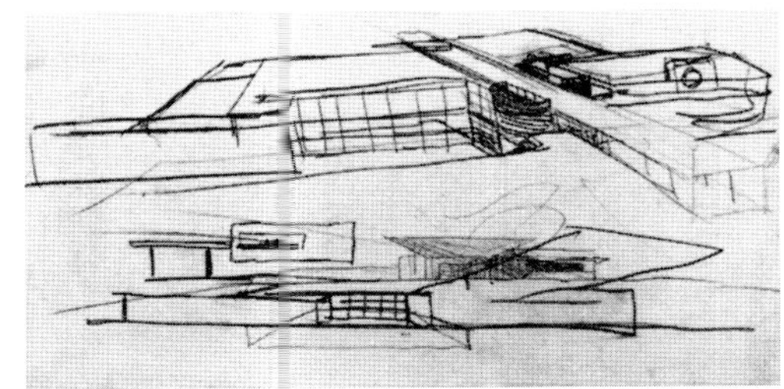

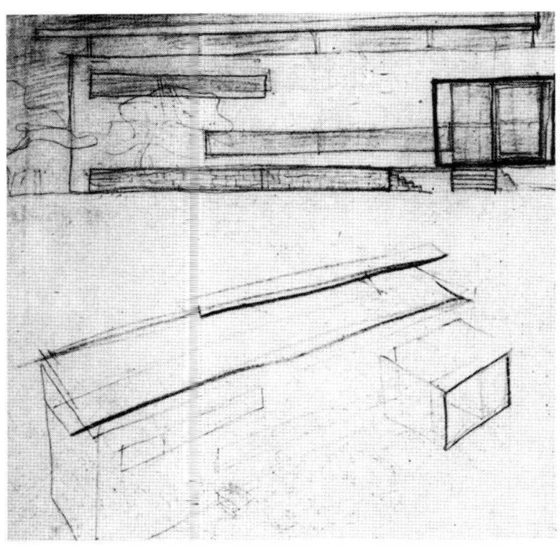

36. Carlo Scarpa. Fondazone Querini Stampalia, Venice, 1961–63. Walkway connecting exhibition spaces. Concrete layer on wall in the front and stone layer applied to the floor.
37. Carlo Scarpa, competition for Licelli Airport on the Lido, Venice, 1934. Sketches.
38. Giuseppe Terragni, Villa Bianca, Seveso, 1936 to 1937. Sketches.

39. Carlo Scarpa. Abatellis Palace, Palermo, 1953 to 1954. Wall panels generating space for exhibited sculpture.
40. Carlo Scarpa. Venezuela Pavilion, Venice, 1954 to 1956. Ceiling detail with sculpted concrete surface and wooden walkway reflected as wood layer in ceiling.
41. Carlo Scarpa. Battuto, vase for Venini, 1940.

exterior walls is striped, like that of textiles. The applied surfaces are clearly delimited. Scarpa later again takes up the motif of the gradated roof edge in plans for the Museo Rivoltella, also in Trieste.

The marble mosaic »carpet« that he later uses as a floor treatment can already be found in his early work. Around 1930, in the »Circolo Ufficiali della Marina Militare« (Venice 1930) he creates a carpetlike floor made up of geometric sections of marble that is considered to be the prototype for the floor in the entrance area of the Fondazione Querini Stampalia and the paneling of the »Sacello« in the Castelvecchio.[24]

In the 1930s Scarpa designs numerous renovations of stores and apartments, such as the Caffè Lavena, Frezzeria (Venice 1931), in which the theme of interior paneling in a mostly traditional aesthetic appearance plays an important role. A store installation designed for the company Cappellin & Co. in Paris (1930) – reminiscent of neoplasticism – illustrates the fact that Scarpa was already forming space from floor, wall, and ceiling elements at this time. The perspective of the project shows a two-story space whose ceiling is paneled with a T-shaped plane that holds the ceiling lamp at its most central point. In contrast to this, there is a ramp rising along the side wall and leading to a gallery. The color and surface treatment of the two wall surfaces visible on the sides is different and the walls have been clearly contrasted against each other.

The intervention in the Ca' Foscari (1935–37 together with Valeriano Pastor) is the first larger renovation by Carlo Scarpa (destroyed). He refurbishes the vice chancellor's office and the other offices and replaces the glazing of the entrance hall and the Great Hall. The high interior walls of the offices are subdivided by horizontal bands. Scarpa redesigns the entrance area, about which G. Mazzariol writes as follows:

»Scarpa sought the interior light values that had been profoundly altered by 18th and 19th century disfigurements. By moving back the fenestration of the entrance in relation to the line of the architrave-like columns, opening up the staircase toward the canal by means of a crystal cube that replaced the double doors, he allowed the light to vibrate along the terracotta walls with soft modulations, vitalizing the portico on the ground floor with shifting shades of color that appear in the changing water in the canal depending on the time of day and the season. The light intensity is regulated by the chromatic atmosphere of the wall paneling, whose function is absorption and which recreates by new expressive means the original effect of this series of spaces. The fashion at the time was histological restoration: Scarpa was the first to propose the organic reestablishment of a historical architecture in Venice, and wanted to bring it back to life in its entirety without recourse to grotesque and funereal prostheses.«[25]

The intervention in Ca' Foscari shows Scarpa's methodology in working with a historical context. The use of fenestration behind the Gothic polyfora of the Great Hall, whose structure remains completely untouched by it, demonstrates the independent nature of the new stratum. The fenestration has a characteristic rhythm of division that does not follow the divisions of its stone external structure. This light curtain of glass, which allows the reflections on the Canal Grande to enter unobstructed and demonstrates the spatial conditions, is in contrast to a somewhat introverted solution that Scarpa used in the renovation of the Sala Manlio Capitolo in the Venice courthouse. This room is »lined« like a suit with wood paneling whose bronze nails constitute the ornamentation of the surface. The function of the wood paneling is to give structure to the space; its precious material (mahogany) creates a dignified atmosphere that is appropriate for court hearings. The paneling is revealed as a separate layer in the cut-out windows and is designed, particularly at the edges, in the form of a hemmed piece of fabric. The door is a cutout of the wooden layer of paneling that is projected outward, an element that stands in front of the space and opens into it with a sweeping, swiveling motion.

### The introduction of an additional layer in designing interiors: exhibitions

Sabine Forsthuber writes about the potential for experimentation in designs for exhibitions in Vienna in 1898 and 1914 (in the chapters that follow I shall go into the relevance of the Viennese designers of that period for Scarpa):

»Unlike the private installation building sites the exhibition buildings offered a field of experimentation welcomed by architects, which made it possible to give a practical demonstration of their skill instead of mere architectural sketches. In turn, the model character of the exhibitions was the condition for varying them every time ... Exhibition designs stir up the public far more than private interiors. Art in the form of modern spatial design provoked a public controversy,

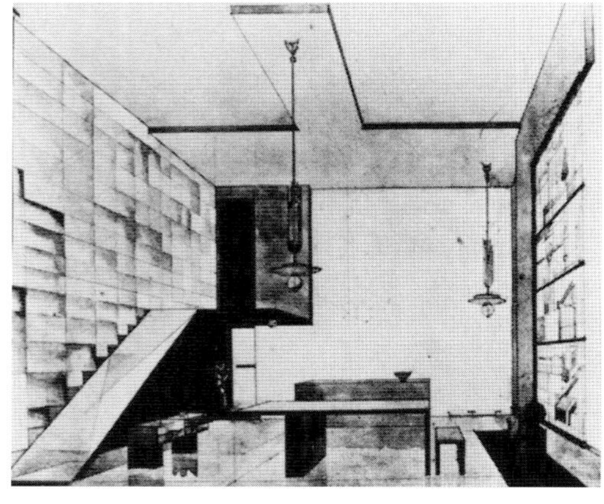

42. Carlo Scarpa, Angelo Velo House, Fontaniva, 1926.
43. Carlo Scarpa, Aldo Martinatti House, Padua, 1926.
44. Carlo Scarpa, study for a social theater, 1927.
45. Carlo Scarpa, study for interior for Murano glassworks, Cappellin & Co., Paris, 1930.
46. Carlo Scarpa, interiors of Café Lavena, Frezzeria, Venice, 1931.
47. Carlo Scarpa, restoration and layout of Ca' Foscari, University of Venice, 1955/56. Glazing behind polyfora.
48. Carlo Scarpa, restoration and layout of Ca' Foscari, University of Venice, 1955/56. Wall paneling.
49. Carlo Scarpa, courtroom Sala Manlio Capitolo, Venice, 1955. Wall paneling.

50. Carlo Scarpa, »Paul Klee«, exhibition, Venice, 14th Biennale, 1948. Plan.
51. Carlo Scarpa, »Paul Klee«, exhibition, Venice, 14th Biennale, 1948. Flexible panels.
52. Carlo Scarpa, Layout of the Galleria dell'Accademia, Venice, from 1945 onward.
53. Carlo Scarpa, »Toulouse Lautrec«, exhibition, Museo Correr, Venice, 1952.

almost counted on being sensational; over and above this it also wished to educate public taste.«[26]

Experiments in designing exhibitions make it possible to test one's own architectural language, serving as an instrument for propagating the prevailing architectonic message.[27] In exhibitions, the theme of the assemblage is an essential component of the design. The designer interprets the exhibits by the way they are presented and can make them stand out or incorporate them in the presence of all the others, producing a total context.

Stratification is automatically a principle in designing temporary and permanent exhibitions. In the exhibitions he designed, Carlo Scarpa determines the path to be taken by visitors, the »percorso«.[28] He defines spatial anticipation and transitions in reference to the exhibits. The stratification of material consists of surfaces that are laid down in front of the existing contour of the room in order to take on the presentation of the works and create an atmospheric reference. These panels, partition walls, or display cases function as the lining of an interior with surfaces or furnishing elements. The innermost layer is formed by the exhibits. In 1945 Scarpa is given the task of reorganizing the Accademia in Venice. Movable panels, into which the works of art can be set, are mounted in front of the existing walls. In 1948 Scarpa designs the retrospective of the works of Paul Klee. His watercolors and oil paintings are presented on panels that are covered with black and white fabric and »function as large passe-partouts that isolate the pictures«.[29] The works do not hang – as is the conventional practice – on the wall in individual frames, but rather are integrated into large panels that react in color and size of cutout area to the type of picture. The visitor's path is guided through the small room by the superimposed surfaces.

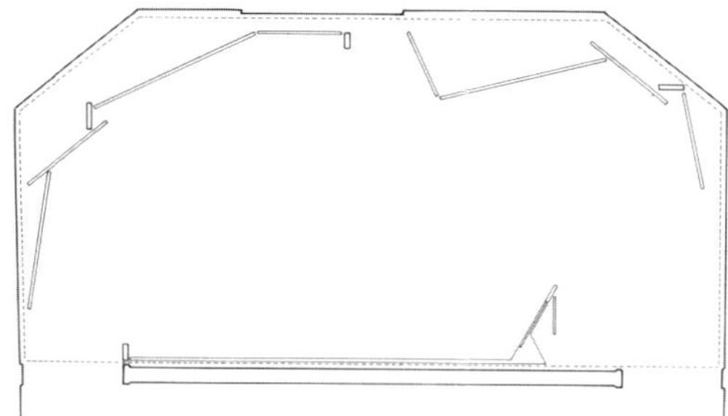

In the same year, on the occasion of the 14th Biennale, Scarpa designs the exhibition »Tre pittori italiani dal 1910 al 1920« in the Italian Pavilion, a retrospective of Arturo Martini and exhibition of the work of Massimo Campigli and Filippo de Pisis. Instead of panels, the side walls, in the upper area, are covered with fabric whose falling folds form differing »shadow zones«.[30] Up above, too, the space is bounded by gathered fabric. The dividers and panels placed in the room divide the room horizontally into two parts. This exhibition is reminiscent of Josef Hoffmann's Secession exhibition.[31] In the exhibition on the occasion of the 26th Biennale in 1952 of the artwork of Toulouse-Lautrec in the Napoleonic wings of the Museo Correr, Scarpa also takes advantage of the effect of large swaths of gathered fabric to redesign the space. He uses the filter effect of a semitransparent layer of cloth that leaves what is behind it effective and is pervious to light yet nonreflective.

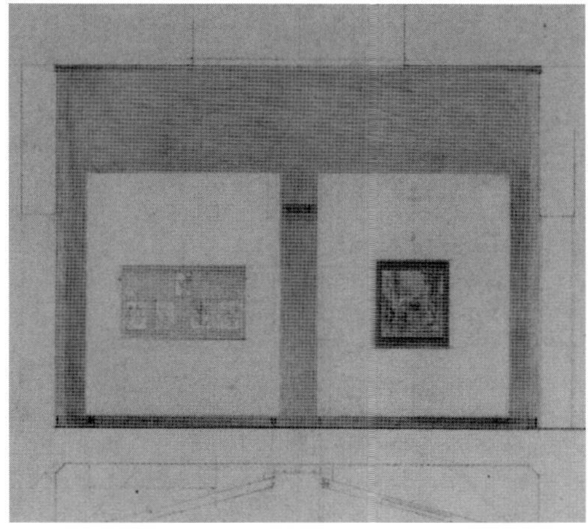

»In the case of Henri de Toulouse-Lautrec's graphics (1952), Scarpa begins by experimenting with curtains affixed close to the windows in order not to lose too much daylight, which is filtered through the almost transparent fabrics. The lower part of the curtain is attached to iron elements arranged in a regular zigzag line. Steel and glass showcases for the display of drawings stand between the windows; they are balanced by tall, cloth-covered panels on the other side of the room; behind them a rich and asymmetric drapery stretches diagonally through the entire hall, covering up its architecture. In several places one is able to recognize the bases or shafts of columns; the heavy 19th century candelabra are still visible under the drapery; as a matter of fact, the time when they were made is not too distant from that which is illustrated by the French artist. It is also natural to imagine the stretched but expressive folds of cloth, which are emphasized even more by the light of the windows behind them, as geometric echoes of the swinging skirts of the ›stars‹ of Paris by night.«[32]

Scarpa designs several exhibitions in the Doges' Palace of Venice. In 1959 he plans the exhibition »Giovanni Bellini«, where his spatial intervention is limited to two semicircular panels placed in the room to correct the space. The exhibition »Ancient Chinese Art« in 1954 intervenes far more in the context; spatial forms and directions of movement are changed by the diagonal positioning of display cases, and a cylindrical element is put in place like a sluice. The exhibit plane that is arranged along the wall continues independently into the central corridor like a material extension. Folded covered surfaces guide the visitor through the exhibition. »Scarpa feels compelled to partition off correspondingly proportioned areas in the exhibition rooms, now by means of colored, smooth swaths of fabric, then of opaque and rough-textured ones, stretched from the ceiling to the floor, in order to house the respective display cases and panels.«[33] The third big exhibition in the Doges' Palace has »Venice and Byzantium« as its theme (1974). In contrast to the previously described exhibition, which still primarily lined the existing rooms, Scarpa now forms a more independent stratum that moves, connected, through the entire story, creating its own spatial forms. The Renaissance ambience is covered up with fabric almost throughout for the presentation of the Byzantine background of the city of Venice. The freestanding partition walls are made of nailed fir boards that overlie the architecture of the Doges' Palace. The height of the ceilings is varied in different places by hanging white planes. Scarpa introduces strata that do not serve to structure the room as a whole but have reference to one or several objects, assigning to the latter a virtual space of their own. Particularly important objects are made to stand out through their position inside the circular gallery by being displayed separately or by forming a special background or special mountings and easels.

The formation of virtual spaces through the use of surfaces that can produce a correspondence to objects or create a space within a space is particularly important when designing an exhibition. In designing exhibitions and museums, floor, wall, or ceiling strata are used for this purpose. A detail from the Italian Pavilion of the Expo in Montréal shows the example of an additive layer on the ceiling, while in the Palazzo Abatellis the wall panels fulfill this function. The city hall of Messina is the location of the 1953 exhibition »Antonello ed i quattrocentisti siciliani«. The spatial characteristics of the city hall demanded a complete rearrangement of the spatial volume. The effect serves »both to conceal and to distribute the light and endeavors to enhance the act of presenting the work of art as much as possible; the architect achieves this by means of the triple draping of a mesh fabric (cencio della nonna) in the colors white, blue, and pink, which produces a beautiful muted light. The swaths of fabric drop diagonally from above, the folds of the drapery are slightly pulled apart and attached almost at floor level, while the ceiling is lowered by means of white, intertwined lengths of cloth in such a way that one does not see the height of the actual ceiling.«[34] Spatial proportions are also corrected by means of textiles that simultaneously control the lighting and the light intensity.

The presentation of an exhibition about Frank Lloyd Wright, organized in Milan in 1969, directs the light by means of draperies indirectly onto the drawings. The high-ceilinged room is structured

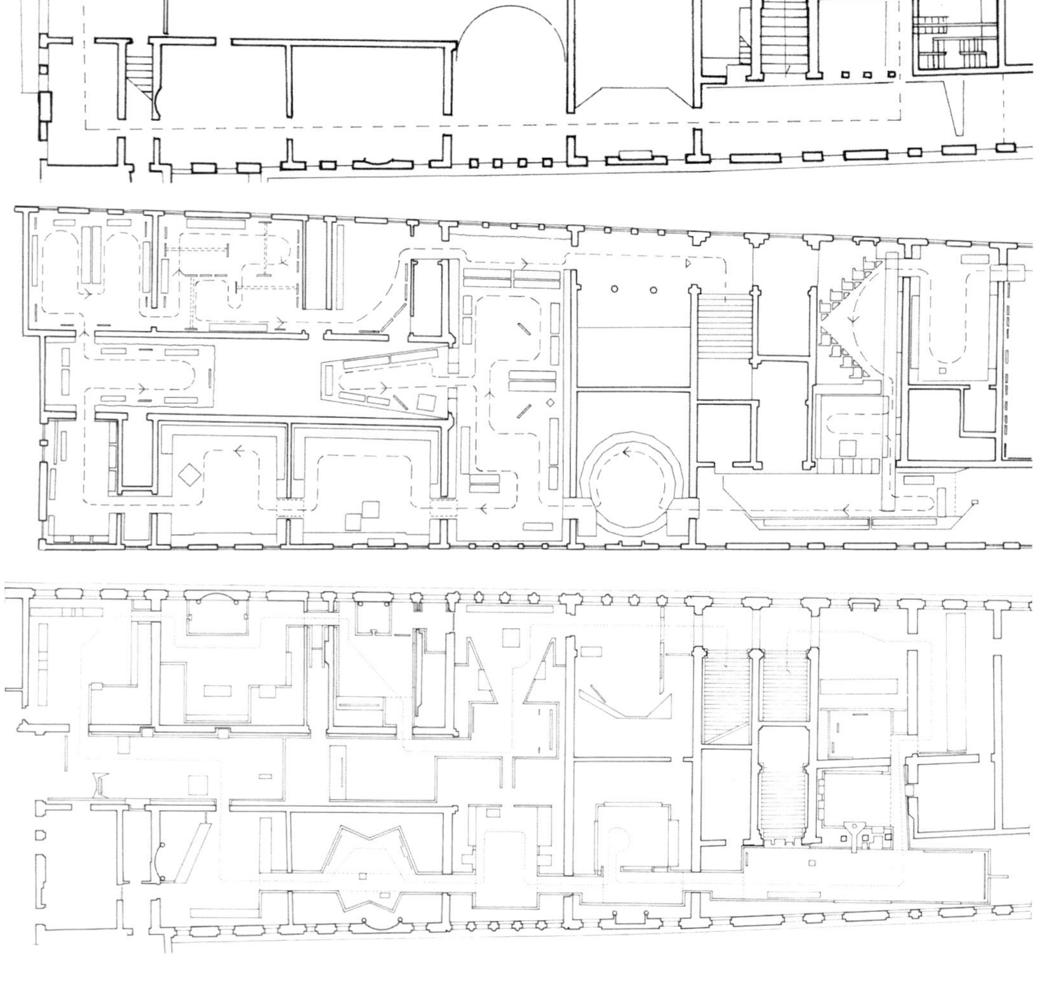

54–56. Carlo Scarpa, designs for exhibitions in the Doges' Palace, Venice. Plans of various layouts,

57. Carlo Scarpa. Italian Pavilion, Expo 1967, Montréal. Ceiling plane treated as independent layer.

58. Carlo Scarpa. »Antonello ed i quattrocentisti siciliani«, exhibition, Messina, 1953. Fabric as new layer within the existing space to define the exhibition space.

by pyramids of gathered fabric and modified by them. By means of the ceiling design, drawings are assigned their own spatial zone. »Instead of lowering the air space, Scarpa here decides to arrange a virtual zone, 3 m above the floor, consisting of a grid made up of large squares; they form the framework for light volumes of folded fabric and, as pyramid frustums, liven up the air space in the hall.«[35]

In 1956 Scarpa designs the exhibition »Piet Mondrian« in the Galleria Nazionale d'Arte Moderna in Rome, whose use of forms corresponds with the art of Mondrian. In the exhibition »Poetry« for the '67 Expo in Montréal the clear separation of architectural elements and their individual strata becomes visible. Scarpa combines closed surfaces with surfaces that are transparent and translucent. The view through the two interpenetrating circles within vertical glasswork gives the visitor a glimpse of Donatello's David, who stands on a detached marble platform.

The long years of work for the Biennale enable Scarpa to establish contact with numerous artists and provide inspiration through many different design projects. Mario de Luigi, with whom he works on the first commissions, and Arturo Martini and Virgilio Guidi are among his friends. In addition to producing a large number of exhibitions, he renovates many exhibition buildings and museums. The Italian Pavilion is remodeled several times: in 1962, between the columns, he erects a construction site consisting of low, unfinished walls that conceal part of the façade. In 1968 he covers up the front with a three-dimensionally very well formed stratum that is reminiscent of Hoffmann's fluted pilasters for the 1911 Austrian Pavilion in Rome. Affinities with Scarpa's Viennese models are discussed further in chapter 2.

59, 60. Carlo Scarpa, »Frank Lloyd Wright«, exhibition, Milan, 1969. Section sketch and plan.
61, 62. Carlo Scarpa, »Piet Mondrian«, exhibition, Rome, 1956. Plan and sketch.

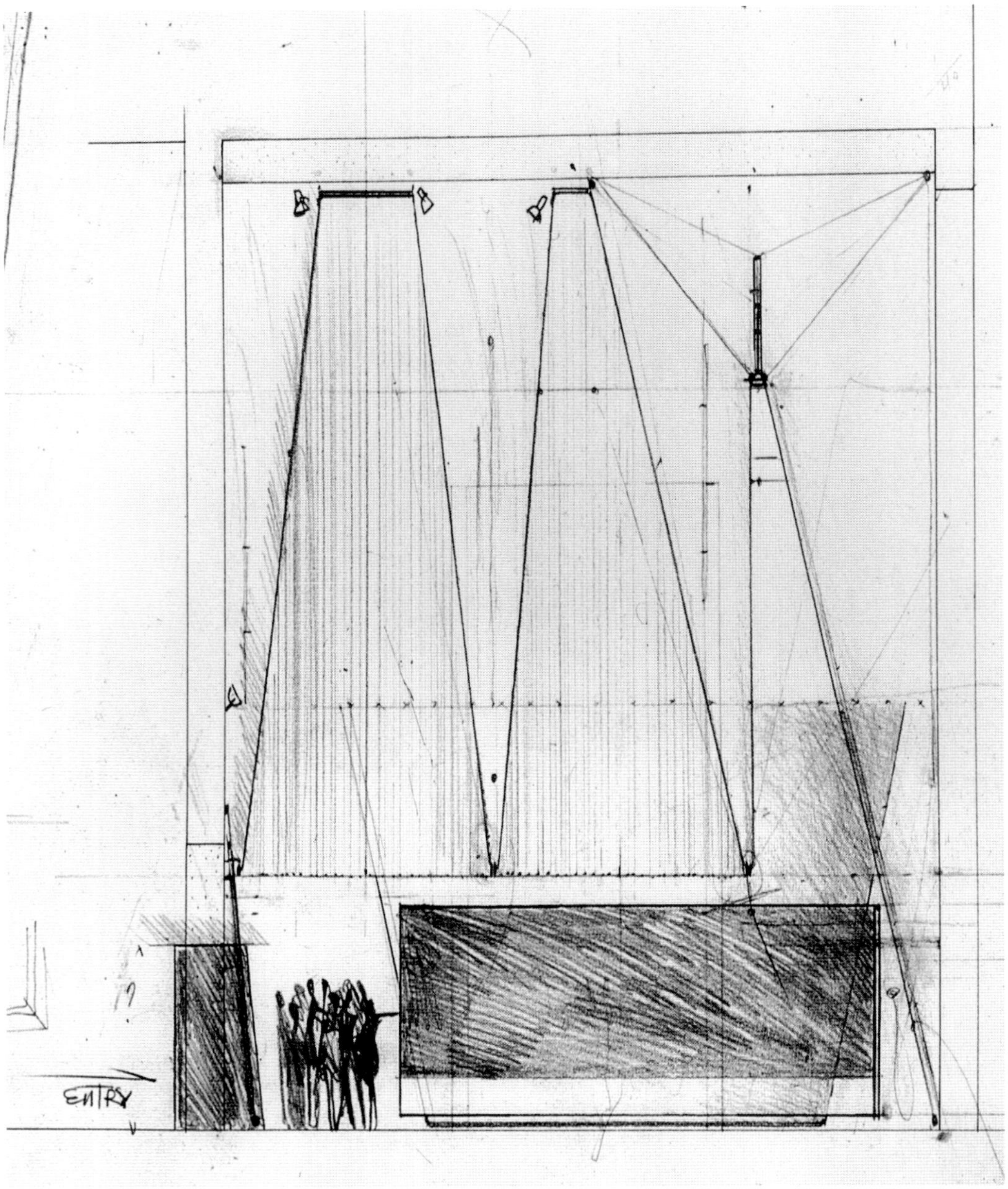

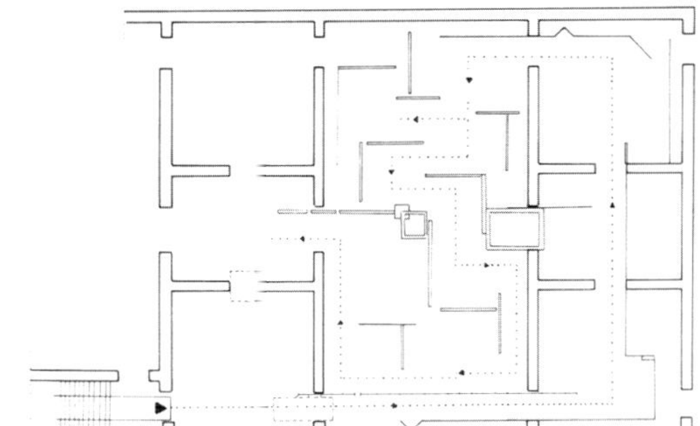

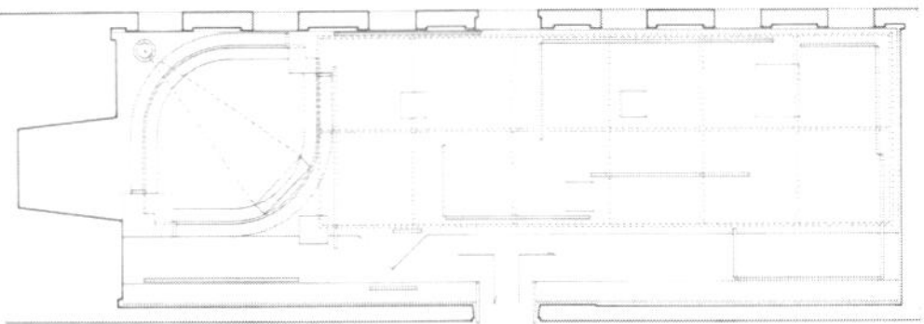

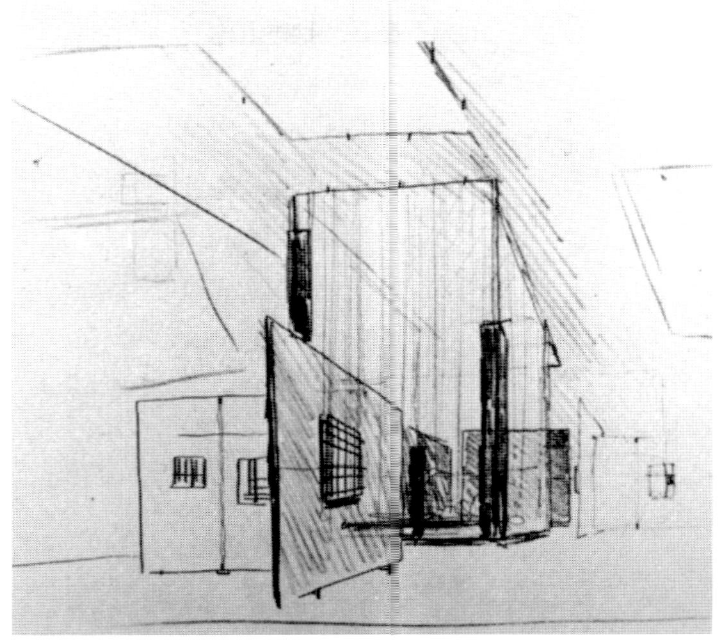

## 1.3. Theoretical foundations of the principle of stratification in the architecture discussion at the turn of the 20th century

The description and analysis of the phenomena of stratification that are discussed in this book with reference to Carlo Scarpa's work originate in the theoretical discussions at the turn of the 20th century. Many of the theorists mentioned here looked into the origin and substance of architectonic elements, intending to work out a universally applicable model for interpreting architectonic form, function, and cultural significance.

In the course of the investigation of stratification, the theoretical background that was elaborated during this period and an aesthetic understanding of the period are important. Definitions of architectonic elements and issues continue to be a valid way of looking at things. As mentioned earlier, Carlo Scarpa probably had limited access to some of these works and, because of his interest in subsequent architectural movements, was indirectly exposed to the reception history discussed in the treatises.

### The polychromy debate

Theoretical foundations relating to the topic of stratification are found in the discussion between architects and art historians about polychromy in the architecture of antiquity that began in France. The polychromy debate[1] goes back, among others, to the sculptor Quatremère de Quincy (1755–1849), who was the lifelong secretary of the Académie des Beaux-Arts and is said to have been the first to use the term polychromy in the context of a conference at the Institut des Beaux-Arts in 1806. In his writings he investigates the use of color in ancient Greek sculpture. In 1814 he publishes his findings under the title *Jupiter Olympien: ou l'art de la sculpture antique considéré sous un nouveau point de vue; ouvrage qui comprend un essai sur le goût de la sculpture polychrome*.[2]

Still without a direct connection with architecture, he refers here to the existence of layers of color on the monumental statue of Jupiter in the temple of Olympia.[3] Hanno Walter Kruft describes his theoretical position: »Like many of his contemporaries, he supports a ›simple normative picture of history according to which the origin, principles, laws, theory, and practice of architecture go back to the Greeks, were supposedly disseminated by the Romans, and are the common property of the world; the Gothic period is ignored‹.«[4]

Quatremère de Quincy's *Dictionnaire d'architecture* worked out definitions of architectonic elements in the format of a dictionary. Starting with the etymology of individual words, he determines the concepts and their use. »Incrustation«,[5] for example, is defined as a metal coating used by goldsmiths and in furniture making and architecture. »Façades»[6] according to his interpretation are accorded different stylistic treatment depending on their structural purpose. He sees »structure»[7] as the vehicle of the poetic language of architecture: it comprises beauty of form and proportions. In contrast to this is the term »construction«,[8] which comprises static, technical, and material-related features. Quatremère de Quincy divides buildings into a technical-material and a poetic-immaterial component. His observations in the area of polychromy referred first of all to large-scale Greek sculpture, but examinations of architecture in Greece and southern Italy yielded traces of particles of color on a number of different ancient temples. The finds prompted discussion about the application of color in architecture.

Jakob Ignaz Hittorff (1792–1867) from Cologne, who spent a lengthy period of time in Sicily, published colored photographs of buildings and, in 1830, presented a *Mémoire sur l'architecture polychrome chez les Grecs* at the Académie des Inscriptions. After his research trips to Italy and his first findings, he organized a regular »press campaign»[9] to make public his views about the ancients' love of color. Hittorff's observations are not only aimed at the research results of his investigations, but also comprise the practical aspect of using colors in the architecture of his time. »For Hittorff, color is a means of protecting the material and therefore, in his eyes, something that needs to be used with greater justification in contemporary Paris than in ancient Athens.«[10] The attempt to activate the architecture discussion of his time with the help of archeological findings was intended to legitimize the use of color in the interior and exterior of a building. Such a transposition shows the beginnings of »stratified« thinking in that a layer of color is accepted as an architectural element.

Auguste Choisy (1841–1909) in his *Histoire d'architecture* wrote a constructive history of building and construction »that traces back the complexity of all architecture to a few simple lines«.[11]

The entire history of architecture is described as the »continuity of a technological development»[12] and deals almost exclusively with construction-related and technical characteristics of various periods. In addition to technical analysis he addresses the aesthetic expression of architectural elements and their proportions. »Stylistic developments, for him, are nothing but the expression of new methods of construction.«[13] His study divides architecture into its elements; thus, he discusses construction, form, proportion, and decoration in separate chapters. While he keeps separate decoration and construction, he examines the various epochs of the history of construction. His study of Greek architecture, for example, shows layers of paint or material being used to clothe construction. Choisy writes: »The custom of covering the stone with a layer of ceramics was the result of a tradition from a time when inadequate tools made it difficult to cut the edges of stone blocks in a regular way.«[14] He traces back the need for a decorative layer to the lack of available stonecutting tools and thus defines it as a means of regulation and leveling. The outer layer can make the construction stand out and elucidate it. Choisy goes on: »The painting of architecture – Hittorff has proved that the Greek monuments were painted.«[15]

Henri Labrouste (1801–1875) spent the years from 1825 through 1829 in Italy. With his watercolor of Agrigento he conjured up an Etruscan-influenced architectural picture of a pre-classical world. Like Hittorff, he tried to deduce practical conclusions from his investigations, such as, for instance, in his Bibliothèque Sainte-Geneviève, which was built between 1845 and 1851 in Paris. The façade contains »reminiscences of many other things he had admired, such as Wren's library in Cambridge, Alberti's Tempio Malatestiano in Rimini, Michelozzo's Banco Mediceo in Milan, and Sansovino's Library of San Marco in Venice. This distillation of knowledge, which we have also found to be at the heart of the work of Duban, was, however, considered to be Labrouste's great contribution.«[16] From a »distillation of knowledge« develop layers of association that conjure up narrative elements not purely as a quotation, but as a reminder that acts as a referent. Beside emphasizing the protective function stucco and paint have for stone, and its significance based on religious interpretation, the architecture of Labrouste has an eloquence that is also present in the work of Scarpa.

»On principle, Labrouste makes a distinction between a building's structural framework and the exterior decorative form – though he would like the forms of decoration to be determined by the construction and the material. This constitutes one of the most important starting points for historicism.«[17]

»In the German-speaking part of Europe, Gottfried Semper continues to move in this direction. At this point architecture is transformed from a monolithic into a many-layered structure whose background can be provided by functional, cultural, and aesthetic aspects.«[18]

In 1935, Franz Kugler (1808–1858) publishes a book about polychromy in Germany. He believes the layers of color are reduced to individual ornamented parts of the Doric temples, such as the frieze above the main ledge.

»In all other methods of construction used in the ancient world that consist of pillars and horizontal lintels, the crowning main ledge is located directly above the architrave: it is only in Greek architecture that a third section is inserted between the two – the frieze, whose purpose is perfectly described by its name, zophorus, ›that which bears the images‹. It is used to give the building a worthy sculptured ornamentation, which would have nullified the laws of architectonic form in the building's lower parts.«[19]

Stratification in the form of painting, according to Kugler, serves a purpose and must be used only in specific areas. The ornamented sections are given the function of conveying information, indicating the importance and cultural position of the building, or clarifying the form and contour of individual parts of the architecture.

»For the special characteristic nature of those components that have a curved profile is not easy to recognize, particularly when they are continued in longer lines; the eye is more apt to notice the effect of the shadows (which, by the way, can only be effective when the lighting is favorable) than the line of the profile. In order to make the line clear to the eye in every section of the component, it was ornamented with color, reproducing that very profile in its main lines – though incidentally appearing to be freely designed in an artistic way.«[20]

He also comments on materials: Metal functions as a connecting element or in the form of shields – booty brought back from the war and triumphantly mounted on the exterior walls. It serves as a kind of second structuring system that overlies the stone construction.

»Of several temples we know that the architrave or frieze was decorated with gilded shields that were generally consecrated by lucky victors from the spoils of victory. Well-known are the twenty-one shields that adorned the temple of Jupiter in Olympia – the votive gifts of Mummius;

63. Quatremère de Quincy, reconstruction of Jupiter Olympien. Colored drawing showing layers of paint on statue and interior space.

64. Jakob Ignaz Hittorff, *Restitution du temple d'Empédocle à Sélinonte ou l'architecture polychrome chez les Grecs*, Paris, 1851. Frontispiz, colored drawing.

in the same way, the temple of Apollo in Delphi was ornamented by the Athenians after the Marathon victory, and the Aetolians after the victory over the Gauls. On the Parthenon in Athens you can still see here and there the holes of the clamps in the architrave and round markings with a roughly 3 1/2-foot diameter, clearly indicating that a similar ornamentation was used.«[21]

## Tectonics

The discovery of the use of color in ancient architecture promoted normative works in architecture theory that discuss the tectonic repercussions of separating decoration and ornamental content from the constructively necessary structure. Carl Boetticher (1806–1889) deals with the tectonics of the Hellenes. Their way of placing structural elements, according to Boetticher, corresponds with the principle of the creative power of nature. The content of each building is expressed in its form. The result is a set of laws that are »high above the arbitrariness of the working subject«.[22]

Bötticher's tectonics divides objects into two elements, the core form and the art form. This is not about separating construction and shell, but rather about a mechanical component that fulfils functions (core form) and a decorative component (art form) that clarifies functions and »symbolizes the essence of the components«. The transport of contents is carried out by strata that serve as a symbol for the invisible structural components.

Boetticher writes: »The realization of the concept of each component may be regarded as being performed by two elements: by the core form, and by the art form. The core form of each component is the mechanically necessary, the statically functioning pattern; the art form of each component on the other hand is only the characteristic of explaining the function. However, this characteristic does not merely symbolize each component's particular essence, but also the way it is related to the adjoining components; it also contains the juncture of those working together with it; and just as all components are already mechanically joined in a static whole, the joining symbols figuratively link all components logically into one inseparable organism. This explanatory characteristic is therefore only a shell of the component, as it were, a symbolic attribute of the latter – decoratio. It comes into being at the same moment that the mechanical schema of the component is conceived: the idea of both is one, they are both born together.«[23]

He continues: »This decorative outer layer or characteristic attribute of the core form therefore never functions materially or structurally, having only an ethical purpose: to represent outwardly the structural function that the core, functioning completely alone, fulfills physically, and to symbolize it vividly. That is why it is symbolic, because actually the notion of a core is described by attributes or characters that, in a metaphorical way, externally denote and seemingly carry out what the core performs in reality.«[24]

In a view of architecture that separates symbol and discourse from the supporting framework, the connecting elements are a fundamental part of the formal statement made by a building. What is meant are both connecting elements between the actual strata, and intellectual connections between the building's characteristics and its structure.

Boetticher calls the art form decoration (decoratio), a shell as it were of the actual component and the symbolic expression of it. These two elements are inseparably connected and come into being simultaneously. The art form ensures that all components are consistently connected into a whole.

Heinrich Hübsch (1795–1863) defines architectonic beauty as the core and the art form working together harmonically: »Let us, then, venture to say it: perfect beauty is virtually a deep fusion of the above-named two sides, whose most extreme characteristics are exactly each other's opposites, and that its dialectical life arises precisely from the union of these two poles; in other words, that the perfectly beautiful form must both express a spiritual content in a characteristic way and present it in a manner pleasing to the eye.«[25] Hübsch puts into words the phenomenon that had been the basis of understanding architecture for Choisy and others – the abstracting of architectural elements into floor, wall, and ceiling as a basis for architectonic organization.

»When we analyze this concept of architecture, we have the following essential components of a complete building: the covering (that which is suspended), the support (that which stands upright), which at the same time forms the lateral boundary, and the substructure, which separates the structure from the natural soil, or the foot (that which lies underneath).

Now, these three main parts, which occur in the monuments of all peoples and times are further subdivided into the following absolute architectonic elements (which may be compared with the principal limbs of the animal body) – the interior ceiling, the exterior roof, whose projecting edge forms the cornice, the external walls with doors and windows, the free individual supports (columns and pillars) with their spans, the main foundation and the interior floor. If upper rooms are added above the lower ones, the result is a building with several stories.«[26]

Carlo Scarpa works with the features of the surfaces that he assigns to the floor, wall, and ceiling, with the characteristics of architectonic elements such as the interior ceiling, the exterior roof, the cornices, the exterior walls, and the supports. Particularly in the Castelvecchio and in the Fondazione Querini these individual architectural motifs are given a distinguished form. Analogies to the models are there as subtle hints, not direct confrontation.

Heinrich Wölfflin (1864–1945) also respects the separation of architecture into elements that fulfill different purposes. »Architecture reaches its peak at the point when individual components have detached themselves from the undivided mass and every part, carrying out solely its own purpose, seems to function without affecting the entire structure detrimentally or being impeded by it.«[27]

## The theory of cladding

In 1834 Gottfried Semper (1803–1879) publishes »Vorläufige Bemerkungen über bemalte Architektur und Plastik bei den Alten« (Preliminary remarks about painted architecture and sculpture among the ancients), an essay that differs from Hittorff's thesis only in the way it interprets the background colors. In this paper there is already a suggestion of the theory of cladding that was further elaborated in his work *Der Stil in den tektonischen Künsten* (Style in the tectonic arts). He describes the need for layers of paint as follows:

»Wood, iron, and all metals require protective layers to protect them from the corrosive effect of the air. It is quite natural that this requirement is met in a way that at the same time contributes to making them more beautiful. Instead of monotonous whitewash, a variety of pleasing colors are chosen. Polychromy becomes natural, necessary.«[28]

»It is quite impossible to think and conceive an architectonic work in its true sense without its correct complement of colors; the essence of the forms is dictated by the colors.«[29]

In his work Semper expounds his interpretation of the development of polychromy among the Greeks: »Their childlike imagination liked vivid colors, bright combinations like those formed by nature everywhere. At the same time people also thought of the usefulness of paint and realized that a protective layer makes wood, clay, indeed even stone, more durable.«[30]

As the concept of religion developed, ornamentation was reserved for the temples of the gods. »Brightly colored distemper« turned into »regular forms«, »contours that stand out, and finally colored reliefs. The next step was probably the attempt to imitate the lines of light and shadow observed in such mezzo-relievos by creating color illusions on a flat surface. This is how the first painted forms with shadow and light came about.«[31] »The vivid colors of textiles explain the polychromy of the wall constructions of antiquity: the German words for wall (Wand) and garment (Gewand) are also etymologically related.«[32] Semper looks for the typological origin of the paint coating ancient temples and develops his »theory of cladding« from it. The division of archi-

65. Gottfried Semper, *Der Stil in den Tektonischen Künsten*. Floor pattern alluding to textile background of stonework in the Pronaos of the Jupiter Temple in Olympia.

tecture into strata is linked to the artisanal origin of all shelter, which is to be found in the use of textiles. Architecture consists of »structure, determined by function, and an aesthetic shell«,[33] which is laid over the supporting structure like something that clothes it, and gives the building its value and its characteristic features.

»These frameworks, which serve to hold, secure, and carry these spatial boundaries, are requirements that have nothing directly to do with space or dividing space. They are alien to the original architectonic idea and initially are not elements that define the forms.«[34] Hans Prinzhorn writes about Semper's theory of clothing: »The prototype of the wall is the mat hung to act as a spatial border, the rug. Later people begin to construct stone buildings: it turns out that the rug or tapestry is retained to cover the wall, which in itself only has the constructional function of supporting the roof. The rug or tapestry still acts as a spatial boundary. Then someone has the idea of covering the wall with costly stone slabs or metal sheets, or with painted stucco, with wood, terracotta, and so forth: all these types of cladding, according to Semper, are modifications of that type of spatial border, the mat, the rug.« [35]

Like his contemporaries, Semper tries to substantiate his theoretical formulations with examples from the history of architecture. Wall coverings have developed differently in different countries, but have a common origin. Regarding Chinese architecture he writes: »The exterior surface of the wall is still materially quite separate from the wall itself here and indeed is mostly movable.«[36] »One can see that the grid forms the basis of Chinese ornamentation, and here it is a natural basis taken directly from reality.«[37] Different materials and requirements accordingly lead to different formal expressions. Egyptian architecture borrows the style of its walls from embroidery: »The sculpture and painting of the Egyptians was a cross-stitch embroidery carried out on walls, with all the stylistic features of cross-stitching; – the technique for painting and sculpture that has been traditional in Asia since time immemorial, on the other hand, completely corresponds with a style associated with satin stitch embroidery.«[38] In connection with Egypt, for instance, cladding becomes autonomous as a consequence of the fact that the core is technically no longer necessary: »We showed how in West Asian art the so-called order of the columns, that is, the art form of the supporting and supported parts of the building, had primarily technical origins; we had deduced it from the principle of hollow body construction, where in gradual transitions the static function of the original wooden core was transferred to the shell that surrounded it. The core became superfluous when the metal shell had gained sufficient strength in itself to act as a support and span. The order retains this hollow body type even after its metamorphosis into the stone style. Its art form emerged both from the shell and from its structure.«[39]

About Greek architecture, Semper writes: »Among these ancient traditional formal elements of Hellenic art none has as profound an effect as the principle of clothing and incrustation, which predominates in all of pre-Hellenic art and by no means weakens or atrophies in the Greek style, but rather lives on, only highly spiritualized and more in the constructional-technical sense, serving beauty and form alone.«[40]

Later he states: »The late Roman style of incrustation that emerged from this – the cladding of already completed architectural arrangements with wall areas, placed before the walls, in which panels with images have been inserted and in front of which the statues and other art treasures find a quiet background – may be called a ›superfoetation‹ of the age-old principle of cladding.«[41]

### Four elements of architecture

Semper divides architecture into four elements. The most important, »moral«[42] element is the hearth, the »first sign of human settling down and rest after the hunt, battle, and roaming in the desert«.[43] »Cultural traditions»[44] are formed around the hearth. Around it are grouped the three other elements of architecture, which serve to protect the fire and the hearth: »the roof, the enclosing wall, and the terrace«.[45] The original technique for creating the enclosing fence or wall is wickerwork and the weaving of rugs; later wickerwork techniques were transferred to other techniques. »Just as wickerwork was the original technique, so later, when the light mat walls were transformed to solid brick or stone block walls, it retained, in fact or figuratively, the whole importance of its former significance, the actual essence of the wall.«[46] Later, too, »the rug or tapestry continued to be the wall, the visible border of the room. The often very strong walls behind it became necessary for other reasons that had nothing to do with spatial matters, such as safety, load-bearing, greater durability, and the like.«[47] The origin of the concept of the »wall« (German

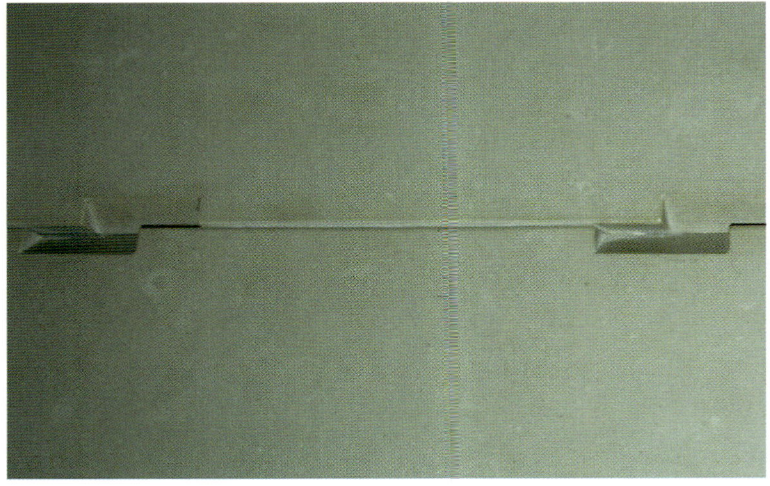

66. Carlo Scarpa, new portal for the Faculty of Literature and Philosophy of the University of Venice, San Sebastiano, Venice, 1976–78
67. Carlo Scarpa, Olivetti store, Venice, 1957 to 1958. Detail of stone radiator cover at window sill.
68. Carlo Scarpa, Querini Foundation, Venice, 1961–63. Framed stucco panels exposing the wall underneath, mosaic flooring with curb acting as boarder for indoor canal allowing water to enter the building.
69. Carlo Scarpa, Zentner House Zurich, 1964 to 1968. Detail of fireplace facing.

70. Carlo Scarpa, Zentner House Zurich, 1964 to 1968. Ground-floor plan.
71. Carlo Scarpa, Zentner House Zurich, 1964 to 1968. Detail of floor, a carpet woven from wood.

Wand), etymologically and evolutionarily, is »garment« (German »Gewand»).[48] Kenneth Frampton points out the connection between Semper's four elements and the architecture of Scarpa: »The main façade of the Banca Popolare is modulated in accordance with Semper's four elements, so that we see a foundation made of cut stone, a facing wall of stucco, and a loggia with a steel frame in the upper part of the building.«[49] In studying Scarpa's work, we find reminiscences of Semper's textile set of rules. These parallels are not based on the direct influence of Semper's writings; rather, they came about via the detour of subsequent architectural styles.[50] Scarpa's independent wall panels suggest tapestries, and his joints and interconnecting details are reminiscent of a carefully thought-out seam. An element must have its »own upper boundary and its termination below. Symbols that art invented, in part in accordance with technical analogies, in order to crown the individual element as something upright and at the same time link it with others into a whole, are valid for all time, – they may be transformed, but not be replaced by anything that is basically new.«[51]

The wall openings, too, follow textile design guidelines. »Thus, for instance, the door frames and window facings are that type of eurhythmic inserts, quite similar to picture frames, except that what is framed is the person who is entering or looking out. This example of the frame clearly shows the difference and the separation of those parts that are part of the frame as such and in which the eurythmic law comes into operation, and of the other parts, which become active partly in a symmetric partly in a proportional sense. As a consequence the frame which includes roofs, consoles and other details, appears as an object to the spectator who is outside of the frame.«[52]

Designs for entrances, such as the entrance of the University of Venice near San Sebastiano seem subconsciously to take a similar position. Not only is the purpose of going through and entering served by an opening, but it is also provided with numerous frames and ornamentation that illustrate the function of entering.

»The frame is one of the most important basic forms of art. There is no self-contained picture without a frame, no scale of size without it. It is only with a frame that eurhythmy is applied – the regularly concentric structuring and ordering of the formal elements that form a unified figure around the framed object.«[53] Scarpa frames sculptures with panels that are themselves edged with wood, and whose colored surface becomes a background for the object and offers it a spatial frame, as it were.

On the treatment of floor and ceiling in the manner of textiles Semper writes: »Like the tapestry, the ceiling symbolizes the concept of a horizontal surface, and both originally exclude the secondary concepts of right and left, of front and back. In the ceiling, too, the concept of the horizontal boundary of space may be thought of as being concentrated on the focal point, and this focal point in both is the starting point and the end of all relationships that can stylistically be produced by subdivisions, lines, and patterns on such a ceiling, which symbolizes the absolute concept of a horizontal plane.«[54] The motifs that are obtained are derived from textile elements as they once existed and are preserved as symbols for that past in their stylistic idiom. »First, some remarks about the border that forms the first part of a tripartite structure, in which every articulated floor must be divided in accordance with its past nature, and thus has a twofold function to cover both cases. Primarily, the border functions statically or mechanically, as it were, by surrounding the carpet or the mosaic incrustation of the floor and encircling it.«[55]

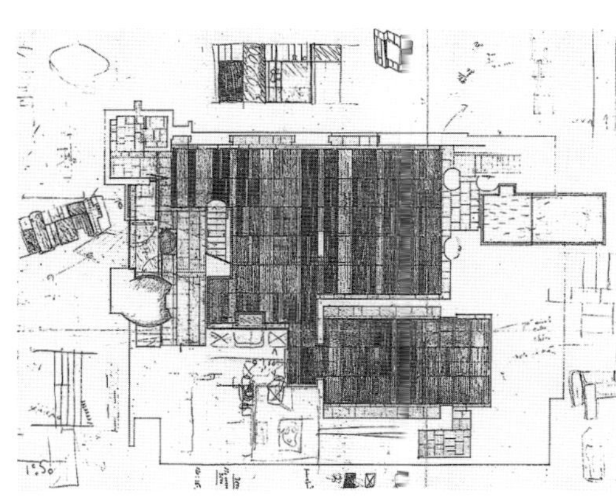

A chief element of textile art is the knot, which, as the most important point of accumulation of various trends in construction, is still used to refer to the connecting elements of a supporting framework. »The knot is perhaps the oldest technical symbol and, as I showed, the expression for the earliest cosmogonic ideas that sprang up among the peoples. A knot primarily serves as the means of tying together the ends of two threads, and whether it is securely tied or not chiefly depends on the resistance of friction. The system that most promotes friction by lateral pressure when both threads are pulled lengthwise in opposite directions is the most secure.«[56] A knot is simultaneously a mechanism and a symbol. The seam functions as a linear connecting element that at the same time becomes a symbol and a decorative element.

Carlo Scarpa seems to be operating within the textile system of expression expounded by Semper. »And what definition can concur better with Scarpa's ›put in place in front of the walls‹ than Gottfried Semper's most sublime conclusions for museum room boundaries that allude to the origins of architecture in a way that is associated with textile art.«[57]

Scarpa's flooring seems to follow textile laws of structure, it is framed or bordered. No surface is left without a border, and the elements of knot, edging, and seam are manifested in the joint,[58] framing, or commissure. Ornaments follow cultural symbolism or illustrate historical or artisanal origins. On the one hand, Semper explains the origin of cladding with paint as a covering that has protective function, while he regards the fact that decoration with motifs became independent as a ritual expression. As soon as the building is covered with layers of stucco or paint, that is, as soon as different layers are formed that serve different functions, as soon as the meaning of individual layers is refined and specifically developed, it becomes singular and separates from other functional sets of facts. Symbolic functions become independent in associative levels that are accessible to those who recognize the references.

An architectural translation of Semper's theoretical ideas takes place above all in Viennese architecture after the turn of the 20th century. Not until architectonic motifs break away from the basic textile significance does architectural design become formally more neutral and lead to the principle of the stratification of surfaces.

72. Carlo Scarpa, Ca' Foscari, University of Venice, 1955/56. Conversion of great hall into lecture theatre, wooden separation wall with mobile shutter panels.
73. Carlo Scarpa, Ca' Foscari, University of Venice, 1955/56. Conversion of great hall into lecture theatre, ceiling detail.

74. Carlo Scarpa, Gavina showroom, Bologna, 1961. Window opening seen from interior showing added concrete layer on exterior of façade.
75. Carlo Scarpa, Gavina showroom, Bologna, 1961. Added layer made of concrete, entrance door.

## 2. Stratification in Scarpa's work: influences

### 2.1. »Cladding« in Viennese architecture

»In the transition from the 19th to the 20th century it (cladding, Author's note) became a central issue in the theoretical debate by architects worldwide about cladding. ›Bekleidung‹ or ›Verkleidung‹, uncovering or masking are concepts related to problems that are becoming more and more relevant, urgent, and dramatic in a changed technical or technological environment. Architects no longer consider only the traditional situation of a continuous wall structure that dissolves the sheath to which cladding adds a degree of material quality and high finish, but also see the inevitable rise to prominence of the iron and concrete structural framework, which exacerbates the differences in the nature and function of the cladding and construction by making their connection inseparable and their true nature no longer transparent though informed by the wish still to preserve a semblance of stone architecture.«[1]

Gottfried Semper's theory of the textile origins of construction is clearly reflected in architecture after the turn of the 20th century. According to Semper, as a result of changing building materials, the textile details went from a framework hung with fabric to a stone house with details that are reminiscent of the former design of textile clothing. Scarpa comes to examine Semper's ideas by way of his reception of Viennese architectural works after the turn of the 20th century. Josef

Gantner writes about his investigation of the the parallels between Semper's world of ideas and modern architecture as exemplified by Le Corbusier: »Yet – once you have grasped this thread by one end, you never let go of it, and then try to shine a light even further into the trains of thought of both books, to leave aside all that is of secondary importance, to observe the thoughts jointly as they arise in their nakedness; then, quite suddenly, you realize that Semper and Le Corbusier both start out from the same basic idea: The demand that form be released from the constraint of ornament, and not only that, but also: that material be released from the constraint of form.«[2]

»And so in the end Gottfried Semper's new demand for a form in architecture and industry that would be appropriate for the material involved and determined by its function was sabotaged almost automtically by Semper's own demand for the reincarnation of historical styles, and his idea first had to be slowly freed from this chain before it was able to discover its own legitimacy and thus fully develop.«[3]

**Otto Wagner**

The translation into architectural terms of Semper's theoretical ideas can be seen particularly in the work of Otto Wagner (1841–1918), who is referred to as Semper's »executor«[4] and his »most consistent disciple«.[5] In his work *Die Erneuerung der Baukunst* Otto Wagner refers several times to Semper's influence and importance.[6] For Wagner, like Semper, the classification of architecture into individual elements is a result of the textile origins of architecture: »The first form built by human beings was a roof, a protective ceiling, no doubt to make up for the lack of caves. A roof demands a support, later a wall, and finally a hearth. The artificial support led to the use of building material, wood and stone; the wall produced wickerwork and masonry.«[7]

In his early works Otto Wagner subscribes to historicism. Then comes an Art Nouveau-oriented phase between 1898 and 1900 during which he cultivates »his modern architectural style – the cladding of the building with thin, but precious material«.[8] Otto Wagner develops his aesthetic architectural idiom on the basis of technical innovations. He uses cladding not only in interiors, but also in the exterior. New technologies have the potential for a formally new statement, as well as the exploitation of constructional necessities as the ornamental design of the house. »Every new style gradually came into being because new designs, new material, new human tasks and points of view demanded a change or innovation of existing forms.«[9] His buildings are a system of clearly defined parts functioning together. »The principle of cladding becomes, for him, a principle of showing, of precise visual definition.«[10] A didactic claim and the making visible of architectonic elements and functions is also one of the principles used by Scarpa. Since Wagner was an important model for Scarpa, Semper's philosophical ideas indirectly became part of his thinking about architecture. In Scarpa the separation of the structure from the cladding is less relevant than the equivalent juxtaposition of elements. He allows historical and contemporary structures to exist side by side and indicates their autonomy by means of respectful joints, which keep the distance. In the design of museums or exhibitions, the »explanatory« claim of the architecture itself is joined to the »percorso« of the presentation of objects whose common and specific features only their planned incorporation in the architectural context makes completely clear. By way of the influence of Gottfried Semper, Otto Wagner is inspired by Byzantinism, which also plays an important role in Scarpa's work in the region around the city of Venice. Going back to Gottfried Semper's Dresden synagogue, Wagner designs the Budapest synagogue (1873–88) in the eclectic style in which he returns to the formal idiom of Byzantium.

»However, it is in the Church am Steinhof that the spirit of Byzantium is felt most strongly. It is the religious quietism of late antiquity and the Orthodox Church that distinguish the space under the starry sky of the inner cupola, flooded with light and directionless, from the directional buildings of the West. It is the term »abstract« that applies to this architecture, the wall appears to be unelastic and rigid ...«[11]

The fact that they were inspired by Byzantium and had a strong interest in history is another important commonality between Otto Wagner and Carlo Scarpa. Traditional motifs and principles form the basis for a modern stylistic idiom that is determined by structure and choice of material. »The architect can draw from the bountiful treasure house of tradition; but there can be no question of this being the copying of what he selects; rather, he must, through reworking that which is traditional, adapt it to his purpose or find out, from the effect of the existing models, the effect intended by him.«[12] For Wagner, the congruence between the development of art, architecture, and cladding is obvious and forms a unified style.[13] Scarpa's work shows the interaction of the development of art and architecture in his professional activity as an architect and designer of exhibitions. Both areas mutually influence each other, and his experience in the world of art is translated as motifs and types in his architecture. Wagner transforms cladding into a layer detached from the main structure – consisting of individual sheets or surfaces, it is attached visibly on its support: »The new architecture will be dominated by sheetlike, slab-type surfaces and by the striking use of materials in their original state.«[14]

Wagner interprets the wall as a plane surface, as in the Haus am Schottenring 23 (1877). »Otto Wagner created an architecture that not only implies, but also clearly expresses a clear change in how we see things, the almost total decline of Romanticism, and an emphasis on functionality that usurps almost everything else.«[15] There is the classic division of a house into base, middle, and roof edge, but the façade has an innovative, two-dimensional design. In the Haus am Schottenring the surface of the main façade consists of different-colored triangles that fuse into one surface and whose motifs are reminiscent of an Oriental rug. Covering layers are made visible as affixed elements or are simulated.

Ákos Moravánszky describes the symbolism of attaching: »The visible attaching of the covering layer is in no case accounted for constructionally – not even in Wagner's work. There, this solution means that the applicative character of the shell is made visible, in the form of a stone cladding, the breaking down of a building into volumes and surfaces.«[16] By being transformed into slabs, the stone is deprived of its fundamental characteristic – heaviness – and symbolizes the duality of symbol and function. Wagner's ties to national or regional history were not very strong. »He tended to experience history as the general ›cultural‹ heritage of humankind, or, to be precise, as a demanding abstraction. In this, too, he was a descendent of Gottfried Semper and of the humanistic tradition.«[17] The only way he strives for local character as an attainable ideal of beauty is by using materials that are available locally. »As a result, buildings made of certain materials predominate in certain regions.«[18] In this, he is the opposite of Scarpa, whose regional ties to Venice and the Veneto region influence almost all his work. He transposes regional traditions of construction and form into a language of his own, and makes them part of their historical and cultural surroundings. In1898/99 Otto Wagner builds the »Majolica House« (Linke Wienzeile 40, Vienna), whose ceramic-clad façade has a continuous pattern of flowers and extends across the entire surface without consideration of the window apertures. The façade is thus given a two-dimensional textile character. Materials and the way they are used achieve not so much a haptic as a visual effect. Wagner emphasizes the »optic sense, not the sense of touch«.[19] Like Wagner in his Villa II in Vienna, Scarpa, too, uses linear elements in the Banca Popolare in Verona or the Negozio Gavina in Bologna, linking windows or giving structure to the surface, for instance, in the garden of the Fondazione Querini Stampalia or the wall enclosing the Brion cemetery.

Like scarcely any other architect, Wagner was influenced by the increasing technical potential of iron architecture, which was also moving in new formal directions. »While for Semper cladding was still the dominant formal element for a building's appearance, Wagner, reacting to the structural developments that had taken place in the meantime, also accepted that which was clad, the supporting structure, as a contributory factor in architecture.«[20] The elements of interior and exterior infill, structuring dictated by the type of construction, become visible. In Wagner's Karlsplatz streetcar stop (1894) he uses an iron structure and suggests that defined individual surfaces developed as infill. »It's the only way architecture can have originated ... All architecture developed from the construction and subsequently became an art form.«[21]

In addition to the direct and inevitable meeting of constructional »structural« sections in the form of structured knots, elements that serve in separating space or as furnishings are set off against each other by forming a transitional space. Double frames for panels create a definite separation that, because it is recessed, emphasizes the distance between elements. Wagner's tendency to structure flat surfaces and his increasing preference for abstraction develop from the very symmetrical design of the Majolica House to the gridlike cladding in his library blueprint, or that of the postal savings bank.

The use of new materials that are not tied to traditional forms, and a cladding-like use of marble that is contrary to its monolithic character, makes possible a break with traditional architectural idiom. Geretsegger writes: »Wagner used whatever new designs were available in such a way that it was possible to see directly the combined effect of the elements. He added elements and materials: he had them intersecting, projecting or receding in relationship to each other, and not merging into each other. The supporting pillars in the large central hall of the postal savings bank break through the glass ceiling; this makes it clear that they support the glass roof above. Wagner avoided a meaningless gentle connection.«[22] The new version of the surfaces brings

olivetti

From left to right

76. Otto Wagner, Villa Wagner II, Vienna, 1912 to 1913. Mosaic frieze connecting the window openings.
77. Carlo Scarpa, Banca Popolare, Verona, 1975 to 1980. Stone frieze connecting the windows at the lower portion of the façade.
78. Otto Wagner, Majolica House, Vienna, 1898 to 1899. Design of transition between the different parts of the building.
79. Carlo Scarpa, Banca Popolare, Verona, 1975 to 1980. Design of transition to the adjacent buildings.
80. Otto Wagner, Karlsplatz streetcar stop, Vienna, 1894. Steel construction with infill layers.
81. Otto Wagner, postal savings bank, Vienna, 1903. Cladding of the exterior façade emphasizing thickness and fasteners.
82. Carlo Scarpa, entrance to the Istituto Universitario di Architettura, Tolentini, Venice, 1966. Detail of the multiple layers of concrete wall elements and a stone door leaf.
83. Carlo Scarpa, Olivetti showroom, Venice, 1957 to 1958. Stone door leaf positioned in a thick layer of stone added to the historic façade.
84. Josef Hoffmann, church am Steinhof, Vienna, 1905–07. Exterior façade detail with pattern of fasteners.
85. Carlo Scarpa, courtroom Sala Manlio Capitolo, Venice, 1955. Wall paneling detail with nailing pattern.

about their separation from each other and thus a reinterpretation of the junctions of elements, giving new importance to these transitions. In Scarpa's work, the importance of the junction is again transformed into motifs that are of an ornamental nature. The »connection« becomes a central theme, just as important as the parts that are the reason for the linking. Because of Scarpa's delight in the play of mechanical connections and the will to clarify mechanical processes, constructional details, becoming independent, take the form of ornaments. For Wagner, the separation of the shell from the building and the emphasis on the fact that they are layered reaches its peak in the postal savings bank in Vienna (competition: 1903). Individual stone slabs provide the cladding elements, both interior and exterior, of the basic architectonic structure. Stratification has become an architectonically used means of expression and implies new methods for creating space.[23] In windows and cross sections, the two-dimensionality of the stone cladding is made visible. The surface of the building is not faux masonry, but enveloping areas of cladding. The design of the façade is completed by the representation of the anchoring bolts, which emphasize, in narrative form, the constructional component of the cladding. In the interior, the cladding of the stairway to the central hall consists of different-sized stone slabs. The way they are affixed is also made visible. The Church am Steinhof (1905/07) also uses the fastening motifs as decoration. In the interior of the church, the motif of the glass canopy again appears as the innermost ceiling layer.

Motifs such as framed zones of walls, ceilings, or surfaces are an integral component of Wagner's canon of forms. »A widespread aesthetic method of emphasizing the slablike, pictorial character of the façade, or of its individual elements, was framing them.«[24] The Neustiftgasse apartment building (1909/10) has a façade whose expressiveness manages completely without ornamental motifs. Above a colored base, the plaster façade extends till just below the cornice. It is subdivided in the form of a grid by a linear structure of plaster joints. The various fields that result are the façade's only »ornament«.

Wagner's initial use of cladded architecture leads to its further development by representatives of the Wagner school. Carlo Scarpa had begun working on Viennese architecture back in his student years. His teacher Guido Cirilli, a devotee of Art Nouveau, promoted research on Josef Hoffmann.

## Josef Hoffmann – contoured planes

Josef Hoffmann (1870–1956), a student of Wagner's, was to have a strong influence on the architectural development that followed. He, too, observes the principle of forming space by means of surfaces, especially as regards exterior façades. The tendency of »breaking up volume that is bordered by massive walls«[25] caused other means to be designated for defining space, such as planes or grids, which can define spatial sequences by displacement or overlaying. This is the basis for the use of the concept of stratification in architecture already sketched out by Semper. Ornament, for Hoffmann, is a legitimately applied part of architecture – Scarpa combined Hoffmann's dictum that ornament could be applied with Loos's understanding that the material is an autonomous element that needs no added ornament.

The architectonic development of Josef Hoffmann took place, like that of Carlo Scarpa, as a result of experimentation with designing exhibitions, which was by no means marginal to his creative work. »There is no doubt that the exhibitions are important stages in Hoffmann's total artistic career. It is even possible to speak without exaggeration of downright experimentation with new means of expression and methods of design: we refer here to a new preoccupation with Classicism in the Rome (1911) and Cologne (1914) pavilions. The ephemeral architecture that we usually encounter within the framework of an exhibition is from the outset a kind of rehearsal that contains a natural element of surprise. There, décor and festivity are completely congruent. The décor is the goal of experimentation, and festivity is the means; the décor is the crystallization of the design, the festivity is the unbridled flexibility of the event, the stage set that does not follow the laws of the durable material.«[26] Similarly, in Scarpa's work, exhibitions are a preparation and experiment with various motifs of stratification. With Hoffmann's Sanatorium Purkersdorf (1903 to 1905), a transition was defined within his work. The entire surface of the façade consists of marble elements that are »no more than vehicles of an architectonic order«.[27] The transition between façade and roof is not achieved by a ledge that conceals the hip of the roof, but only by a simple line. Openings are cut into the wall space, as it were, and their contours are accentuated by majolica frames.

Wagner's strategy of a balance between tradition and modernity was adopted by Hoffmann. Both Scarpa and Hoffmann planned exhibitions, designed furniture and tableware. Hoffmann's innovation – the »elementariness of the rooms« and open exposure of a concrete structure – differs in the design of interiors, great selectivity, and a high degree of detailing. Cladding as a theme emerges in a more sophisticated form in the interior, and differentiated strata become more clearly visible as a result of varying motifs and utilization of space. The processing of architectonic experience and models is a determining factor of the design process in the work of both Scarpa and Hoffmann. Hoffmann »analyzes the historical model, breaks it down into its constituents, and then redesigns it in accordance with his own carefully thought-out worldview. The final result is that the object in question is completely permeated by a characteristic Hoffmann aura.«[28]

Josef Hoffmann's Palais Stoclet in Brussels (1905–11) is, down to the last detail, an example of the systematic disassembling of the classical order of the building's elevation. The façades are clad with marble slabs, the edges of the planes are framed with bronze relief. This creates the impression that the whole building, like a house of cards, is made up of thin plates, something that is emphasized even more by the doubling of strips of relief at the corners. The windows under the roof have been shifted upward so far that they »protrude« from the surface of the wall near the ledge, which makes it impossible to recognize the wall as a three-dimensional body. The fact that the extremely thin plate of the canopy is supported by broad pillars indicates that Hoffmann not only avoids the forms of historical architecture, but also destroys the visual logic of the traditional context of architectural elements. In spite of the lack of ornamentation on the planes of the façade, the building by no means appears bare; quite the contrary, it looks as though it were pure cladding, a shell that conceals what it contains only in places; often, however, several strata of the shell are shown superimposed on each other, als though the planes were movable.

William R. Curtis writes the following about the Palais Stoclet: »The forms were coated in thin stone slab veneers detailed with linear mouldings to accentuate the planarity. On the interior materials were stern, rectilinear, and precise, and included polished marbles and rich wood finishes.«[29]

The volumes of the Palais Stoclet exhibit a thin marble veneer whose planes are framed with three-dimensional profiles of gilded metal. Certain aspects of Carlo Scarpa's Zentner House in Zurich (1964–68), with the framed contours of its exterior façade, are reminiscent of the Palais Stoclet. In the exterior façades, Scarpa clearly shows the additive character of the upper level of the façade. The new façade follows its own rules of design and looks as though it were attached to its supporting stratum in such a way that it can be dismounted. In the Gavina store in Bologna, Scarpa leans a concrete slab in front of the existing façade of the historic palace. The use of the wall paneling as a regular, continuous surface can be seen in Scarpa's interior. Doors are »cut out« of the material of the wall paneling, leaving a unified surface when they are closed. Because cabinets, shelves, and other furnishings are also integrated, the wall appears as a continuous surface that, in addition to the function of partitioning space, may also comprise other functions such as cabinets, shelves, or pictures.

In several respects Hoffmann was a precursor of the de Stijl movement,[30] which definitively separated surfaces from each other, using them as individual elements. In Italy, Josef Hoffmann was relevant for the architects of the Stile Liberty, and thus his influence on later architects was already established.[31] Scarpa knew Hoffmann's work and, as he said himself, was inspired by a number of Hoffmann's motifs.[32] He met Josef Hoffmann in 1933 in Venice, where the latter was planning the Austrian Pavilion for the Biennale. Three-dimensionally grouped rectangular forms, a motif Hoffmann used to structure planes, would later, together with multiply stepped framing, be a basic design motif of the Brion cemetery in San Vito di Altivole (1970–75). Hoffmann uses this play with rectangular forms for the first time in 1902 in the supraportas in the right-hand hall of the Secession Exhibition. The motif of multiple framing is a theme found in Byzantine brick construction or in the coffered ceilings of the temples of antiquity. Multiple frames form the gable of the Knips Summerhouse in Carinthia (1903). The project for the Austrian Pavilion of the International Art Exhibition in Rome (1911) also works with this motif; like those later used by Scarpa in the Brion cemetery, pillars and roof edge are designed in the form of a labyrinth by means of a kind of graduated fluting.[33]

In the process of simplifying forms Hoffmann turned to the abstract geometry of »cubical and crystalline«[34] forms. »What this means, however, is that in his work even decorative enrichment was carried out in a puritanically strictly limited manner – by repeating the simplest formal gestures, such as frames and the uncovering or adding of layers.«[35] The multiple frame illustrates stratification within a material and simulates substantial depth and three-dimensionality.

From left to right

86. Josef Hoffmann, supraportas relief, Secession Exhibition, Vienna, 1903. Relief ornament.
87. Carlo Scarpa, Brion cemetery, San Vito di Altivole, 1970–75. Relief ornament in concrete façade.
88. Josef Hoffmann, Austrian Pavilion for the International Art Exhibition, Rome, 1911. Linear ornamentation along building edges.
89. Carlo Scarpa, Brion cemetery, San Vito di Altivole, 1970–75. Façade of the chapel, linear ornamentation along openings and edges of façade.
90. Josef Hoffmann, Sanatorium Purkersdorf, Vienna, 1903–05. Framed façade planes.
91. Josef Hoffmann, Palais Stoclet, Brussels, 1905 to 1911. Framed façade planes.
92. Carlo Scarpa, Zentner House, Zurich, 1964 to 1968. Framed façade planes emphasizing building edges.

NEUSTIFT
GASSE 40

VENEZUEL

From left to right

93. Adolf Loos, Haus am Michaelerplatz, Vienna, 1909–11. Stone cladding on façade.
94. Carlo Scarpa, Museo Rivoltella, Trieste, 1963. Façade cladding.
95. Adolf Loos, Müller House, Prague, 1930. Bodouir, built-in furniture defines space.
96. Carlo Scarpa, Sereni apartment, former Ambrosini, Venice, 1952/53. Living room, built-in furniture.
97. Carlo Scarpa, Olivetti showroom, Venice, 1957 to 1958. Stairway as spatial sculpture.
98. Otto Wagner, Neustiftgasse 40, Vienna, 1909 to 1910. Cladding elements act as decorative pattern.
99. Carlo Scarpa, Venezuela Pavilion, Venice, 1954 to 1956. Panels and glass layers wrapping over roof and façade.

## Adolf Loos

Adolf Loos (1870–1933) concentrated completely on emphasizing the importance of materials. »If ornaments, molded parts, and curves are totally banished, we are still left with the secret of fine materials and the play of proportions« – an idea he adopted. Loos attacked the way architects overemphasize the decorative.

»Since ornament no longer has an organic connection with our culture, it is also no longer the expression of our culture. The ornament that is created nowadays has no human connections, no connection with world order.«[36]

Although in 1897/98 Loos did not yet have an explicitly negative attitude toward the Secession, he later increasingly becomes its critic. The divergent interpretation held by Loos of what is represented by ornamentation had already been formulated by Semper, in his earlier essay »Wissenschaft, Industrie und Kunst« (»Science, industry, and art«). »The most general requirement is that all ornaments must be decoration of surface areas, and this characteristic is already clear from our definition that all that is textile forms a sheath, a cover.«[37]

Loos writes that an appropriate stylistic idiom does not become possible until the old stylistic forms have been »definitively subverted by their use as ornaments«.[38] Though he implements ideas differently, Loos, too, develops his ideas on the basis of the treatises of the turn of the 20th century and adopts Semper's separation of surfaces into the floor, wall, and ceiling typology and agrees with the thesis of the textile origins of surface and space formation. When rugs are spread and hung, a space becomes habitable, and the nature of such rugs requires a structural framework. »To invent such a framework is the second task of the architect.«[39] The cladding is the nucleus of architecture, and »the ceiling is the oldest architectural detail.«[40] That fact also determines the rules of design that must be used. The actual carpeting of living spaces corresponds to the original concept of building when these carpets want to be simply carpets, not building stones.[41] In addition to making a space habitable, cladding – in the form of coats of paint and the like – can fulfill other functions, such as protection against the weather (paints on wood) or hygiene, for instance, tiles in bathrooms.[42] Loos's »law of cladding» goes as follows: »The possibility that the clad material might be mistaken for the cladding should be excluded in any case.«[43] Here, Semper's understanding of material plays an important role. Stratification in the form of »nailing on«[44] façades that merely satisfy people's sense of style is inconsistent with the principle that the material chosen should be appropriate to its use.

About the Baroque palaces of Vienna, Loos writes as follows: »Their ornamental details, their brackets, garlands of fruit, cartouches, and denticulations are nailed-on cast cement. No doubt this practice, which has only come to be used in this century, is completely justified. But it is quite out of the question to use it on forms whose origin is closely tied to the nature of a particular material simply because their use presents no technical difficulties. It would have been the artist's task to find a new stylistic idiom for the material. Anything else is imitation.«[45]

Adolf Loos passionately believes that materials must be used in accordance with their nature. He condemns materials that purport to be something else, or try to represent something else. »Matter must once again be seen as divine. Materials are almost mysterious substances. We need to feel deep awe and amazement that something like this was ever created. The idea of ›improving‹ a beautiful material that is perfect in itself with ornaments is a crime!«[46] Material, and its use and finish in a form appropriate to it, is to replace ornament, which has predominated so far.[47]

The use of new materials also gives rise to new formal modes of expression. Loos writes about the influence of materials on the use of forms: »Every material has its own stylistic idiom, and no material can claim the forms of another material for itself. For the forms have emerged from the usability and manufacturing method of each material, they have come into being with the material and through the material.«[48]

Carlo Scarpa, too, »idolizes the material and uses the specific colors and tactile qualities of a material as something that creates form and atmosphere«.[49] The characteristics of the material are used in the form of dimension, surface, and color in the formal design process. Added to this, there is the way the material was processed. Here, Scarpa also takes certain liberties and resorts to apparently paradoxical procedures. In the Fondazione Querini Stampalia, stone is treated like wood and thus covers two sets of circumstances. The characteristics of the material contain the information for stone, while its processing suggests slabs of wood. Scarpa regarded material as a substance that needed to be shaped, having a historical and cultural history, while Loos »never used these materials as pieces that were to be shaped«, »but always as smooth, connected surfaces, always as smooth as possible and always emphasizing their own material nature, almost as though they themselves were a kind of ornament«.[50] The apotheosis of material and color is a fundamental component of Scarpa's architectural idiom. Parallel to considering the material aspects of architecture, its associative interpretation must not be neglected, for when a form or a particular material is used, memories and associations are evoked.

»Scarpa's typical method is visible, especially in the travertine walls in the exhibition room which, apart from the traditional reuse of stone, recalls the picture of a metonymic change between wood and brick wall, for example between the wood of the bridge and the railing.«[51]

Adolf Loos uses structural elements that have associative power. In the Kärntner Bar, an establishment Carlo Scarpa was familiar with, he installs coffered ceilings,whose structure suggests the dignity of a Greek temple. »The forms Loos uses in the bar comprise elements that have appeared in his earlier work and recur in his later work: the classical pillar, mirrors set between the pillars, the high gloss of the wood-paneled walls and the marble coffered ceiling. The treatment of the marble – panels cut from a single block and regularly framed by brass bead borders – indicates various interpretive approaches: on the one hand the repetition of the coffer form, on the other the principle of ›cladding‹ characteristic of Gottfried Semper (1803–1879).«[52]

»He by no means rejects the historical roots, but seeks a new way of integrating historical values. »You check to see which buildings in earlier times were already capable of producing these feelings. Those are the ones you have to use as your starting point. Because human beings have spent their lives praying in certain kinds of spaces, drinking in certain kinds of spaces. Feelings are matter of nurture, not nature. Consequently architects, if they're serious about their art at all, need to show consideration for these feelings that have been instilled in people.«[53]

Loos's understanding of space is manifested in the way he develops his »Raumplan« (space plan), which allocates to each interior its own specific properties – height and width; Loos's plans indicate that he worked in the third dimension and had strong powers of imagination when it came to creating volume.

»However, so far we've seen concepts that are basically two-dimensional, like those of a painter. The three dimensions are not experienced simultaneously, but in succession. In reality what has been visualized is the layout, elevation, and sections: in other words, planes, and perhaps a very rapid sequence of two-dimensional strata may come quite close to a unified three-dimensional view. That's how I can imagine it myself to some degree, and that is why I feel the difference with a great sculptor's building's unassembled, immediate, three-dimensional conception, which can be completely understood perhaps only by someone who has the same type of talent. Here, he has thought, invented, composed, designed in space, without makeshift devices, without auxiliary levels, elevations and sections; directly, as though all solids were transparent; the way our mind's eye has space before it in all its parts and simultaneously as a whole.«[54]

»I do not design ground plans, façades, sections, I design space. Actually, in my work there is neither a ground floor, upper floor, nor a basement, there are only connected spaces, vestibules, terraces. Every room has to be a certain height – the dining rom different from the pantry – and that is why the ceilings are on different levels. Afterward, these rooms need to be connected in such a way that the transition is unnoticeable and natural but also as functional as possible. I realize others consider that a mystery, while it is self-evident to me.«[55] The space plan is a concept that allows each room to have its specific characteristics and whose goal is the differentiation of the interior.

An important element of spatial design are stairways, a connection between floors. »In all of Loos's buildings, the stairway as a connecting link and as part of the room constitutes an important organizing element in the way rooms are interconnected.«[56] Loos integrates spatial elements such as stairways as built-in furniture into the apartment unit. Scarpa uses stairways sculpturally as connecting elements, for instance in the Taddei apartment, or in the Olivetti store, where the stairways stand in space as autonomous objects.

Walls in contrast to the stairway create the character of the individual room as an overarching element. As in Scarpa's work as well, the wall consists of various forms of cladding and is frequently divided into three in the classic way. Manlio Brusatin describes the connection between Scarpa and Loos: »In many details of the furnishings and the remodeling a latent interest in Adolf Loos can be detected.«[57]

Johannes Spalt writes: »The wainscoting often chosen by Loos, wooden wall paneling (mahogany or painted white), is subdivided into various heights. In its lower level it incorporates bookcases or shelves, display cases, radiators, and the typical upholstered corner bench.«[58] Wall cladding need not be a two-dimensional layer of fabric or paint, but may take over the function of furnishing. In the miniscule Ambrosini (now Sereni) apartment the inner wall covering provides almost the entire furnishings, down to the folding tables, radiator covers, etc. Loos integrates pictures as panels in his wall cladding in order to preserve the character of a wall layer.[59] Borders and transitions are formed by ledges. For Loos stratification meant total cladding, the layers that are superimposed on each other are not shown by being laid bare. They lie on the same plane, separated by ledges or butt joints.

»Loos's interventions in existing structure no longer correspond to this hierarchy of scale of the classic metropolis. They are not interpretations but reinterpretations, not conversions but modifications. This kind of modification affects the building's ›substance‹ by calling it into question – but not by eliminating it. Loos's interventions fall into a few categories.One of them might be described as the adding of spatial layers: in the case of the Villa Karma on the exterior, but generally in the interior, the architect introduces not only a covered layer of material, but a layer of space that enters into relation with the rest of the space. The original spatial configuration is thus modified or counteracted in the service of new, often axial spatial connections; the layer of space itself provides small rooms, connecting passages, or built-in cabinets.«[60]

## 2.2. Frank Lloyd Wright the model

Frank Lloyd Wright was an important model for Scarpa, and unlike Scarpa he made a large number of statements about his view of architecture. In spite of the geographical distance between them, Scarpa's and Wright's architectural and cultural spheres of influence have a great deal in common. Wright works with elements of historical and folkloric aesthetics, keeps one eye on Japan, and is aware of contemporary European trends. During a stay in Italy he had the opportunity to study Florentine architects, sculptors, and painters such as Giotto, Arnolfo, Pisano, Brunelleschi, Bramante, Sansovino, and Michelangelo.[1] Wright got to know Japan as early as 1905 during his first trip there. Later this affinity was to be deepened when, in 1915–20, Wright was commissioned to design the Imperial Hotel in Tokyo. Wright, too, valued the Vienna Secession, and in 1909, during his European journey, discovered that he was referred to as »the American Olbrich«.[2] Scarpa had extensive documents about the work of Frank Lloyd Wright.[3] He met him in Venice in 1951 when an honorary doctor's degree was bestowed on Wright by the faculty of architecture of the University of Venice, and an exibition Scarpa had helped design took place in Florence. Francesco Dal Co describes the meeting of the two architects as follows:

»But the meeting with Wright, unavoidable for many reasons, was not motivated by formal considerations alone. Intellectual curiosity is the driving force behind Wright's language as well. The American architect's forms are intended to awaken and control suggestions that come from cultural traditions of different origins, destined in turn to leave their sediments in planned experiments. Like Scarpa, Wright is a collector of images and an acute observer. Though both of them worked in such different milieux and certainly with opposite goals, they attribute, in their own work, a great deal of importance to the problem of tradition, in the meantime giving free expression to compositional hypothesis, aware that all stylistic rules have been profaned.«[4]

In addition to designing various exhibitions[5] that are reminiscent of Wright's formal idiom, projects that were completed during the period of close collaboration with a young architect Angelo Masieri (up to 1952), such as the Casa Romanelli in Udine (1950–55), are evidence of the inspiration exerted by the American master. The openings in the roof, which corbels outwards horizontally a long way, and the arrangement of air volumes and organization of the building's interior reveal their models.

The sketches of the ground plan for the Villa Zoppas (1952/53) are reminiscent of Frank Lloyd Wright's graphics. In 1967, during a trip to the US, Scarpa visits some of Frank Lloyd Wright's buildings and is disappointed that »nothing about Wright's architecture is true«.[6] The organic architecture in the context of which Zevi speaks both of Scarpa and of Wright[7] attempts to remain in keeping with the nature of the building. Frank Lloyd Wright himself writes as follows about organic architecture: »In organic architecture it is completely impossible to regard the building as one thing, the furnishings as another, and the location and surroundings as something else again. The spirit in which these buildings are conceived sees all this together as one thing.«[8]

A building by Wright functions as an organism in which such factors as outside and inside, character and functionality, method of production, place and time, are congruous.[9] »In organic architecture every conception of a building qua building starts at the beginning and proceeds to a secondary expression as an image; it does not begin with some secondary expression as an image and then move backward. That isn't modern.«[10] Scarpa, in Venice, achieves the integration

100. Carlo Scarpa, Angelo Masieri, Romanelli House, Udine, 1950–55. Partial exterior façade and roof overhang with perforations.
101. Frank Lloyd Wright, Coonley House, Riverside, Illinois, 1907–09. Partial exterior façade and roof overhang with perforations.

of architecture into his context by using local materials and bringing in the historical motifs and technologies of his geographical region. The ground floor of the Fondazione Querini Stampalia reacts to the given conditions of high tide and in response forms architectonic elements – gutters – that control high tide instead of excluding it.

With regard to integrating a building in the landscape, Wright himself writes that architecture cannot be set »on a hill«, but must be »part of the hill«, »belong to it, so that the hill and the house could live together, each of them made all the happier because of the other«.[11] Building thus becomes »four-dimensional«,as »the space surrounding the building becomes a natural part of space«.[12]

Wright builds the Hotel Imperial in Tokyo from lava stone, which he had seen »in Tokyo and in the earth«.[13] Even Wright's orientation towards historical architecture corresponds with Scarpa's interests: »In those early days I was fascinated by the vestiges of the Mayas, Incas, and Egyptians, and I loved the Byzantine ... I loved the Byzantine of the Hagia Sophia – a genuine domed building in contrast to Michelangelo's mixed cupola.«[14] In Wright's opinion the ancient peoples come close to the ideal of »organic architecture»and the »beautiful»: Mongols, Indians, Arabs, Egyptians, Greeks, and Goths had the right idea of the beautiful. »They had the knowl-

edge of beauty in a highly developed sense.«[15] On this point his view resembles that of Gottfried Semper, who feels that his ideal picture of textile architecture was made a reality primarily by the ancients. Style is created by organic elaboration, for all individuals have style in them. Style is a product of nature and the »result of a project in character,and an emotional state«.[16]

Edward Ford writes: »Although Otto Wagner and Auguste Perret were basically classicists, Wagner built in layers and Perret built monolithically. Others, including Frank Lloyd Wright, used both systems at different periods of their careers. (Julien Guadet, the chief theoretician of the Beaux-Arts at the end of the 19th century, recognized both systems as acceptable methods of construction, and many architects employed both systems simultaneously.)«[17] The use of spatial stratification enabled Wright to develop new wall-less floor-plan forms with fluid transitions in lieu of abrupt separation. Wright uses material stratification as a possibility for applying material that allows the architect to form desired ambiences intentionally and to combine materials and colors that give the elements dynamic force. Cladding in the work of Wright is an atectonic masking of the structures, which achieves the classical tripartite façade on the exterior, while inside it creates a characteristic space and elucidates or symbolizes the nonvisible construction.[18] Wright differentiates the elements of floor, wall, and ceiling (for instance, in the first Jacobs House in Westmorland, Wisconsin, 1936/37) by means of different materials or technical formulation. He overcomes the role of a homogeneous wall, which limits space, by transforming it into screens. Here is what he says about a model of the Larkin Building: »Suddenly the model was in the middle of the room on the studio table. I came in and saw what needed to be done. I took the four corners and pulled them away from the building, made them into independent elements, positioned them. And that was the beginning of what I was trying to achieve ... I now had characteristics instead of walls. I pursued this further with the Unity Church, where there were no actual walls any more but only determining elements, namely screens arranged to form the interior.«[19]

»Organic architecture, to put it briefly, never regards the third dimension as weight or mere thickness, but always as depth. Depth is a spatial element; the third dimension is transformed into a spatial dimension. Penetrating the inner depths of space becomes an architectonic and valid design motif. This depth perception that penetrates the depths causes to bloom a freedom of design never heretofore known by architects, who can now use it in their blueprints – a true liberation of life and light inside the building; new structural integrity; the outside comes inside; and space in which we live is projected outward.«[20]

Spatial depth is an important effect that can be achieved by spatial stratification. Wright employs various mechanisms in order to create space. As an alternative to buildings with boxlike enclosed rooms, he works with fluid space.

»The interior consisted of boxes side by side with other boxes called rooms. All the boxes were in turn contained in a complicated box. Every »function« of a house lay tiditly in box after box. I didn't see much sense in these barriers, this cell-like isolation, which reminded me of my predecessors, who were familiar with prison cells – except for the seclusion of the bedrooms on the top floor. These were possibly useful as »sleep boxes«. That is why I declared the whole lower floor to be a single room, cut the kitchen off as a laboratory, placed the bedrooms and living rooms of the servants next to the kitchen, but somewhat removed from it, on the ground floor, screened off various parts of the big room for certain purposes – such as for eating, reading, or receiving a formal visitor ... The house became ›freer‹ as a space, as well as more habitable. The time of inner expanse began.«[21]

The additional dimension that is important for Wright is the »feeling of space«.[22] Wright quotes Lao-tzu, who »was the first to declare that the reality of a building is inherent not in the four walls and the roof but the interior, the space in which one lives. Floor, wall, and ceiling are thus means of illustrating the desired space, which, however, is independent of them. Space is an active medium, can »leave or enter wherever life happens to be lived at the moment«.[23] Otto Maria Graf calls spatial structure »space in the process of becoming«, an evolving process. The Avery Coonley House (1907) shows the far-reaching principle of the »open ground plan«, the surroundings are »enclosed, included in the building« and the ground plan of the house develops with the uses it is put to.[24]

A noticeable horizontal stacking of elements can be seen especially in the Kaufmann House (Fallingwater 1935/36). The massive balustrades of the cantilevered terraces form square blocks that are partly overlapped by the narrower bands of the projecting ceilings, which are partly massive and partly perforated. The horizontal stratification of elements achieves the vertical integration of the buildings in the landscape. Like tableaux, the terraces, pergola structures, and ceilings that

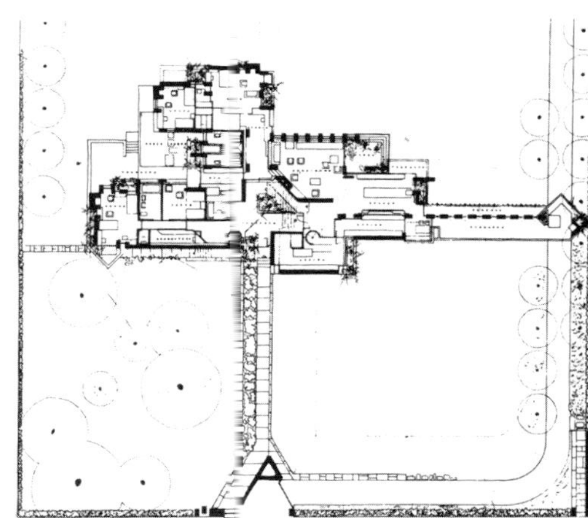

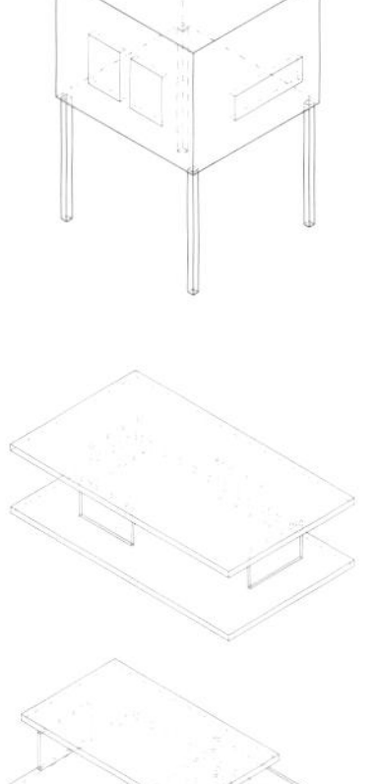

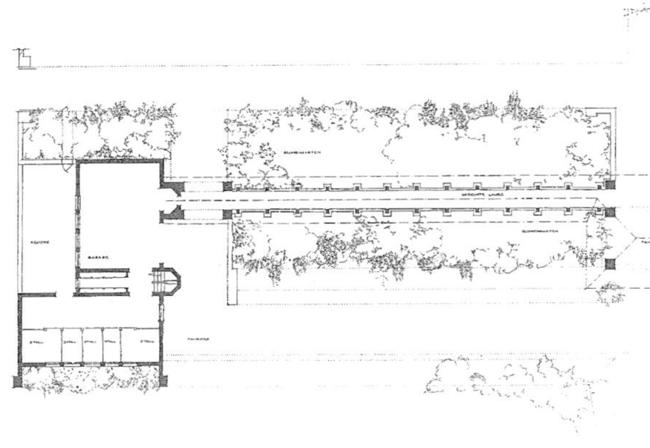

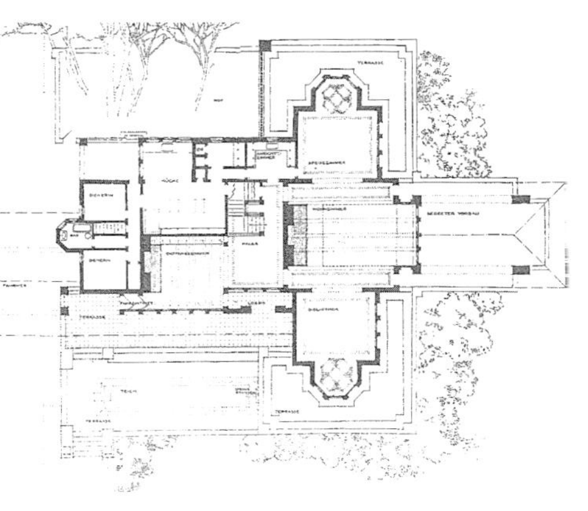

From left to right

102. Frank Lloyd Wright, Taliesin, Spring Green, Wisconsin, 1911–25. Exterior blending with surrounding vegetation.
103. Carlo Scarpa, Ottolenghi House, Bardolino, 1974–78. Exterior integrated into hillside and vegetation.
104. Frank Lloyd Wright, Kaufmann House, Bear Run, Pennsylvania, 1935/36. Exterior view of cantilevering volumes.
105. Carlo Scarpa, Hotel Bauer, Venice, 1949. Sketch of exterior showing cantilievering volumes.
106. After Frank Lloyd Wright, diagram showing the decomposition of the box into separate planes.
107. Frank Lloyd Wright, Villa Metzger, Sault Ste. Marie, Michigan. Floor plan.
108. Carlo Scarpa, Villa Zoppas, Conegliano, 1952 to 1953. Floor plan.

project from the living spaces overlap. There are also the monolithic rocks of the waterfall, with the house towering over it. The natural stone walls were once part of the land and connect the remaining parts with the ground on which they stand.

Frank Lloyd Wright strives for constructed harmony created by a compositional balance of the elements. Balance is the basic principle of designing with space and cladding. He speaks of the »grammar«[25] of a style and of the material, a structure behind his working method and certain givens that characterize the language and applicability of materials. Regarding the Kaufmann House (Fallingwater) he states: »Each will have its own grammar, appropriate for the material involved, such as in a new ›grammar‹ of ›Fallingwater‹, my first reinforced concrete home. If the simple knowledge of the grammar, the syntax of the organic design were turned into a reality, every building would show its essence in an honest differentiation of form – of a type that a sensitive architect could accomplish for a bright, knowledgeable owner.«[26] The Pew House (1940) also radiates the horizontal stratification of the balustrades and ceilings, reinforced by the duality of the natural stone walls and wood paneling. In the Pausan House (Phoenix, Arizona, 1939/40), the wooden parts of the façades seem to move apart, while the stone elements are anchored in the earth.

The influence of the type of vertical volume formation and horizontal stratification is discernible in Scarpa's 1949 design for an apartment house in Feltre. The volume is determined by horizontal stratification consisting of balcony balustrades and projecting ceiling slabs. The blueprint for the Bauer Hotel in Venice (1949) also has a horizontal volume structure.

The fusion of the interior and exterior that Wright was striving for is produced by the overlapping of inner and outer areas. Overhanging walls incorporate space and interweave the structures. Covered porches tie outside space to the living areas, as in the villa for Victor Metzger in Sault Ste. Marie (Michigan): A covered porch connects the outdoors with the living room; the quality of the space becomes more permeable from inside (stove) to outside; terraced levels and a pond form the transition of the floor elements; pergolas and scaffolds are the connecting link with the walls. The Coonley House (1907) shows the development from the Semper element of the hearth as the center of the house outward to more open areas. It also shows the separation of ceiling elements, walls, and floor elements.

Scarpa's project for the Villa Zoppas in Conegliano (project 1952/53) experiments with the principle of the open ground plan and with the fluid transitions from interior to exterior. The fusion is also produced by way of Mies's principle of overhanging walls that connect and string together interior and exterior spatial layers. Maria Antonietta Crippa writes: »The Villa Zoppas in Conegliano was planned in three different phases. In these Scarpa moved from a very open ground plan, expanded, still mindful of Mies van der Rohe's interiors and exteriors, into a compact arrangement, linked primarily to the study of Wright's rhomboid forms ... The space was articulated around the entrance, a pivot of the whole and point of connection of the orthogonal planes and the diagonal in the plan and elevation. In this project the decorative elements in the style of Wright are clearly defined: from the round pillars that are repeated at every nodal point of the plan, to the mirrors on the edges of the high central part, to the design of the large circular openings in the solid masonry wall, to the way a natural element enters the atrium in the form of large planters.«[27]

In the work of Frank Lloyd Wright, spatial stratification is extremely important – an interior that can be experienced three-dimensionally. Two-story air volumes connect spatial planes and at the same time make it possible to experience the various floors simultaneously. Linear ledges structure the height of a room at two different levels, which are emphasized by different lighting and treatment of material. For instance, Neil Levine writes about the Willits House (1902/03): »Conceived as a series of layers permeating and permeated by space, the Willits House becomes an enveloping presence in its urban context.«[28]

In several of the »Usonian Houses«, for instance, the Palmer House in Ann Arbor, Wright uses pillars to give the house structure. Scarpa also adopts this principle in the Negozio Gavina, in Bologna, whose interior is structured by massive, different-colored pillars. Scarpa's Veritti House (1955/61) is evidence that Scarpa on occasion followed Wright's three-dimensonality and stylistic idiom.[29] The arrangement of pillars defines the space and extension of the building, while varying room heights emphasize the third dimension. The Casa Veritti quotes not only the construction method of the structured concrete in the pillars of the house, but also their arrangement. Here Scarpa tries, by means of air volume in the living area, to achieve the three-dimensionality present in Wright's spaces. »Scarpa's intentions in Udine continued to be associated with Wright's geometric theme.«[30] The entrance floor consists of one large room, with various parts of the room screened off for their respective uses. The circular shape of the largely closed back wall of the

Casa Veritti is completed by a pond, which is part of the garden design. A transparent winter garden creates an open transition from the inside to the outside. At the same time the fireplace area and the winter garden obtain their effect from the central day room. The exterior façade is structured by ornamented concrete elements, which again are reminiscent of Wright's models. In the Ottolenghi House, too, Scarpa achieves the fluid integration of the interior and exterior space by pillars positioned in both areas.

### Strata of material

In Wright's buildings, material is stratified in order to cover the load-bearing structure. »It never occurred to either Wright or to Sullivan that they could lay bare these construction systems. Ornaments and décor were what Wright called the ›blooming‹, which expressed the character of that building.«[31] The Winslow House demonstrates horizontally articulated exterior clothing.[32] It is classically subdivided into a base (stone cladding), a middle (textile-like terracotta cladding), and the roof. The construction is in accordance with prevailing conditions and is transformed by the cladding to be the expression of the building. In this context, Fanelli speaks of stratification from below to above: »Very frequently he uses cladding in forms that are tantamount to masking the structure completely and that follow the law of stratification from below to above, always indicating that the wall is tectonically rooted in the ground, never showing that the cladding is actually an applied or suspended layer. Usually what seems to be brick or stone structure is really clad-ding. And as late as this century's first decade, wood construction is resolved in the continuity of a plaster surface that produces the visual effect of traditional masonry or concrete.«[33]

»The walls of the ›Miniatura‹ (Millard House, Pasadena, California, 1922/23) are formed from two ›textile‹ walls that are connected by steel reinforcement and consist of concrete blocks that are in turn woven together with steel grid reinforcements. The walls have become small but reinforced concrete panels, decorated with embossed concrete panels duing manufacture. Because of the rich inlaid work of the moulds, the stone wall of the »Miniatura« is slightly corrugated. In part, the cement blocks have been made pervious to light by inset glass panes; in this way the interior wall is animated by an incredible play of light such as no architect has ever imagined.«[34]

In the Millard House, one of the »Maya Houses« (Passadena 1921–23) the textile concept is not only applied externally as a reminiscence, but also provides the constructional solution. The building consists of two frameworks and was erected without foundation walls, standing on the ground like a giant, artificial monolith. The ornamentation in Scarpa's Brion cemetery brings up associations with Wright's concrete ornamentation.

The »lining« of interiors with two-dimensional planes that also had the function of being furnishings simplifies the usability of small spaces and obviates the excessive use of furniture. In the Scatturin House in Venice, Scarpa designed wooden wall paneling that, depending on its position in the apartment, turns into a shelf, cabinet, or door. Material layers on the ceiling emphasize the directions of movements created by the way rooms are used. The cladding of the ceiling – reflected in the floor – forms an independent space within a space, embodies an illustrated independence from the immovable historical substance of the building. Its colors echo those of the surrounding roofs of Venice. In the Ambrosini Apartment (1952/53; from 1995: Sereni Apartment) a stratum of furnishings that is layered in front of the walls and corresponds to the furnishings of a yacht provides a complete interior skin. Because of the alternating use of different types of woods and surfaces, the furnishings have a differentiated haptic quality. Metal joints and details such as integrated folding tables call up nautical associations from shipbuilding, celebrating the fact that the apartment is located in Venice. Frank Lloyd Wright strives for perfect paneling – for instance, in the wooden fittings of the Kaufmann Office. In Scarpa's paneled rooms there is the didactic factor, when the paneling reveals its backing or shows its character where there is an opening.

Wright states: »There is no difference between the floor and the masonry.«[35] His late Prairie houses quote the invisible roof construction in their ceiling design. Double wall frames or ceiling frames, such as those in the Darwin D. Martin House, 1904, differentiate elements from each other. The ceilings contain references to the actual construction, represented by clothing that is installed atectonically. Their character is visibly two-dimensional, and they are set off from the wall by framing.

For Wright, abstraction is the »innermost essence of a thing, its pattern«. For him the core of an object lies in eliminating everything that is not essential; »if this is done well: the linear and spa-

From left to right

109. Frank Lloyd Wright, Davidson House, Buffalo, New York, 1908. Space stratification horizontally oriented.
110. Carlo Scarpa, Casa Veritti, Udine, 1955–61. Space stratification horizontally oriented.
111. Frank Lloyd Wright, Pew House, Shorewood Hills, Wisconsin, 1940. Cantilevering volumes with wood siding.
112. Carlo Scarpa, Apartment building, Feltre, 1949. Sketches showing cantilevering volumes with wood siding.
113. Frank Lloyd Wright, Palmer House, Ann Arbor, Michigan, 1950. Floor plan.
114. Carlo Scarpa, Casa Veritti, Udine, 1955–61. Floor plan.
115. Frank Lloyd Wright, German Warehouse, Richland Center, Wisconsin, 1916–21. Ornamented cornice element.
116. Carlo Scarpa, Casa Veritti, Udine, 1955–61. Façade ornaments.

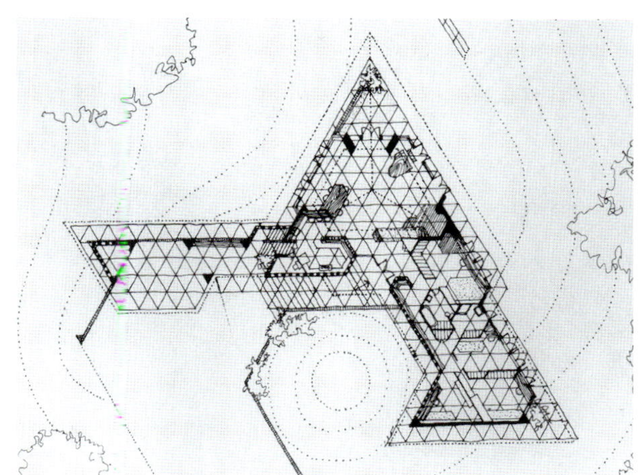
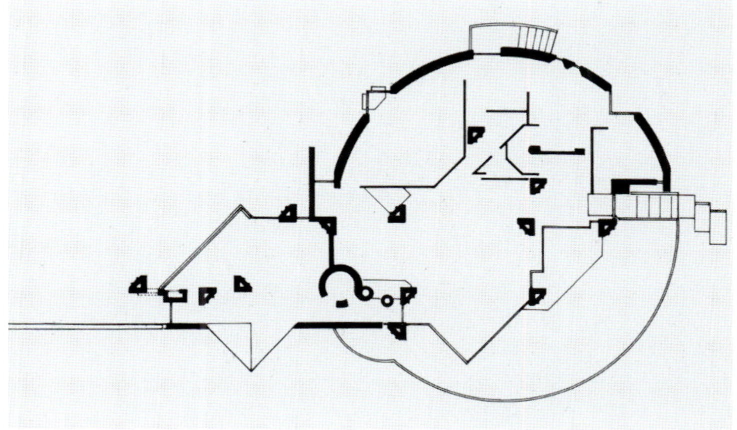

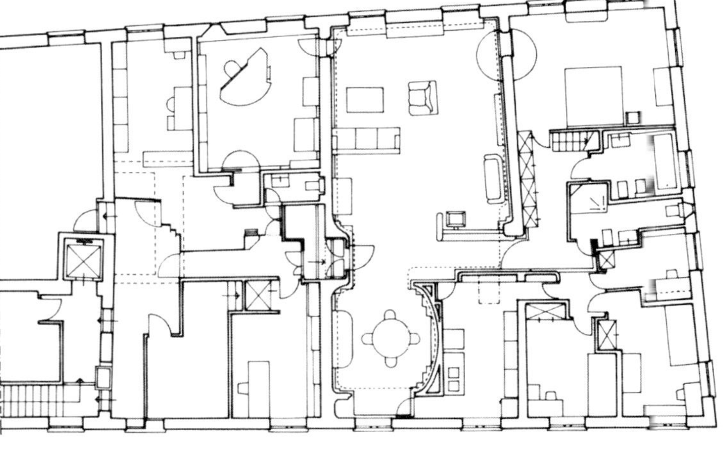

From left to right

117. Carlo Scarpa, Brion cemetery, San Vito di Altivole, 1970–75. Decorative concrete treatment on exterior.
118. Frank Lloyd Wright, La Miniatura, Pasadena, California, 1921–23. Concrete blocks with decorative treatment on exterior of building.
119. Frank Lloyd Wright, Jacobs House, Westmorland, Wisconsin, 1936/37. Layer of ceiling paneling.
120. Frank Lloyd Wright, Coonley House, Riverside, Illinois, 1906–09. Resolution of ceiling layers into individual areas.
121. Carlo Scarpa, Scatturin House, Venice, 1962/1963. Ceiling being made of a colored layer of plaster detached from the walls floating above the space.
122. Carlo Scarpa, Scatturin House, Venice, 1962/1963. Floor plan showing ceiling outline.

tial meaning of inner reality – that is what must be brought into form.«[36] Clarity of the right idea is the search for the true meaning of the elements: »The real meaning of a line, color, and form is now the only true method of construction.«[37]

### Materiality

Parallels between the two masters appear in the apotheosis of the material: in accordance with the principles of organic architecture, Wright uses material as is appropriate to its nature. The beauty of individual materials lies in their characteristics. Wright develops the ideal that every material must be used in accordance with its nature on the basis of a characteristic grammar that honors the material and its own striving for form. Characteristics such as grain, structure, and color determine design and use. Accordingly new materials bring into use new forms and structures: »New expressiveness in architecture means that new materials determine the form and structures, and demands a new outlook that in the end characterizes both as ornament.«[38] He was impressed by how Japanese architecture treated material: »No Western nation has ever used wood with such understanding as did the Japanese in their buildings, where wood always appeared and stood out in noble beauty.«[39] Glass, for Wright, is the embodiment of the new freedom of space, which leads to organic architecture. Wright describes his attitude regarding the use of materials as follows: »But I learned to see a brick as a brick. I learned to see wood as wood, and concrete, glass, or metal each by itself and as what it was.«[40]

## 2.3. Japanese aesthetics: mobile layers

»Later I found that Japanese art and architecture really did have organic character. Their art was nearer to the earth and a more indigenous product of native conditions of life and work, therefore more nearly modern as I saw it, than any European civilization alive or dead.«[1]

As Frank Lloyd Wright writes above, traditional Japanese architecture held great interest for many early-20th-century architects. Bruno Taut, for instance, »discovered« the Katsura Imperial Palace as a source of inspiration and an example of the successful harmony of proportions and geometries; he admired »the reduction of architecture to a combination of surfaces that implied the idea of a montage of simple elements«.[2]

Walter Gropius, too, values the culture of Japanese architecture, its beauty and simplicity: »I have never seen a better example of an integrated culture than Japan ... Beauty, for instance, a cultural factor of great importance more and more lacking in the Western world, is still a basic requirement of life for the Japanese.«[3]

Searching for flexibility and exploring the possibilities of industrial prefabrication, Gropius discovers an already fully developed modular system based on flexibility, modular design, and standardized products that imply problem solutions that are still being sought in Western architecture. »I had found, if only in illustrations, that the old handmade Japanese houses had already all the essential features required today for a modern prefabricated house, namely, modular coordination – the standard mat, a unit of about 3 x 6'– and movable wall panels.«[4]

The relation between inside and outside produced by the flexibility of interior and exterior walls, the multifunctional rooms, and the balance between individuality and subordination to a general principle become a model for the development of modern architecture. Kenzo Tange writes about the structural principles of the Katsura Palace in Kyoto: »Instead of defying gravity, they have preferred to seek space in which to spread out horizontally. Thus, in the Japanese concept of architectural space, the organization and balance of forces is reduced to two dimensions; what one has is a succession of planes. The proportions of structural members are governed not only by physical principles but simply by aesthetic sensibility.«[5]

The principles of modern architecture were combined with the Japanese conception of creating space. Arata Isozaki also traces the curve from traditional Japanese architecture to the architecture of the 20th century: »Thus, in the large buildings that had now become free of load-bearing walls, movable partitions and curtain-wall façades, comparable to fusuma and shoji, can be installed, whereby interior design became more transparent.«[6]

Yasuhiro Ishimoto traces the curve to Chicago: »It was amazing to me that in this Shoin architecture I rediscovered all the basic elements of the modern architecture of Chicago that was so familiar to me, for my vocation as an artist had first come to light as I contemplated the pure geometry of the glass surfaces and metal structures of Mies van der Rohe's buildings in Chicago. It was an inspiring experience for me when, in this monument of the classical architecture of my country of origin, I discovered not only approximations or reminiscences of modern architecture, but rather its sources.«[7]

Traditional Japanese architecture strives for the unity of nature, building, and use. The Japanese garden frequently works in a small area with space markings, elements that as a part point to a more distant whole. Elements serve as symbolic markers for another context. Thus a stone can represent the mountain that is incorporated in the artificial landscape of the garden. It is a narrative »pars pro toto« that extends the space of the garden in imagination and raises it to the level of an associative landscape. The delimitation of space is proposed, complexity and distance are suggested by multiple planes. »In contrast to the medieval walled city or cloister in the West, Japanese sacred spaces were usually suggested or implied rather than enclosed ... For the Japanese, gates (torii), fences, straw ropes, and even cloth banners acted as signs to demarcate spaces. Shrines were thus more a mental construct than a tangible compound, a place which existed in the mind rather than a place that could be seen.«[8]

The commonalities between Japanese architecture and Carlo Scarpa's architectonic work are based on active interest, which, once discovered, continues to develop and grow. In an interview Carlo Scarpa describes this as follows: »Yes, I've been strongly influenced by Japan, not only because I was there, but even before I went there I admired their essentiality and above all their supreme good taste. What we call good taste, they have everywhere. It is an unsophisticated taste, plain, not exactly peasant, but almost. Many have also looked in the direction of China, but in their personal virtues the Japanese are simple and have an incredible purity.«[9]

The intentional treatment of materials, the deliberate use of the effects of light and shadow, the poeticizing and symbolic function of spaces and elements are commonalities that have to do primarily with an attitude of mind. The fact that Scarpa owned several books about Japanese architecture and horticulture attests to his interest.[10] Scarpa first traveled to Japan in 1967, not many years before his work on the Brion cemetery. His second trip to Japan, during which he died in an accident, took place in 1978.

Influenced by Zen Buddhism, the Japanese searched for the principle of the »deepest silence, a connection with the eternal and infinite«.[11] It may be explained as a »striving for the beauty of imperfection». It is true that a perfect thing may be beautiful, but »it is without poetic charm and leaves no room for the imagination«.[12]

The strongest parallel in Scarpa's work with Japanese architectural culture are factors that transcend matter, which are hard to describe. In addition to related motifs like stepping stones, which create associative connections, the reference of objects to something beyond them and the treatment of materials is shaped by the interest in Japan. The nonphysical level of Scarpa's designs allows us associations and accounts for the fact that his buildings can be openly interpreted: imperfection in the sense of lack of completion is the principle of his building modifications, which with their partly fragmentary interventions give rise to the aesthetics of sedimentative assemblage. What characterizes Scarpa's poetics are references to a wider sphere, to cultural associations that go beyond the physical form and the treatment of elements. The complexity of indirect and nonphysical relationships is the subject of this book, the reason why I attempt to construct the different possible spheres of Scarpa's influence as connections.

In Japanese culture imaginative space comprises detaching one segment of the space from its context; this is distinguished from the rest of the world as a holy and power-laden element.

»The prototype of such a space may be a stone or a post. Detached from its original surroundings, it receives a definite place, character, by being erected or positioned. As a result the stone expresses more than its original and natural accidental form. Wishes are projected into matter, making spirit out of stone. In other words, the stone is space for spirit. It is animated by a meaning projected by human beings.«[13]

Scarpa's motifs are given life by this type of projection of meaning. They include references to traditional building elements and to the aestheticized process of production and manufacture. Scarpa's power of imagination, which enables him to present not only the object itself but also a circle of association surrounding it, is what creates the much-described poetic charm of his works, elevating the work above the arbitrariness of the forms he has used.

Symbolic elements – like the column of a Japanese farmhouse – form an imaginary space. »The symbolic column in the Japanese farm house demonstrates this twofold visualization of the imagined space object. Being symbolic it has no structural or load bearing function, but it is the

123. Carlo Scarpa, Brion cemetery, San Vito di Altivole, 1970–75. Door in the chapel reminiscent of Japanese shoji screens.

124. Carlo Scarpa, Brion cemetery, San Vito di Altivole, 1970–75. Spatial layering in chapel.

most important element in the house because its placement in a room makes that the most important room in the house.«[14] The central pillar of the house, as the material manifestation of the roof support, is a symbol for the protection of the family. Scarpa's Brion cemetery has atmospheric and physical suggestions of the ceremonially influenced architecture of Japan. In the cemetery, too, visitors walk alongside it rather than enter it. Contemplation and meditation are more important than haptic experience and an active walk through the cemetery. The path to the meditation pavilion leads through the entrance gateway (propylaea), through a covered passage to a footbridge across the pond, where there is a meditation pavilion. From this secluded place one can overlook part of the cemetery grounds, whose formal elements, in spite of the enclosing wall, remind the visitor of the mood of a Japanese garden. The door elements inside the chapel refer to Japanese paper walls with their translucent glass panels and gridlike metal frames.

As a result of the type of construction – framework without diagonals – straight lines are predominant,[15] and the interstices are filled in with panels that have differing characteristics. In contrast to the web of lines that Frank Lloyd Wright creates in his spaces, which functions as an integrated ornament, a visible structural framework predominates in Japanese architecture. Traditional Japanese architecture is also very close to Semper's basic idea. It creates space by means of a wooden framework clad with wooden, grid, and paper panels. The framework remains visible and determines the proportions of the fill elements. Scarpa uses the stylistic idiom of the panels that delimit the space without being tied to the basic constructional conditions of wood construction. He alienates their use, from that of a fill element to an independent element that can have spatial and expositive functions and follows its own laws of design. He uses the gridlike web with its Japanese overtones as a literal quote in the ceiling design of an exhibition space on the top floor of the Caserma in the Castelvecchio in Verona.

The additive type of room layout that can be observed in the Katsura-rikyu imperial country residence shows that rooms have been connected over the diagonal, resulting in a seemingly fluid, infinitely expandable ground plan. This type of design produces a large number of exterior surfaces that make communication with the garden and surrounding area possible.[16]

»If we observe birds of passage in flight, we see that they take their place on both sides of the lead bird, slightly staggered each time in relation to each other, in the flock that seems to trace the two arms of an angle in the sky. In architecture we use the expression ›sawtooth‹ for this type of arrangement. You find it very often in Japan, and, as in Katsura, it is mostly developed only on one side. This principle of composition was occasionally interpreted from a functional perspective. Every one of the buildings arranged in this way enjoyed a maximum of light and air.«[17]

Ashihara Yoshinobu writes as follows about the creation of space: »Architectural space may be created in two ways: by addition and subtraction. In some kinds of sculpture you start with nothing and create a work of art by adding on clay, bit by bit. In other kinds you start with a block of stone or wood and hew it down, discarding unnecessary parts until the desired form takes shape. Likewise, there is one kind of architectural space that is created centrifugally, ordering the space from the inside out – this may be called architecture by addition. And there is another kind in which the space is created centripetally – by subtraction. The distinction depends on the relationship between the whole and the parts: whether you start with the parts or with the whole.«[18]

125. Perspective section of a typical one-story home.
126. Katsura Imperial Palace, Kyoto, Japan. Ground-floor plan.
127. Carlo Scarpa, Brion cemetery, San Vito di Altivole, 1970–75. Ground-floor plan.

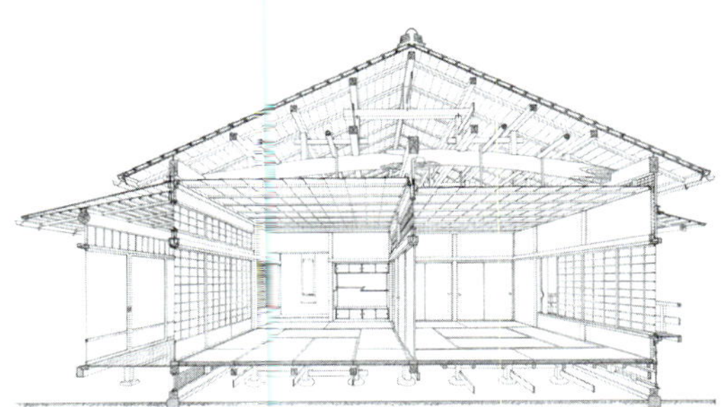

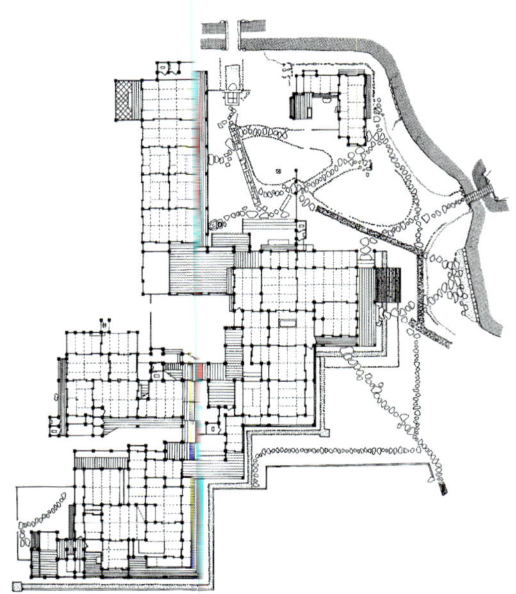

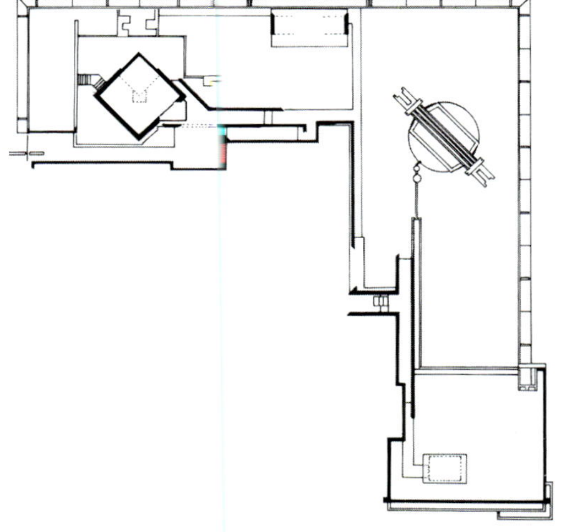

#### Stratification of space

The arrangement of the rooms one behind the other or diagonally to each other, noticeable through apertures, attests to the principle of the stratification of space. This is made visible through changeable openings – sliding elements that can remove or close off entire wall sequences. The uniform floor covering with tatami mats joins together the larger space into a complex that is organized by means of differently permeable surfaces. About the Shoin architecture of the Katsura Palace, Arata Isozaki writes as follows: »Directly after entering the Old Shoin Building, the visitor is surprised by the impression of transparency radiated by the whole. The light, which is dimmed by the shoji, pervades the five rooms.«[19]

The sequencing of rooms one after the other and, consequently, their simultaneity produces the nonhierarchical flexibility of the ground plans. The way rooms are used is not forcibly dictated, as it is in European culture, but changes with the time of day. The use of solid walls is kept to a minimum. »Sliding and, if need be, completely removable doors serve to separate the rooms. That means that to a large extent the living spaces can be altered. By opening or removing the sliding doors, the house can be transformed to an extent into a single large room from which there is a direct transition into the garden.«[20] In its form the house follows the lives of its inhabitants and is a flexible organism.

Scarpa's modification of the Taddei House in Venice (1959–61) works with the principle of sliding walls that can divide the large living hall into zones.

The arrangement of space in the open hallways, which are located outside, preserves close contact with the outdoors. »Duality is a common principle in the daily life of Japan and it comes from Lao Tzu's teaching about space. This important Chinese philosopher taught that space contained both inside and outside and that it maintained dynamic balance between these opposite elements. With the aid of the principle duality, one can see the infinite of all things.«[21]

Edward Morse compares Japanese and American architecture: »One of the main distinguishing characteristics in a comparison between a Japanese and an American (author's note: Western-style) house is the treatment of the interior and exterior walls: in our country they are solid and unmovable, they are a firm component of the load-bearing structure. In the Japanese house, however, two or more exterior sides remain without a solid wall, and inside only few walls are unmovable. Instead, they can be moved like sliding doors on tracks along the ceiling and floor. These tracks are the demarcation of each room.«[22] Because of the additive arrangement of rooms the form of the ground plan is free and exploded. »The rooms are quite naturally linked together in accordance with their purposes, without starting out with a particular idea of form.«[23] The result is free, nonsymmetrical compositions that grow in the landscape. Vertically rooms are divided into three strata. »The lowest is only a surface – the tatami, which gives all activities and possessions a firm foundation. The next stratum extends up to a height of approximately 40 cm

From left to right

128. Carlo Scarpa, Fondazione Querini Stampalia, Venice, 1961–63. Birds eye view of garden.
129. Carlo Scarpa, Italian Pavilion, Castello Gardens, Venice, 1952. Biennale sculpture garden.
130. Katsura Imperial Palace, Kyoto, Japan, Old Shoin Building. Spatial stratification.
131. Carlo Scarpa, Taddei Apartment, Venice, 1959 to 1962. Sliding and layered wall segments in the interior.
132. Katsura Imperial Palace, Kyoto, Japan. Shitaji-mado and round window in the house of tea ceremony master.
133. Carlo Scarpa, Brion cemetery, San Vito di Altivole, 1970–75. Double round opening in covered hallway.
134. Katsura Imperial Palace, Kyoto, Japan, Shokatei Pavilion. Garden with step stones.
135. Carlo Scarpa, Fondazione Querini Stampalia, Venice, 1961–63. Garden with step stones and water basin.

above the floor; it is the stratum in which the face and hands of the person sitting on the tatami are located – that is, the stratum in which most activities in the room are carried out. That is why this stratum is supplied with enough light; the solid lower part of the shoji and the wall below the windows are rarely higher than 26 cm. The next spatial stratum belongs to the person who is standing and walking around in the room.[24]

»The Japanese Garden is in essence a vastly enlarged box garden, and though the Japanese house is open to the garden, it is by no means open to the wide outdoors. Nor is it open in the social sense. Japanese tradition reveals little that could compare with the agoras and piazzas of European cities.«[25] The exhibition hall of the Fondazione Querini Stampalia in Venice is expanded by the addition of a garden room. Not only is the garden reminiscent of the compact and controlled quality of Japanese gardens, evoked by the design of stepping-stone trails and stone paths, but also with its mini-canal and the pond it is a tribute to the city of Venice. The sculpture garden that Scarpa designed inside the Italian Pavilion of the Biennale in 1952 arose from an interior space that now functions as an open caesura in the percorso of the exhibition. Three pillars with a lenticular cross section support a roof that has circular segments cut out of it. Here, too, the natural-seeming artificiality evokes the Japanese stylistic idiom.

### Stratification of material

In Japanese architecture the floor is defined by the arrangement of tatami mats in standardized sizes. This modular system defines the size of the room and the arrangement of the mats determines the direction of the room. Often rooms have no specifically assigned function, but are used in various ways. The absence of heavy, solidly installed furnishings, for instance, makes it possible to use each room as a sleeping room.[26] Solid walls are limited to a minimum. Rooms are separated by means of sliding and removable doors. Zones are created with the help of screens. Mats are the basic design module, a space consists of several virtual individual rooms that are formed by the edged mats. Arranging the mats and moving them provides orientation and geometry.

»The floor of the house is not a floor in the western sense, but a platform upon which one sits or walks. The view of the world from a sitting position on the floor level is quite different from a chairlevel position.«[27]

Scarpa takes up the idea of the tatami-like module as a floor covering element and transforms it into stone or terracotta. The approach to the Castelvecchio consists of stone »mats«, each of which is individually edged and thus, in spite of the solid material, embodies a basic textile concept. In the Fondazione Querini the floor of the exhibition space, which extends into the garden, is similarly structured. The »mats« here not only remain in one plane, but become three-dimensional elements, which, when they lie above each other or side by side, can produce differences in levels. In designing the floor of the exhibition »Arturo Martini« in Treviso (1967 in the Convento Santa Caterina di Treviso) Scarpa uses the opportunity to give direction through the orientation of the stone floor slabs.

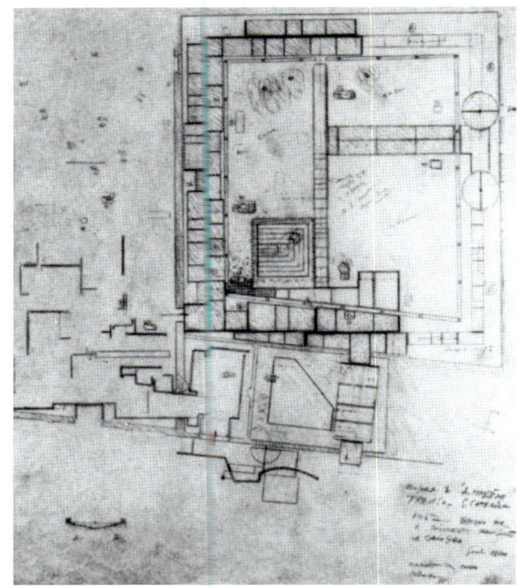

The wall framework of traditional wood construction can consist of various materials. The walls are formed of paper-covered panels, while the furnishings, such as shelves or cabinets, are integrated in the room dividers.

»A European room is only given its solidity by the furniture. The wallpaper tends to negate rather than confirm the fact that the wall is a solid spatial boundary; above it soars the ceiling, an incorporeal surface at an incalculable distance. Several pieces of furniture compete with each other for the right to draw the axis of the room toward them so that a clear direction can develop. For Europeans this is a meaningful order of the things around them they use every day.«[28]

As window and door panels the Japanese use different types of latticework that formerly used to be covered with glued-on layers of paper, while nowadays they are mostly glazed on the outside. Screens of various kinds, whose function is to structure space and provide visual separation, form mobile ways of creating spatial zones. Special interior design features include integrated furniture that is part of the room and the »tokonoma«, the cult niche, a motif originating in the Buddhist ritual that has been incorporated in the construction of homes. »The seat in front of the tokonoma is the seat of honor, and no one must enter the tokonoma niche. It is usually placed in the center of the wall, that is, it is not symmetrically arranged.«[29] The tana is a wall niche next to the tokonoma; consisting of small cabinets and boards, it does not actually have a practical purpose, but chiefly serves interior design and helps break up the space.[30] The third element of spatial organization is the reading niche (shoin). »Shoin as a reading niche consists of a bay-

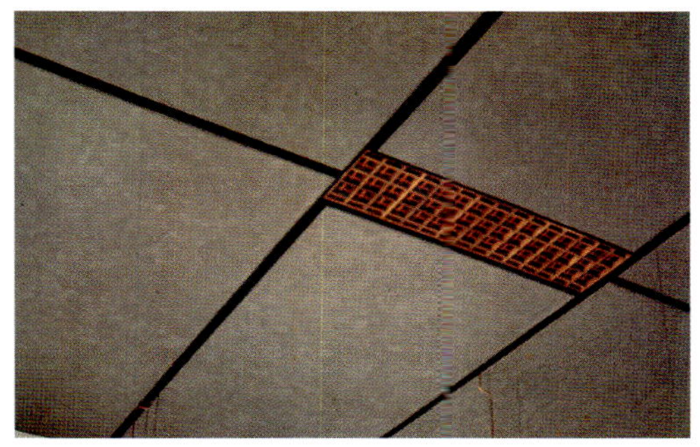

type, built-out transparent paper window whose wide windowsill was used as a lectern. The space below the windowsill is also made into a wall cabinet.«[31]

Differently shaped wall apertures paneled with a lattice structure form a connection with the outdoors. Tetsuro Yoshida writes: »The difference between Japanese and European windows lies mainly in their form. Japanese windows are low and wide, while European ones are high and narrow.«[32] Big, round apertures are a motif of transition into the garden area. Depending on the season, bamboo curtains and hanging roofs are added as protection from the sun. Thus the appearance of the house changes from season to season. The interior walls can be divided into two areas: the area for movement, as tall as a person, and the contrasting area of the skylights. In the inside rooms shelves and cabinets, with few exceptions, are part of the wall clothing, a stratum of furnishings that makes free interior design possible. Surfaces whose function is to protect the building from rain or sun are also affixed to the façade. »Rain shutters – amado – are closed at night and during inclement weather; they consist of light wooden walls and their size corresponds with that of the shoji. They are made of thin pieces of wood held together by a light frame and additionally supported by a few crossbeams.«[33] Elements are autonomous, and this is also made clear by the fact that each has its own border and contour, or by the different treatment of surfaces. The wall coatings of the Brion cemetery, attached to the surface of the concrete walls like pinned-on papers, attest to an understanding of the independent surface, which, used as an ornament and reflector of light, is what gives the outside shell its characteristic look.[34]

The roof is practically the most important element of the Japanese construction style; it dominates and emphasizes the horizontality of the buildings and, because it projects for quite a distance, creates the space for verandahs in front of the house. In the Katsura Imperial Palace the ceilings of interior rooms are mostly simple wood paneling, or bottom views of the roof made of layers of bamboo poles.

Materials are mostly used untreated. In particular elements like furniture, lacquered surfaces are used as well because of the lighting effect. Builders strive to bring out the effect of properties specific to the material and to show them off to advantage. Water is used as a two-dimensional and restless element in exterior design. The atmosphere of movement and the sound associated with it reflects closeness to nature.

The effect of the rooms of the Katsura, described here as a representative example for traditional Japanese architecture, is based on the differentiated effect of light and dark and the search for harmonious proportions. Various sequences of rooms are seen simultaneously because of spatial stratification even while their specific qualities are not revealed at first glance, and form a texture of atmospheres, a microcosm. Through the care taken in creating detail and in placement, respect is shown to the element and the user. The duality of inside and outside, light and dark can be felt clearly and creates the poetic charm of the rooms. Jun'ichiro writes about the aesthetics: »Looking at Japanese rooms, Westerners are surprised at their simplicity and have the impression there is nothing there but grey walls without the least bit of ornamentation. Seen from their point of view that is quite plausible; but it shows that they have not understood the mystery of shadow. We, on the other hand, install additional protective roofs or verandahs on the outside of rooms that sunlight penetrates with difficulty as it is, keeping the light out even more, so that only the diffuse reflection from the garden can steal into the interior through the shoji. Thus the aesthetic element of our rooms consists in nothing other than this indirect, dimmed lighting effect. And so that this weak, limited, vague light can lie quiet and familiar on the walls of the rooms, we deliberately give these walls a sand coating in reserved, subtle colors ... Presumably by the ›mystery of the Orient‹ that Westerners talk about they mean the eerie silence that such darkness conceals ...Then where is the key to the mystery? I shall reveal the secret: Its source is the magic of shadows. If we chased away the shadows lurking in all the corners, the wall niche would instantly become nothing than empty space. Thus the genius of our forebears has given a mysterious aesthetic expression to the world of shadows that is automatically created by purposefully screening off an empty space; wall painting or decoration can hardly match this effect.«[35]

Scarpa reproduces the views described above, such as the careful attention to detail and the play with light, which lead to a congruent but not equivalent architectonic atmosphere. He controls light and uses shadows in his museum designs as material components that support the staging of the exhibits and the zoning of sections of space. Particularly in the Gipsoteca in Possagno, where the exhibits are Canova's plaster statues, he uses various types of lighting together with the corresponding shadow they cast.

»If you look at Scarpa's works, it is possible to perceive a taste in them that is not unlike comparable details that can be observed in many parts of the building and garden of the Kyoto urban

136. Carlo Scarpa, extension of the Canova plaster cast gallery, Possagno, Treviso 1955–57. Spatial layering in the interior.
137. Carlo Scarpa, »Arturo Martini«, exhibition, Treviso, 1967. Floor design in the formal language of modular tatami mats.
138. Carlo Scarpa, »Arturo Martini«, exhibition, Treviso, 1967. Floor-plan sketch.
139. Carlo Scarpa, book pavilion, Castello gardens, Venice, 1950. Exterior.

140. Carlo Scarpa, Castelvecchio, Verona, 1958 to 1964. Ceiling made of different panels with wood grille element in the center.
141. Katsura Imperial Palace, Kyoto, Japan. Step stone at the main entrance.
142. Carlo Scarpa, Castelvecchio, Verona, 1958 to 1964. Step-stone detail.

house. From the combination of geometric forms that can be observed in the details of his buildings it is possible to get the impression that there is a certain distant correspondence with Frank Lloyd Wright: but that is natural, since he respected and admired the American architect. However, he insisted that Wright's taste could not be defined as oriental. It is conceivable that he bases his assertion on observations of Japanese architecture formed during a trip to Kyoto. No doubt he thought that his work, compared to that of Wright, had a stronger bond to the Orient. For me the aspect of the works of Carlo Scarpa that resembles the painstaking care typical of the urban house in Kyoto is primarily the meticulous sensitivity with which he is able to combine materials. Among urban Japanese houses, those which show the influence of the sukiya (a pavilion for the tea ceremony) present a combination of materials of very different kinds. Today, the Japanese create a sense of harmonious fusion by their masterly introduction of stylistic fragments of diverse origins. To me, this seems to be precisely the technique that is found in Carlo Scarpa's entire work, from the beginnings to his last projects.«[36]

Scarpa detaches elements from their historical and constructed context, such as the motifs of the round windows, or the exposed wall panels, and integrates them in his cultural milieu. He is aware of the tension between the surroundings, the cultural milieu, and the artificial creation of elements that are integrated in a preexisting context, and elaborates a dialogue between them. Yasuhiro Ishimoto writes the following about the Katsura: »I was struck even more forcibly by the extent to which Katsura is an architectonic illustration of the aesthetic philosophy of the kirei sabi,[37] which was in high esteem at the beginning of the Edo period.«[38] Scarpa's buildings illustrate the cultural soil on which they developed and the intellectual attitude toward material and locale.

### 2.4. The De Stijl movement: an architecture of surfaces and planes

The De Stijl movement influenced and inspired Carlo Scarpa by way of its publications and his own designs of exhibitions (see chapter 2).[1] In 1956 Scarpa designs the exhibition »Piet Mondrian« in the Galleria Nazionale d'Arte Moderna in Rome. The influence of the two-dimensional designs of the proponents of De Stijl becomes noticeable in Scarpa's early projects, such as in the blueprint for a salesroom for the Cappellin glassworks. The De Stijl movement, founded in 1917 by Theo van Doesburg, adopted Frank Lloyd Wright and his view of space in Europe, thus touching on Scarpa's fields of interest. In 1914, the architect Robert van't Hoff had returned from a stay in the United States and was incorporating the impressions of Wright's architecture in various projects in the vicinity of Utrecht (1914 and 1915). The principles of the American architect, who had become known in Europe as a result of two publications of his projects by the Wasmuth publishing house in 1910 and 1911 in Berlin, are integrated, in Holland, in the idea of the »New Design«[2] of architecture, painting, and sculpture. Hendrik P. Berlage, one of the movement's precursors, also drew attention, in Europe, to Frank Lloyd Wright with his writings after 1911. He also studied the theories of Gottfried Semper, whom he regarded very highly. Semper's views regarding the elements of architecture, and a rudimentary form of the concept that materials should be appropriate to their function left their mark on his work. The actual conditions associated with the construction of a building are to be made visible, they are themselves an ornamental element and must not be falsified by decorative concealment. »One must not try, in constructional combinations, to eliminate the necessary joint; on the contrary, one should make it into a virtue, that is, an ornamental motif; therefore, you artists, use the various inconvenient aspects of construction as decorative motifs.«[3] Construction offers a sufficient number of reasons and possibilities for embellishing a building with architecturally necessary details. Berlage considers artificially superimposed decorative elements to be wrong. The »naked wall« must again be shown in »all its simple beauty«, and »ornate clutter« must be avoided at all costs.[4]

Berlage attaches a great deal of importance to the study of the frame – the skeleton – which, like nature, gives the building the »correct form«.[5] Covering the skeleton is, as it were, the »exact playback of the inner framework ... where the logical principle of construction predominates and the actual cladding part does not sit on the structure like a loose shell that completely negates it, or like a cover, but is completely fused with the inner construction, since it is, after all, ornamented structure; and so let us try to find the body once more«.[6]

The goal of the Neo-plasticism movement was to reduce design to its elementary basic components: form and color, order, connection, and material structure. The movement dealt theoretically and experimentally with the problem of creating space by means of surfaces and colors; it

143. Carlo Scarpa, Brion cemetery, San Vito di Altivole, 1970–75. Layers of white paint on concrete walls, reflecting light and defining the hallway space.

formulated spatial phenomena that had already been used previously and thus exposed them to architectural theory. The then-prevailing architecture and its use of ornament to conceal formal imbalances was criticized. J. J. P. Oud comments: »An architecture without ornaments requires the greatest possible purity of architectonic composition. Ornament is the universal panacea for architectural impotence!«[7] This programmatically expressed lack of ornamentation in buildings demands balance in the design of architectonic elements and »purity of architectural composition«.[8] In contrast to symmetry, the design principles developed here represent a »balance of the parts«. Oud propagates the principle of »balancing«, an active process as opposed to predetermined rules of design. He replaces a static harmony of the parts with »the process of mise en scène«.[9] Scarpa's compositions also primarily worked with the balance of the parts, instead of a fixed canon of design. This balancing makes it possible to integrate the most varying parts, which fit together without formal harmony, into one composition.

»It is the principle of the scale, whose pans are constantly in motion and where balance appears only momentarily, only to shift again immediately. It is true that harmony is the inherent hope to achieve balance, and also everything is happening in the direction of harmony – but nothing is set at rest, no final state is reached. Underlying this is a different idea of time: time as process, as something that connects, as the unfolding of complexity and anticipation.«[10]

The strived-for balance is the result of the fact that individual parts are without hierarchy. »There is no dominance. Even minute details are seen as having value, respected for their singularity – they rank as equally important.«[11] Details and joints are as important as the design of the overall context. Scarpa himself celebrates the places where the smallest elements of his architectural works are joined together. Play with the »small« and the »large«, »aspects of the small as points of connection«[12] are important design elements in his architecture. His additive way of proceeding comprises the principle of stratification. »For observers this means they are being challenged to read traces of the past, to uncover many strata and the connections among them.«[13] Tensions between forces become noticeable in the divisions of windows, and the way elements are detached from each other makes it possible to produce compositional balance.

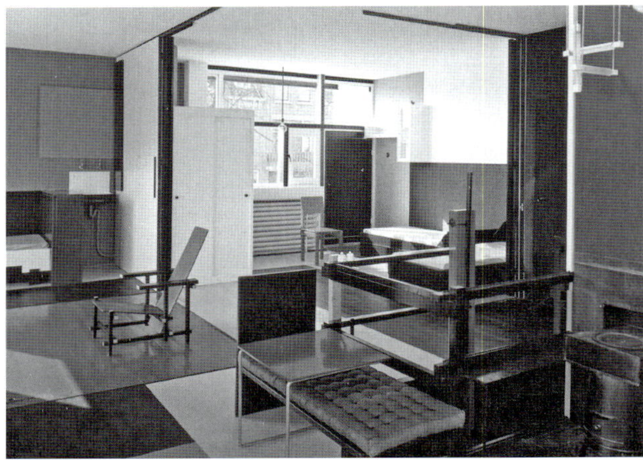

From left to right

144. Carlo Scarpa, »Piet Mondrian«, exhibition, Rome, 1956. Panel detail.
145. Carlo Scarpa, study for interior for Murano glassworks, Cappellin & Co., Paris, 1930. Layering on ceiling.
146. Carlo Scarpa, Ottolenghi House, Bardolino, 1975–78. Façade detail.
147. Gerrit Rietveld, Schröder House, Utrecht, 1924. Spatial stratification, sequence of interiors on second floor.
148. Gerrit Rietveld, Schröder House, Utrecht, 1924. View of entrance side, planar elements forming space.
149. Carlo Scarpa, Olivetti showroom, Venice, 1957/58. Staircase composed out of stone blocks.
150. Carlo Scarpa, Italian Pavilion, Castello gardens, Venice, 1960–62. Staircase.
151. Carlo Scarpa, Taddei House, Venice, 1959 to 1962. Staircase.
152. Carlo Scarpa, Castelvecchio, Verona, 1958 to 1964. Roof potruding out from courtyard façade.

The principles described above are congruent with the characteristics of an architectonic concept of stratification like that described in this book: It comprises lack of hierarchy among elements, simultaneous perceptibility, and a compositional balance of the parts as well as freedom from formal and stylistic norms.

### Spatial stratification

Van Doesburg titles work in the areas of art and architecture as the »New Visual Arts« or »Spatial Design«[14] and views it very holistically. The principles he puts forward apply to different artistic genres and strive to have general validity. The artists of the De Stijl movement frequently dealt with both painting and sculpture as well as architecture. The fusion of architecture and art is made possible by formulating a building as a composition of various surfaces. The combined effect is thus based on the same fundamental element, the »wall or canvas«.[15] Yves Alain Bois writes: »It is the level surface that conveys the continuity of space ... painting is architectonic today because painting itself and its methods serve the same concept as architecture – namely, space and surface – and therefore express ›the same thing‹, only in a different way.«[16]

In Scarpa's work, art and architecture in the intellectual sense are combined. He uses formal principles of art, which, as a designer of exhibitions, he examines intensively in his architecture, and he was able to distil usable principles and mechanisms from a large number of different creative themes. He worked holistically without, at the same time, working full-time as a painter,[17] and deals with the same topics as Rietveld, Mondrian, and van Doesburg. The creation and design of sculptures, furniture, interiors, flatware, glasses, and buildings are evidence for the view that creative problem solving can be used for a large range of projects. The De Stijl movement decomposes the elements that limit space and abstracts them into their individual parts. In contrast with Loos's room plan, which constructs the volumes inside each other and designs their form on the basis of their use, a procedure in accordance with surfaces is less space-related. Moravánsky calls the view of space held by the De Stijl movement the »negation of space«;[18] space is not automatically seen as volume, it consists of surfaces that give form through their treatment with color. Since space is composed of surfaces, its clear, volumelike boundaries are abolished: »We have abolished the duality between inside and outside by breaking through what is closed (walls).«[19] Referring to Rietveld, Scarpa speaks about the abstraction of the wall and the abolishing of inside and outside: »In fact, it would be my dream to design a house for a rich gentleman who was so wealthy he could afford to dissolve the walls ... indeed, there are panels that move in many directions, the Rietveld House (author's note: he means the Schröder House, by Gerrit Rietveld) is made entirely with panels that move. They close off a room, but suddenly they open and everything is one single room.«[20]

As in Frank Lloyd Wright's architecture, inside and outside merge, and the architecture meshes with the surroundings and the landscape. Theo van Doesburg's »principles of modern (creative) architecture«[21] describe the formal beginnings of the new architecture: »The new architecture is without form, though it is definite, that is, it rejects any aesthetic formal pattern adopted a priori; in other words, it does not strive for a form into which to force the functional rooms that arise from practical residential needs. Unlike the earlier style, the new architecture knows neither a self-contained type nor a basic form.«[22]

The requirements that arise from the way a building or interior is to be used determine its form, the concept of »spatial continuum« develops; this continuum creates an overall context, with spaces that merge into each other. The Schröder House (1924) in Utrecht, mentioned above, may be regarded as a model of the conception of architecture and space as practiced by De Stijl. What is significant here above all is the projection of the open form on architectonic space: The building itself or its interior rooms are no longer seen as self-contained bodies, but as elements that can flexibly merge into each other. The two-dimensional, slab-shaped elements of modern architecture are arranged in such a way that they are in a direct relationship of tension to the open space in the outside world.

Mies van der Rohe also perfected the system of integrating inside and outside by working directly with slabs, no longer starting out with a box. Bruno Zevi connects the working method of the De Stijl group with Mies van der Rohe's blueprints: »Unlike van Doesburg and Rietveld, Mies no longer needs to start with the structural box by taking apart corners, differentiating the walls, and dividing them into rectangles that are more or less connected and painted in different colors, with the deep-seated fear that he is leaving the spatial rhythm unchanged. For Mies the box does not exist: Wright has destroyed it, and therefore it is not necessary to fly into a rage over its disintegration. He uses the gestures of a continuous space, with no interruption between inside and outside, never limited by four walls, and he guides the influences by means of partitions which, extending beyond the areas of the floor and of the roof, stabilize an incessant dialogue between the open building and the surrounding environment.«[23]

»K. H. Hüter coined the word ›planoplastik‹ to describe it. The interiors are no longer self-contained cells of space, but merge into each other. They are no longer housed in a predetermined basic form, but rather a continuum is being developed from the inside out.«[24]

Windows function as apertures that connect inside and outside and form the interface of individual strata. They are also seen as a positive area, like corresponding wall spaces. Here, too, we see the nonhierarchical equality of the strata, which are part of an overall composition. Glass and plaster form differing surfaces whose interplay produces the totality of the façade. (see chapter Banca Popolare). Rietveld's Schröder House shows the composition of an architectonic building that appears to be put together from individual parts, such as discs and rods. The vertical and horizontal elements overlap and thus demonstrate their additive structure. All forms are subject to an orthogonal geometry, and curves are rarely found in the repertory of forms. The shell of the house simultaneously appears to be both »put together and taken apart«.[25] The furnishings and construction elements are treated according to the same methodology and thus produce the effect of being a unified structure. The spatial stratification of the interior may be manipulated by means of sliding elements. The design of the surfaces – floor, wall, and ceiling – differentiates the zones: instead of clear »virtual« spaces created by individual surfaces, Rietveld creates multiple surface relationships that intercommunicate flexibly. Walter Eugen Ehrmann, in his dissertation, also speaks of »spatial strata« formed by individual slabs.[26] In Scarpa's 1956 Mondrian exhibition in Rome the walls of the stands form spaces that merge into each other by the typical mechanism of overlaying. Scarpa works with the formal principles of the painter Piet Mondrian in the form of a reminiscence within the architectonic design of the exhibition space.[27]

In the renovation of the Castelvecchio, Scarpa uses the addition of horizontal and vertical slabs. The architectonic history of the Castelvecchio already showed that it was the result of adding a range of different elements. Behind the side exit of the Caserma, Scarpa creates an entrance that is independent of the three arches; it is lower and toward the exterior is gradated in a differentiated way. A vertically placed wall slab and the continuous floor covering achieve visual connection and a transition from inside to outside. When it comes to smaller objects as well, Scarpa uses the principle of overlaying addition characteristic of Neo-plasticism. The staircase in the Olivetti store, like the staircase in the Italian Pavilion, works with stone elements lying one on top of the other, while the staircase in the Taddei Apartment is the addition of wood planes. He makes visible the separation of individual parts by clearly contrasting them with each other. The elements are either separated by a joint or the transition is marked by an additional element.

The architecture of the De Stijl group is also – as in the early work of the Secession – separated into a structural framework and its cladding, an approach reminiscent of Semper's »theory of cladding« that is also publicized in Berlage's 1904 book *Over stijl in bouw- en meubelkunst* (Concerning style in the art of architecture and furniture making) for Dutch readers.

Paul Overy writes: »The name ›De Stij‹ probably originated from the interest they shared in the work and ideas of Berlage. In 1904 Berlage had published a book entitled *Over stijl in bouw- en meubelkunst*, where he introduced to Dutch readers ideas derived from the writings of the German architect and design theorist Gottfried Semper. Semper's monumental two-volume study of form and applied arts, *Der Stil*, had originally been published in Germany between 1860 and 1863. Berlage developed and adapted Semper's ideas in terms of his own utopian socialist beliefs. Following Semper, he placed great emphasis on the walls as both plane and definer of space. This was to be absorbed into De Stijl architectural theory where ›unity in plurality‹ was represented by the configuration of individual elements from which De Stjil buildings, furniture, sculpture and paintings were constructed, perceived simultaneously both as complete wholes and as assemblages of individual elements.«[28]

Van Doesburg, too, defines space with the help of a composition of orthogonal floating surfaces that glide one behind the other. Structure tends to be negated in favor of de-hierarchizing the elements, and is overlaid by the cladding of the surfaces. The »blurring of the ›structural framework‹« was a necessary concealment »if one wanted to show the interior off to advantage as a nonhierarchical, abstract whole«.[29] Color serves as decoration that builds no relationship to the structural framework of the building and whose purpose is, rather, to hide the construction. Color and construction exist side by side instead of existing one for the other.[30]

»In principle, architectonic space is to be regarded only as a formless and blind vacuum, as long as color does not actually organize it into space. In the end only the surface is crucial for architecture, people do not live in the structure, but in the atmosphere evoked by the surface. When dealing with the problem of the exterior surface there is one more thing to consider: only the surface is of significance for people. They do not live in the construction, in the ›skeleton‹ of the architecture, but rather come into direct contact with it only through its surface (outside as a cityscape, inside as an interior) ... Houses are like people. It is by their facial features, their posture, their walk, their clothing, in short: by their ›surface‹ that we are able to read their thoughts, their inner life.«[31]

Theo van Doesburg writes about the relationship between construction and surface: »The outer surface is also a result of the construction. The construction is expressed in the surface. Poor construction results in a poor surface. Good construction has an intact, tight surface. The perfection of architecture is actually due to the perfection of the surface, both inside and outside. From the first stone to the last brushstroke, the development of the surface is of essential significance.«[32]

### Stratification of material

Surfaces are intended to represent functional and ideational content and to create atmosphere. Choice of material and tactile qualities can provide information about the use and origin of a space. They have no tectonic function. Theo van Doesburg, in contrast to the above-mentioned views of Berlage, denies that cladding has the direct function of illustrating the construction underlying it. The connections lie deeper than in sheer reproduction. Semper's concept of polychromy as the basis of the principle of stratification here has some influence on the architecture. S. Umberto Barbieri describes the origins of designing with color in the De Stijl movement: »The concept of colour as an independent element in architectonic design stemmed from the interpretation of archaeological discoveries and the subsequent reconstruction of ancient settlements in Italy and Greece.«[33] He distinguishes »pictorial polychromy«,[34] which covers the architectonic surface as an independent layer, from »structural polychromy«,[35] which is based on the construction and illustrates it. Scarpa does not work exclusively with primary colors, as De Stijl dictated, but rather adapts his choice of colors to the surroundings in order to successfully integrate the new spaces in the existing context. As with most of his influences, Scarpa does not directly adopt the principles he uses, but integrates them in his formal idiom and cultural circle. Vincent Scully describes Scarpa's relationship to De Stijl as follows: »But Scarpa actually tames De Stijl, in Italian marble – the weight itself, the strength, the clear, cold permanence are kept in subordination, reinterpreted with profoundly authentic expression.«[36] Parallels in the design of surfaces produce results that are visually very similar. Floor surfaces such as that at the Fondazione Querini Stampalia, the Il Torresino church in Padua, or the Casino of the Marina Militare in Venice seem related to Mondrian's painting *Checkerboard*, and Oud's floor design in the holiday center in Noordwijderhout.

The colors contribute to the creation of space. The juxtaposition or combination of colors, their use on the basic architectonic substance is necessary to create a whole. Bruno Zevi writes about color in Neo-plasticism: »Color is indispensable for human beings – like light. In modern architecture, surfaces must be brought to life, that is, must be composed with the help of pure color.«[37] Architectonic space is regarded as sheer volume, which is brought to life only through the use of color.[38] The different fields enter into relation with each other. »The use of rectangular surfaces and pure colors in architecture and in interiors should, according to Bart van der Leck, have the effect of ›creating space, in contrast to the colorless two-dimensionality of architecture‹ ... As early as 1917 Vilmos Huszár implemented these principles in an interior. In painting a bedroom for Cornelis Bruynzeel, he used combinations of yellow, white, blue, and grey rectangular areas to accentuate wall sections and sets of furniture. By reversing color combinations on facing walls, a new feeling for the volume of the room was evoked, and the walls and furniture placed in front of them were connected into a harmonious whole.«[39] The use of color makes possible the invention of a new element, »the indivisible unity of the wall slab«.[40] For the exterior this means detaching the façade from the volume, it is regarded as a separate architectural element whose use makes it possible for a house to communicate with its surroundings. In 1924 Huszár together with Gerrit Rietveld develops a model for an exhibition space. Rectangles in primary colors, white, or black structure the interior surfaces of the room. What is striking is that the floor, wall, and ceiling are treated nonhierarchically in the same manner. The planes enter into communication with each

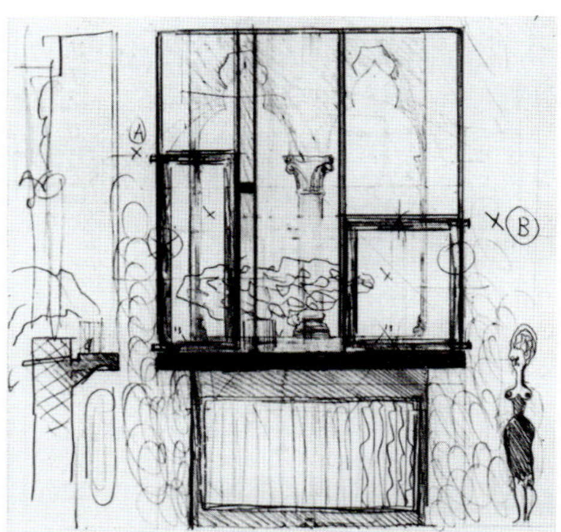
A
B
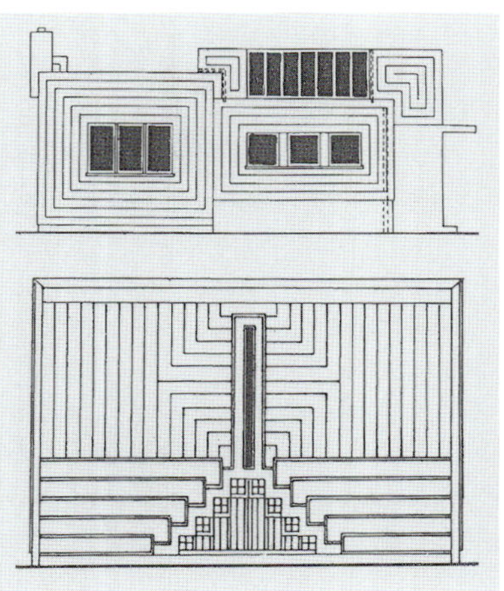

IVAV

From left to right

153. Piet Mondrian, *Checkerboard*, The Hague, Gemeentemuseum, 1919.
154. J. J. Oud, vacation vamp, De Vonk, vacation camp, Noorwijderhout, 1917/18.
155. Carlo Scarpa, church of Torresino, Padua, 1978. Altar and paving.
156. Vilmos Huszár, Gerrit Rietveld, model for exhibition space, 1924. Layers of color and paint defining space.
157. Carlo Scarpa, Palazzo Abatellis, Palermo, 1953/54. Colored panels provide defined space for sculptures within the exhibition space.
158. Piet Mondrian, *Composition in Red, Yellow and Blue*, 1922.
159. Carlo Scarpa, Castelvecchio, Verona, 1958 to 1964. Sketch with window divisions.
160. J. P. Oud, residential complex Oud-Mathenesse, Rotterdam, 1923. Façade drawing.
161. Carlo Scarpa, entrance to the Istituto Universitario di Architettura, Tolentini, Venice, 1966. View of the entrance portal with parallel recessed frame pattern on concrete walls.

other, and by orthogonal overlapping at the corners of the room negate the actual geometry of the interior – they form a »sub space«. Between individual planes, virtual spaces are formed within the total volume. Layers of color are used to form spatial zones within the physical contours of the interior.

Scarpa uses the principle of organizing space described above primarily in his exhibition designs. In the Correr Museum in Venice he introduces strata of material that provide a background for the paintings and form a sub space of the desired size and proportion. The room of Antonello da Messina has travertine panels, which reduce the effect of height. The paneling is a link joining art and architecture into a single unit. The works of Antonello da Messina are surrounded by frames that enclose them like a showcase at a distance, fitted into the travertine panels. The travertine panels are given rhythm by an ebony panel. The black panels and the paintings communicate with the Pietà, placed on an easel, which creates the impression of being a single soaring plane. An important difference between the neutrally abstracted two-dimensional elements of the De Stijl movement and Scarpa's treatment of surfaces is that material and surfaces, in spite of their formal abstraction, have metaphoric reference.

In Scarpa's building modifications the structural framework in most situations is clad but keeps its value and is emphasized in some places by the type of cladding or the partial absence of cladding (see analysis of the Banca Popolare, chapter 3). Impressions of surfaces in Scarpa's work do not consist of an assortment of primary colors, but are closely interwoven with their surroundings both in terms of color and material. The interrelationship of the surfaces is just as important as their relation to the incidence of light and to elements in the surroundings. They act communicatively, establish connections, and stimulate associations (often through colors taken from the paintings). In the Palazzo Abatellis in Palermo sculptures are mounted on colored panels of varying sizes that communicate among themselves and form »virtual spaces« around the sculptures. The colored areas provide a clearly defined scenic background for the objects and respectfully honor their value.

Ákos Moravánsky writes: »In our imagination space is created from impressions of surfaces – that was Mondrian's conviction as well. His Paris studio, whose spatial boundaries consist of orthogonal canvases that soar on light easels, is in keeping with this vision.«[41]

On the relation between Carlo Scarpa and Piet Mondrian, as well as other De Stijl architects, Maria Antonietta Crippa writes: »From the Dutch painter, from his language (programmatically stripped of subjective yet figurative components by a puritanical iconoclasm in which theosophical and pseudosocialistic positions converge), from his search for rhythms and harmonies in open geometric textures, where every hint of curve forms had been eliminated, he took the idea that it was possible to structure each plane element of architecture without fixed rules on the basis of a small number of compositional data. From the neoplastic architects – both those who were still sensitive to the influence of Wright and Berlage, like van 't Hoff, Wils, Oud, and those who were more formalistic, like Lissitzky, Richter, and especially Rietveld – he learned to organize formal values of the surface in space, the result being that the entire volume is kept open and animated by rhythmic correspondences. From them he also took over the use of color as an essential compositional element, but he distanced himself from a programmatic emphasis on the primary colors, instead opting for the natural coloration of the building tradition of Venice and, in plaster and stucco, wide-ranging, varied, often costly chromatics. Especially in the restoration of historical buildings, as is clearly evident in the Castelvecchio in Verona, Scarpa used the figurative possibilities of Neo-plasticism, transforming the compactness and self-contained nature of the historical buildings into spatial continuity connecting inside and outside through visible axes, window openings, and subtle and complex geometric structuring of the whole, which individually are often not immediately perceptible.«[42] The design of the windows of the Castelvecchio (1958–61) quotes Mondrianesque geometric principles of division. From the exact analysis of the genesis of the works of art he dealt with,[43] Carlo Scarpa often adopts mechanisms of form and design.

### Reduction and abstraction

The »creed« to which the members of the group had undertaken to adhere reads as follows: »Perfect abstraction – in other words, the perfect exclusion of the entire sphere of direct perception – and limiting the graphic means of expression to straight lines and right angles – that is, to the horizontal and vertical line – and to the three primary colors (red, yellow, and blue) and the primary non-colors (black, grey, and white).«[44]

»For architectonic design as well, geometric abstractionism brought important new ideas. What is crucial is that design moved forward to new notions of space. Though the ›New Design‹ may initially appear to be two-dimensional, its purpose is, after all, interior design – not in an illusionistic, perspective sense derived from natural corporeality, but with its specific means: the line, rectangles, and colors. ›These planes are capable of structuring space both by their dimension (line) and by tone values (color) without expressing space in a perspectively individual way. Because dimensions and tone values shape relations clearly, space is represented in a balanced way: breadth and height face each other uncurtailed, and depth appears as a result of the distance effect of the color differentiation of the surfaces‹ (Mondrian). Hence the term Neo-plasticism. And so, in the practice of design there are transitions to spatial design, similar to Malevich's ›Architektona‹ or Lissitzky's ›Prounen‹ – again, stages in the transition from painting to architecture: van Doesburg's perspective paintings, ›relations between vertical and horizontal planes‹ that seem like modern buildings represented from a bird's-eye view.«[45]

Color, according to van Doesburg, becomes a »building material«.[46] The surface of the wall is »dematerialized thanks to the color«.[47] Beside color, surface design and choice of material is important for the special aura and effect of the buildings. Motifs such as the multiple frame, which can be found repeatedly in Oud's work, are used as a central theme in the Brion cemetery and the entrance of the Tolentini School of Architecture.

In order to differentiate planes from each other, the edges were emphasized, both in architecture and in painting. »Thus, painting generally represents the three-dimensional by stressing angles. The three-dimensional is essential in painting, since it creates space. Since painting forms space on a level surface, a different corporeality than the natural one becomes necessary for it.«[48]

The motif of the multiple frame is a surface treatment that suggests something multilayered or massive and at the same time serves as surface decoration. Instead of pure coats of color that lie on the wall as if incorporeal, Scarpa frequently uses the Venetian stucco lustro, which, however, he frequently applies on the wall like a framed picture. Beside color, he also emphasizes the existence of an additional layer, which is given its own corporeality.

#### Materiality

Materials, believes Theo van Doesburg, have their own energy and atmosphere, a fact that is heightened by their proper use. A use that does not take into account the character of the material results in loss of energy and thus of beauty. »When reinforced concrete was first used correctly (I think by F. L. Wright), the tension, the energy of the concrete came into its own in such a way that architecture was unintentionally, without aesthetic ulterior motives, enriched by a new kind of beauty. The same is true of plate glass, seamless floor coverings and other single-textile material surfaces, which mirror the spirit of modern times through their flawlessness, simplicity, and tautness.«[49] The appropriate use of material has to do with correct processing and with avoiding the »rape of the material through wrong use, as a result of which a large part of the energy is lost«.[50] For instance, wood has the property of »shrinking«, while concrete represents »tension«.[51]

Accordingly it is particularly the combination of materials that depends on their qualities; mechanical aesthetics is a balance between artistic creation and utilitarian constructional design. Scarpa's main concern in design was the selection and treatment of materials, their apotheosis, as it were. In the Fondazione Querini Stampalia in Venice, Scarpa modifies the properties of travertine by working it like wood, cutting it like a panel, which suggests the atmosphere of both materials in space. Kenneth Frampton describes the stone wall paneling in the Fondazione Querini: »Scarpa's typical method of cladding comes in especially useful in the travertine walls of the great hall, in which, except when he reverts to the traditional stone, there is the illusion of a metonymic exchange between wood and masonry, that is, between the wood of the floor of the bridge and the railing, and the travertine on the wall of the exhibition area. The stone is perceived in two forms – first, as simple cladding, and then as a kind of ›wood‹, carved, inlaid, and connected by a hinge, as though this was cabinetwork transferred to stone.«[52]

162. Venice, view of canal reflecting buildings and a bridge, strong effect of light, shadow and reflection.

## 2.5. Venice

### Regional affinities – examples of stratification in Venice

In addition to the new ideas Scarpa received from the study of contemporary architecture, he was profoundly influenced by his direct local environment. Scarpa used the surroundings of his projects as a formal connecting link and source of inspiration. Mazzariol calls him a »sensitive reader of the locales and the situation of his reality«.[1] The surroundings serve as an underlay for new design ideas, like a blank page that can be written on.

»In choosing Venice as his spiritual home, Scarpa affirmed his identity as magister ludi of fragmentary architecture. In this type of architecture the possibilities of innovation and invention reside in the building elements and in the manipulation of the visual and kinesic relationships among the various fragments and artefacts. Hence this architecture is the product of the resolution, substitution and design of elements, whereas technology, with its double faced role as techne and logos and logos of techne, forms the basis for an understanding of the interplay of elements and in the dialogue set up among them by their replacement in the fabric of the building.«[2]

IVAV

ANNO DOMINI
·M·D·XLVIII·

From left to right

163. Palazzo in Cannareggio, Venice. Façades exposing different layers of materials.
164. Palazzo Flangini, Venice, Canal Grande. Side view of representative façade layer facing the canal.
165. Santa Maria dei Miracoli, Venice, 1481–89. Exterior façade, multicolored stone cladding.
166. Carlo Scarpa, entrance to the Istituto Universitario di Architettura, Tolentini, Venice, 1966. View of the entrance portal with expressed layers.
167. Carlo Scarpa, new portal for the Faculty of Literature and Philosophy of the University of Venice, San Sebastiano, Venice 1976–78. Pronounced additional layer at entrance.
168. Andrea Palladio, San Giorgio Maggiore, Venice, 1560–80. Mosaic floor.
169. Carlo Scarpa, Castelvecchio, Verona, 1958 to 1964. Sacello, exterior mosaic façade.
170. Carlo Scarpa, Fondazione Querini Stampalia, Venice, 1961–63. Mosaic floor.
171. Palazzo Soranzo, Venice. Gothic window imbedded in rectangular layer of stone.
172. Carlo Scarpa, entrance to the Istituto Universitario di Architettura, Tolentini, Venice, 1966. View from the interior courtyard towards entrance wall.

Scarpa was born in Venice and spent a large part of his life in this city, whose character and history is reflected in his work. Almost all of his professional life, he was a member of the Faculty of Architecture in Venice, beginning in 1926 as the assistant of Prof. Cirilli, and later as a lecturer at various institutes until 1978. His work as a consultant for the Biennale put him in touch with the most well-known artists and architects of his time. His isolation in Murano (1929–47) probably played an important part in his involvement with the region of the lagoon and its islands. Eduardo Detti, with whom he collaborated over a long period, writes about Scarpa as follows: »Carlo Scarpa had a ›sense of place‹. Even though his works and projects were primarily related to Venice and the Veneto, we must, perhaps, modify the attribute of ›venezianità‹, which, even if it need not be regarded as a mere stylistic characteristic, makes him appear to be an anomalous, almost indefinable person.«[3] In spite of his years of work for various institutions in Venice, Scarpa was not able to bequeath a new building to the city; he planned primarily renovations and extensions of buildings, additional strata, like the two entrances for university buildings.

### Stratifications within the context of the city

In Venice, as in other historic cities, stratification[4] is a fundamental principle of city and building development. In an environment where access is difficult, where all procurement and disposal of material is very time-consuming and costly, the additive principle of building is promoted, such as the reuse of existing buildings by adding new uses and spaces. Sergio Bettini writes that this is »the characteristic procedure of medieval Venetian builders: reworking, integrating in the new buildings that which one was able to transport across the lagoon, and keeping anything worth preserving from the old buildings that had already been torn down or were in the process of demolition. The reclaimed material consisted primarily of marble relics, recycled building components: that is, columns, capitals, architraves, ledges, etc.; but perhaps unfinished as well ...«[5]

The architecture of Venice consists of structural and imaginary strata. The structural strata bear witness to the various periods experienced by a building or square (locale), while the imaginary or associative strata refer to other epochs and influences and thus make possible a parallelity of events. Because the city has gone through so many changes in its history, the associative stratum appears frequently and becomes a regular component of Scarpa's architecture. Elements that have narrative components give an architecture a deeper meaning, which goes beyond merely fulfilling functions. Symbols and details link buildings with their historical and local context.

Vittorio Magnago Lampugnani writes about Scarpa's affinity for Venice: »The deep affinity between an architect and a place results in a more intense mimesis between the building and its surroundings, between redefinition and genius loci. Scarpa's refurbishing of the Fondazione Querini Stampalia is work that bears his trademark like almost no other; at the same time, it represents an unmistakable artistic metaphor of the city of Venice.«[6]

The layout of Venice itself makes it a stratified city. The palaces, in spite of their external stone appearance, are supported by countless wooden piles. Buildings consist of different strata that undergo more and more additions as time goes by. Stratification in the form of layers of representative cladding is one of the main themes of façade design. The fact that the façades face the canals was often the reason that only the side that showed was clad with lavishly designed layers, since only on that side the observer was sure to be close enough. On the sides the thickness of the layer is quite apparent.

Cladding dominates the spatial design of many Venetian churches, such as the church Santa Maria dei Miracoli, which was begun in 1480. Clad outside and lined on the inside, it has the identical many-colored marble cladding on its external and internal façade. According to Ennio Concina the subdivided surfaces made up of multicolored marble slabs are a reminiscence of the chromatics of Florentine buildings.[7] The use of different types of cladding is flexible with regard to their placement. On the Palazzo Dario on the Canal Grande motifs that were originally limited to floor design are used on the façade. »In the Palazzo Dario they are encircled by a ring of small disks in interlaced patterns. These were obviously inspired by inlaid mosaic floors like those found, for example, in St. Mark's and in the churches of Murano and Torcello.«[8] A similar transformation of a floor into a wall can be studied at the entrance of the Tolentini Faculty of Architecture in Venice. A floor surface in the forecourt rises up to become a wall and thus forms the rear of the portal. The motif of the floor mosaic in the Fondazione Querini Stampalia (1961–63) in Venice is the wall cladding of the »Sacello« of the Castelvecchio (1958–66) in changed chromatics. The polychromy reminds one of traditional colors of church floors. The prototype of this multicolored flooring is found in the Circolo Ufficiali della Marina Militare in Venice, designed around 1930. Scarpa's models appear in his work on another »level of reality«,[9] like the stone shutters of the cathedral of Torcello, which continue the tradition in travertine gates of the Fondazione Querini or the stone gate in the Olivetti store on the Piazza San Marco. Carlo Ragghianti writes that Scarpa's inspiration comes from the ambience he has in his blood, from the structures and forms originating in the history of Venetian architecture.[10]

### Water and light as materials

Its unique location on the water means that in Venice special conditions create the atmosphere of the city. The constant presence of reflections, and their duplicating effect, the light that is reflected on the façades, the transparency and the shimmering of the air go to make up the character of the city. Because water is present in all its different states, the city's architecture is perceived differently at different times. The surface and color of the water in the canals and the open sea constantly change as a result of light and weather and thus also change the appearance of façades and surroundings. Because of the climatic conditions of the various islands, architecture frequently manifests in the form of silhouettes. Water as a reflecting layer that expands space both nonmaterially and physically appears in almost all of Scarpa's works, either as a two-dimensional element, framed in a pool, or linear like a symbol of a canal.

For the Brion cemetery, water plays a central symbolic role: it functions as a metaphor for the Styx and as the source of life in its turbulent form, appears in a detail as a dried-out riverbed, symbolizing death. There is a deep pool with objects under the water while its surface reflects the meditation pavilion. The funerary chapel is adjacent to another pool, and is accessible from the outside by stepping-stones in the water. The sarcophagi are overarched by the »Arcosolio«, a bridge whose underside is lined with tiles in different shades of green and blue that look like reflections of water.

Pier Carlo Santini writes about the cemetery as follows: »The water is now no longer a reflecting mirror, or is not only that. It is no longer a fine crystalline veil or a thin layer. In the pond near the pavilion, which should have had a natural clay bottom, there is an opaque liquid containing microorganisms, insects, water plants, and water lilies. The weather and the seasons are reflected there, leaving visible traces. But time, the sense of time passing, is one of the most vibrant components in San Vito, and its implacable and fatal passage cannot be held back.«[11]

In the Brion cemetery stratification consists of a structure of terraced underwater concrete elements, the surface of the water itself, and planes accessible on foot that are a little above the water level. The reflection of the encircling wall and the buildings forms a fourth virtual stratum, which changes depending on the weather and light. In Venice the occurrence of floods causes Scarpa to work with soil stratification, for instance, in the Fondazione Querini, where the soil is separated from the walls by floodwater channels to respond to different water levels.

Giovanni Klaus König writes: »Floods are a natural phenomenon to which Venice has been accustomed for centuries now and which it can therefore anticipate when they arrive ... In the Fondazione Querini Stampalia, Scarpa feels it is absurd to try to fight the floods; once the water flows inside, it encounters the outlet in the interior, is channeled, and runs off into areas designed for the purpose.«[12]

The presence of the water unifies the transition between the interior and exterior. The transition becomes »fluid« in the truest sense of the word. In the entrances of buildings, the floor of the entrance room is overlapped by the sheet of water that comes through under the gates. The mobility of water and light responds to materials and planes that let them have their effect. Translucent surfaces, glass tiles, or glass surfaces make this possible in Scarpa's architecture.

Italo Furlan writes: »The native taste of the Venetians was clearly for color, living color, fluid, open to experience, open to time – time in natural and in human terms. That is to say, feeling, including feeling that embraces what we call nature, and seeks and finds a response there. Here on these islands the Venetians found a nature that lacks plasticity – no mountains or hills or masses of trees – only water and air: pure elements, immaterial, colored. And as for the form of this city, wholly constructed by human beings, to begin with the same terrain on which it is located – the Venetians' dream made it bloom between the water and the air: created on the elusive, almost indistinguishable line where water and air touch: as dimensions these are unlimited: these are pure qualitative values that cannot be formed, that is, dominated and arranged, except in the order of time.«[13]

From left to right

173. Carlo Scarpa, Brion cemetery, San Vito di Altivole, 1970–75. Water basin with partial view of meditation pavilion.
174. Carlo Scarpa, Brion cemetery, San Vito di Altivole, 1970–75. Canal along »propylaea«.
175. Carlo Scarpa, Gipsoteca, Possagno, 1956 to 1957. Water basin in front of glass façade.
176. Carlo Scarpa, Brion cemetery, San Vito di Altivole, 1970–75. Post of meditation pavilion anchored on a concrete cantilever in the water, »built« concrete reflections in the water.
177. Carlo Scarpa, Brion cemetery, San Vito di Altivole, 1970–75. Arcosolium, colored mosaic tiles acting like water reflections.
178. Carlo Scarpa, Venezuela Pavilion, Venice, 1954–56. Vertical and horizontal glazing merging exterior light and interior space.
179. Carlo Scarpa, Banca Popolare, Verona, 1973 to 1980. Double wall acting as light reflector.
180. Carlo Scarpa, Brion cemetery, San Vito di Altivole, 1970–75. Mosaic edge of concrete wall.

From left to right

181. Basilica Santa Maria Assunta, Torcello. Stone shutters.
182. Carlo Scarpa, Olivetti showroom, Venice, 1957/58. Exterior door leaf made out of stone.
183. Basilica Santa Maria Assunta, Torcello. Detail of the mosaic *Last Judgement*.
184. Carlo Scarpa, Fondazione Querini Stampalia, Venice, 1961–63. Wall in garden area with mosaic accent strip.
185. Carlo Scarpa, Fondazione Querini Stampalia, Venice, 1961–63. Entry bridge, detail of wood connection.
186. Venice, Stone bridge railing. Detail of metal connector between stone elements.
187. Santa Fosca Church, Torcello. Window detail on the exterior façade.
188. Carlo Scarpa, Banca Popolare, Verona, 1973 to 1980. Window detail on the interior.
189. House on Torcello. Double circle window shape, exterior stone trim.
190. Carlo Scarpa, Brion cemetery, San Vito di Altivole, 1970–75. Double circle opening with mosaic surround.

On three-dimensionally treated façades the effect of typically Venetian light in a combination of direct light and the light reflections of the water creates the characteristic impression of »chiaroscuro« (clear darkness),[14] and details are thrown into relief by the intense effect of light and shadow. In Scarpa's works the immaterial elements of light and glass function as matter that has corporeal properties, forms atmosphere, and is able to connect elements. In this connection, Plummer refers to the Japanese author Tanizaki: »Translucid surfaces constructed by Carlo Scarpa possess some of the pearly qualities evoked by Tanizaki. We find intricately layered surfaces that soak up the light, employing old Venetian techniques reminiscent of the city's shimmering atmosphere. Some of these optical properties may derive from Scarpa's early work as a glassmaker for Venini, where he developed ingenious methods for locking light inside glass by means of vitreous pastes, layered washes of contrasting colors, the use of murrhine and milkglass, and the pitting, dimpling, cutting, engraving, and ›weaving‹ of the glass-surface.«[15] Scarpa uses stratification of material in order to capture light, tame it in containers, and thus demonstrate that his designs are differentiated. He draws attention to situations like the centrally located Venetian garden, with its green oases within a stone city, in designs like the garden in the Italian Pavilion at the Biennale, or the garden of the Fondazione Querini Stampalia. In the Banca Popolare he builds a layered wall that serves as a light catcher. The design for the exhibition »Il senso del colore e il dominio delle acque« (1961 in Turin), specifically makes visual the element of water. What makes the Venezuela Pavilion in the Giardini come to life is the light supply thanks to openings that are laid like carpets over the pavilion's wall and roof. The light filters make noticeable the spatial stratification of the exhibition halls and admit the presence of the park, its light, and its atmosphere.

### Motifs and symbols

The typology of Venetian houses is based on conditions resulting from the city's situation. Projections of the second floor, so-called barbacani, allow builders to maximize the areas above the ground floor. The fact that houses are subdivided into a central hall and two side tracts influences the structure of the façade and is a result of the circumstance that buildings are used for industry and trade, and that the purpose of the upper floors is residential and representational. Architectonic symbols of the city are paths of access such as bridges and the calle, the counterpart of the canal on solid ground. An important component of the Venetians' lifestyle was and continues to be seafaring – hence the presence of navigation and elements pertaining to its practice in daily life. Wood, the basic material of shipbuilding, at the same time forms the foundation for the entire city, and wood products also play an important role in interior construction. Scarpa's designs of detail and part of the conversion of an interior are reminiscent of shipbuilding. The renovation of what is now the Casa Sereni, a very small apartment near the Piazza San Marco (formerly known as the Casa Ambrosini) has playful allusions to shipbuilding in the form of folding tables and teak furniture; the same is true of the fittings of the furniture and the workmanship of the details. Here stratification is not only a means of creating association – all the walls are paneled with wood, the ambiente is »lined« like a suit. The inner lining contains all the functions necessary for the rooms: shelf space, radiator covers, cabinet space, bay windows, folding tables, and lamps. The entrance pavilion of the Biennale works with associations to shipbuilding – masts with a sail.

In addition to the influence of the city's atmosphere and typology it is possible to find specific parallel motifs. Venice offers Scarpa a glimpse of various historical epochs in a limited space. His fondness for Byzantine architecture increases in these surroundings. A work that was important for Scarpa on which he had already worked while a student was the Byzantine basilica on Torcello, which influenced him in many ways. »How lovely are these stone slabs, and the hinges. I'm sure they are there so they can be turned to shut during the night; I wonder who did that, or maybe they were there for defense ... I remember them so clearly that I often amuse myself with what I can use from all this, only in details ... I enjoy using them whenever possible.«[16]

Scarpa transforms the above-mentioned casements of the church nave, made of Istrian stone, whose purpose was to prevent flaming arrows from reaching the interior of the church, into stone doors, like those at the Olivetti store on the Piazza San Marco, or the door of the exhibition space of the Fondazione Querini Stampalia. The vivid colors of the mosaics of the *Last Judgment* appear in the borderlike strips of ornamentation made of glass mosaic stones, for instance in Brion. The doubling of architectonic elements, which are thus joined together into a figured unit, can be seen in the external façade of the Torcello Cathedral. Scarpa uses this doubling not only with pillars, but also with other architectonic objects. It becomes an established term for specifying the value of the object. The mosaic floor of recurring geometric forms that can also be found in the Basilica San Marco, the »momento massimo del bizantinismo veneziano»[17] according to Italo Furlan, occurs as a reminiscence in the floor of the entrance room of the Fondazione Querini Stampalia.

»In the meantime it also seems clear that the façade of San Marco is part and parcel of the square, is the most important wall, the most expressive, the one that sums up its value. The entire square is surface, color, and rhythm; but on the façade of San Marco is centered the most intensive and best-articulated color, the highest and most decisive rhythm. The close-standing marble pillars of the bases color the pilasters between the doors and unfold, in the vast light from the sea, a deliberate abundance of precious materials. Above them, marbles and mosaics cover the entire surface. It is a magnificent panel, a cloth with marble intarsia, made of multicolored golden stones.«[18]

The mosaics have the characteristics of an iridescent fabric, a textile covering. Double pillars also appear in the 12th century church of San Donato in Murano, which Scarpa must have known very well, having stayed on Murano for a long time while he worked with Venini. In Scarpa's work the motif of multiple framing of windows found in Byzantine churches and buildings becomes a sculptural element, which is not limited to the framing of surfaces, but occurs as a symbol in the most various forms (Brion cemetery), as a ledge (Banca Popolare in Verona) or on door handles (Brion) and other objects. In modifications such as the Taddei Apartment, Scarpa is confronted with Venice's Gothic past. He supplements the transparency of the fine polyfores, which filter the light as if through a lace curtain, with independent fenestration, a procedure he already used in the renovation of the Ca' Foscari.

The textilelike structure of the Doges' Palace with its chromatics is an example of a stone »carpet« on the façade that stretches over the outside surface like a tapestry. The façade of the Ca' d'Oro (for which Scarpa created a design as part of the interior design of the Galleria Franchetti that he did not carry out) is an example for the carpetlike application of isolated areas of stone; edgings form transitions and façade borders at the corners. The polyfores with the loggias behind them are detached from the unified outside wall; they are an open transitional link between inside and outside and function as a detached ornamental shield. Scarpa visually shows the detaching of the façade stratum in the courtyard façade of the Banca Popolare. The mosaics in the inner courtyard of the Ca' d'Oro have the effect of Oriental rugs turned to stone. Semper writes about why the idea of textiles is valid: »Thus textile art does not include actual fabrics alone, as will become apparent from the following. Tectonics also comprise a vast area; beside the wooden roof structure and the pillars that support it this area includes a large part of the household equipment. In a certain respect they also comprise a part of stone construction and a particular system of metal construction. Stereotomy includes more than the skill of the mason and excavator; the mosaic worker, the carver of wood, ivory, and metal is also a cutter of solids.«[19]

In his projects, Scarpa also addresses a typically Venetian construction project – the bridge: The stylistic idiom of the access bridge to the Fondazione Querini Stampalia in Venice is reminiscent of a bridge on Murano, the effect of whose metal structure is also produced in combination with its wooden steps. Scarpa emphasizes elements like the handrail standards by doubling them. The double handrail presents the duality of metal and wood – the linear elements are formed differently; the end of the wooden rail is set and protected by metal. The mounting consists of double flat bars, and the rail, too, seems to consist of a metal base and a wooden rail layer. The part that echoes the stone bridges of Venice is the initial stone steps and the reversed detail that fastens the material.

The resemblance of the façade of the Palazzo Ducale to Oriental carpets – taking the form of a floor mosaic on the wall – appears in its chromatic quality in the »Sacello« of the Castelvecchio. The circle as a theme representing openings appears in buildings, particularly churches, as front or side windows. Scarpa doubles the element and uses the resulting figure eight as an aperture (Brion, Banca Popolare in Verona) or decorative symbol.

### Materiality and color

The specific materials available in Venice offer the basis for the use of colors and materials in designing new buildings. One important element is Istrian marble, employed to reinforce edges or as a two-dimensional cladding. In Scarpa, the stabilization of edges and corners of buildings be-

191. Torcello Museum. Corner detail of solid stone in brick wall.
192. Carlo Scarpa, Fondazione Querini Stampalia, Venice, 1961–63. Corner detail of solid stone in concrete elements.

193. San Zaccaria Church, Venice. Corner detail.
194. Carlo Scarpa, Gipsoteca, Possagno, 1955 to 1957. Corner detail of window and skylight.

comes a geometric motif and corner detail in the garden of the Fondazione Querini Stampalia. »Because an effect of depth needed to be produced by shadows, Istrian marble was preferred even after finer types of marble became easier to obtain. In the Istrian stone, exposed surfaces that are protected from the weather turn black, which accentuates the shadows, while those that are exposed to the weather turn white.«[20] The corner profiles made of Istrian marble are partly covered by plaster, which made it possible to form the corners more precisely. The intensification of the corners as the point where two surfaces meet is a motif found everywhere in Venice.

Istrian stone, marble, plaster, and bricks are in contrast with the color of water and sky. The carpetlike layer of plaster in the house of his lawyer and friend Luigi Scatturin (1961–63) in Venice again reflects these colors and gives substance to a fleeting glance out of the window over the roofscape of Venice. Scarpa utilizes the artisanal techniques of marmorino and stucco lustro, develops them further, and experiments with the craftsmen.[21] Plummer writes about this as follows: »His architectural materials are worked into similar glowing lattices. Plaster is made luminescent by mixing it with marble dust, colorful pigments, and oil, by a layered and permeable brushwork reminiscent of Titian's canvases, as well as by scratches and induced patinas that form a primordial accumulation of slightly translucent films and ›stains‹. Walls of corroded mosaic are assembled into luminous wavelets, loosely and imprecisely aligned, with chips and surface defects that thicken their glow. Polished marble and glass are laced with networks of gold foil that seem to float in the air, like sun glinting off water, and burnt horizons at sundown. Glass sheets overlap stone walls in a kind of displaced glaze, while concrete remnants and tissues can be seen under shallow ponds whose transparency has been dyed green by algae.«[22]

The color scheme of the mosaic in the entrance area of the Fondazione Querini Stampalia reflects the typical triad of colors in the floor mosaics of a number of Venetian churches. Colored glass as a material typical of Venice, one with which Scarpa worked for a long time, reappears in his architectural work, particularly as a linear element made of mosaic tiles. Again, here is Italo Furlan describing characteristics of Venetian architecture: »Venetian architecture thus had to become light and diaphanous, be transformed into values of color, light, and rhythm, break up the masses, to become, in the end, an image without weight, almost immaterial, assuming the entire responsibility for expression, becoming more and more rich and valuable. – And this is how it happened that the whole form of Venice is color, or, one might say, surface. That is why Venetian palaces, regardless during which period they were built, are, from a formal perspective, nothing but façades: the entire expanse of these façades, subtly perforated and open to reflections, forms a system not of volumes and planes, but of shadows and lights, engravings and fine reliefs, which makes almost no demands on what is volumetrically evident.«[23]

The more intensively one studies the architectonic phenomena of the city and their details, the more apparent the sphere from which Scarpa drew his inspiration becomes. Scarpa was able to absorb all that he saw and integrate it into his creative process. He was convinced of the importance of the genesis of a work and tried to understand how not only architectonic works but art works as well had developed.[24] In his projects in Venice he also uses the principle of the palimpsest – modifying spaces and complexes without completely deleting all traces of his predecessors. He makes room for something new, which earned him the sharp criticism of conservators, but preserves trails to the past with the help of fragments and newly constructed reminiscences. The city's architectonic motifs and its specific atmospheric situations leave their mark on Scarpa's work.

## 3. A detailed analysis of layering in three examples

### 3.1. Castelvecchio, Verona (1958–64)

#### History

The renovation of the Castelvecchio began at a time when Scarpa had already completed several museum projects and exhibitions. Having remodeled the Galleria dell'Accademia in Venice (1952 to 1955), done the interior design of the Museo Correr in Venice (1953), worked on remodeling the Uffizi Gallery in Florence (1954), and built the Venezuela Pavilion for the Biennale in the Giardini (1954–65), he had gathered experience in the didactic presentation of exhibits in a historical context.

The varied history of the Castelvecchio goes back to Roman times. The first written documents date back to 1162, when Verona was a free commune.[1] Between 1354 and 1356 the Scaligeri built the actual Castelvecchio and the bridge over the Adige, which divides the complex in two. The purpose of this fortress was not to enable the citizens of Verona to withdraw into it, but rather to be protected against them. This also explains the orientation of the fortifications (interior and exterior ditch) in the direction of the city. The Scaligeri built the reggia as a closed complex around a central inner courtyard on the west side of the grounds, and a courtyard used for military purposes on the east side that was open toward the river. They closed the Porta del Morbio, which came from the period in which Verona had been a commune, in order to build an access road to the bridge. Under the rule of the »Serenissima« (1405–1797), under whose protection Verona had placed itself, the building was also used for military purposes. After the French took over in 1799 it was named Castelvecchio instead of Castello di San Martino (after the church located in the inner courtyard). The French expanded the fortificaton structures in a northern direction against a threat from Austria. In 1806 they built the L-shaped building of the Caserma and, in the northwest corner of the courtyard, a connecting staircase to the ambulatories around the walls. In order to widen the road, they reduced the size of the surrounding wall and razed the church of San Martino. Later the access road to the bridge, which had previously been reserved for the fort, was opened to the public. In 1923 it was decided that the Castelvecchio would house the city's collection of paintings, and Antonio Avena, librarian and archivist, who was at the same time the director of the city's museums, was given the task of restoring and refurbishing it. Together with the architect Forlatti, Avena carried out a historicizing intervention, which imitated medieval structures such as towers and crenelated walls, as did the interior decorations that, in the Reggia, were done in the style of the Scaligeri frescoes. The façade of the Napoleonic barracks was completely replaced by an assortment of elements such as Gothic windows and columns, originating in the Palazzo Camerlenghi (15th/16th century), which had been destroyed by a flood in 1882. The façade was divided symmetrically, while the courtyard was transformed into an Italian garden.

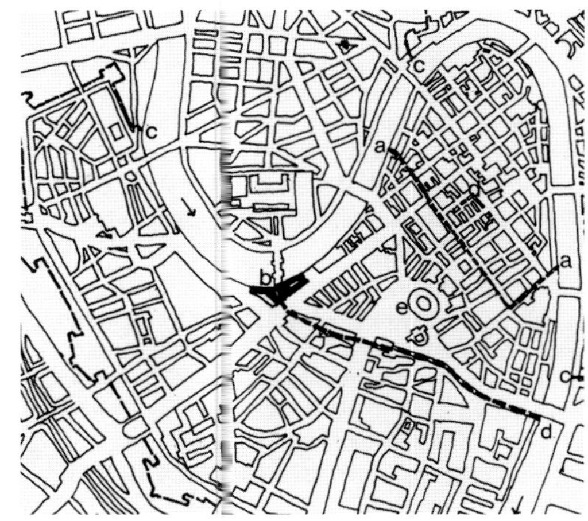


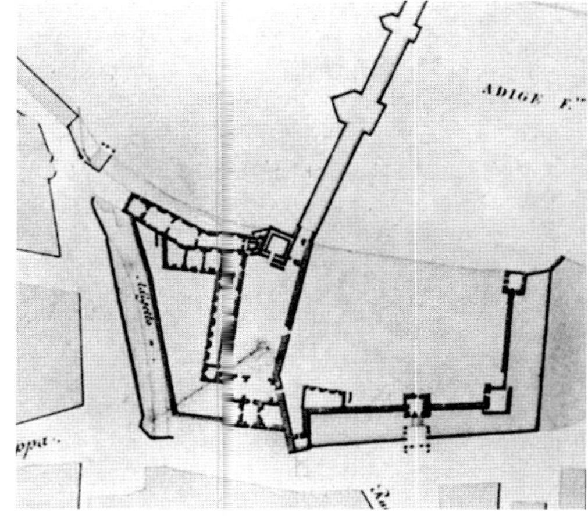


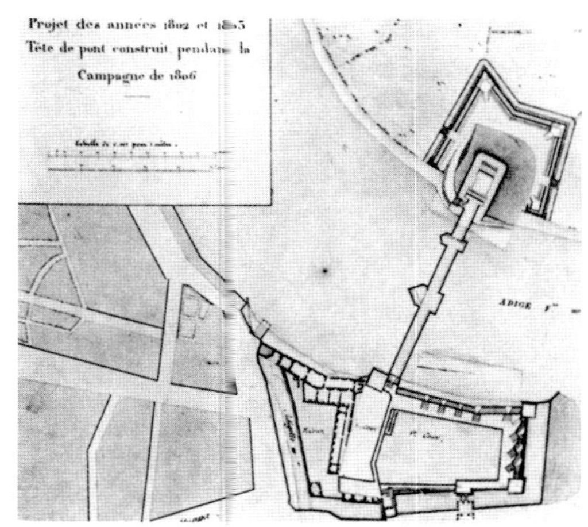


Only the historical development of the architecture of the Castelvecchio can explain the process-oriented intervention of Scarpa, who found a building consisting of more or less historical fragments that had already been altered several times. The rediscovery of the Porta del Morbio and of the inner moat had considerable influence on the development of the renovation. On the occasion of the 1958 exhibition, the oldest area of the Reggia in particular was redesigned. The Reggia was given a forecourt, a new access staircase was built for it in the Torre del Mastio, as well as a connection on the second floor between the tower and the Reggia. In remodeling the Reggia Scarpa took a critical look at a building of consistent age, from which he merely removed Forlatti's and Avena's historicizing paintings. As early as 1958, he moved the exit from the ground floor of the Caserma one room over deeper into the building and redesigned the floor of the sixth hall, which has now become the exterior, or transitional, room. Before new levels were added, he took back the architecture to its original basis. L. Magagnato describes the intervention: »In particular, in a manner that must not be confused with postmodernist eclecticism because he renounced theorizing, Scarpa researched the individual concrete case in its specific historical situation, which he had studied objectively and stripped clean down to the authentic layer, though without destroying the most valuable interventions; in turn, he worked among these preexisting givens with combinations of modular and differentiated elements, in accordance with a Neo-plasticist syntax that is always the fundamental basis of his cultural training.«[2]

Which of the architectural relics inside the fortification would be considered to be worth keeping was definitely the architect's personal decision. Scarpa removes the layers of color of the ar-

195–199. Carlo Scarpa, Castelvecchio, Verona, 1958–64.

195. Plan of the center of Verona illustrating the systems of fortresses.
196. Plan of Castelvecchio in 1801 with the major courtyard being open towards the river.
197. Plan of Castelvecchio and fortifications in 1802 and 1803.

198. Exterior view of the fortification walls seen from north-east.
199. Courtyard façade of the Napoleonic barracks.

chitect Forlatti and has the Napoleonic staircase in the northwestern part of the courtyard torn down. In planning the garden, he decides not to consider the position of the Church of San Martino. Beside bringing out various epochs in the building's history, Scarpa adds one more sediment of interpretive layers in his own stylistic idiom. Stabenow and Plecnik call this way of didactically dealing with historic buildings the »didactic appropriation of the monument«.[3]

In this building stratification has a historical and didactic component. Adding horizontal and vertical surfaces makes it possible for Scarpa to insert new parts in the existing spaces, to change the proportions in accordance with his ideas, and to form transitions between rooms and sequences. The rooms of the complex are not covered with a single »modernized« layer; rather, fragments that span the building's history until well into the 20th century are added to them at historical nodes. A critical examination of the building, and the decision for or against existing structures, demonstrate the subjectivity of such a project. In 1959 Scarpa remodels the ground floor of the Caserma, configuring a new entrance and items of furniture for displaying the exhibits. Stylistically, many of the principles of Neo-plasticism can be found in Scarpa's intervention.[4] The organization of the spatial structure into horizontal and vertical planes, which may in turn consist of individual strata, makes it possible for Scarpa to subdivide walls, floors, and ceilings into fields, to do partial interventions, to leave elements visible, or, in some cases, to cover them completely. He works with cladding that is applied to the floor or wall; the fact that these are detached is clearly revealed by the formation of detail, such as framing or surface structure. The theme of the joint has central significance for the autonomy of the elements and becomes the symbol of connection and separation alike.

## The complex as a whole

Scarpa makes visible the separation of the individual buildings by means of selective interventions. He creates negative spaces between the Caserma and the city wall in the direction of the Reggia, and between the library tract and that of the Caserma – a strategy that exposes the northeast tower. Interior rooms are transformed into exterior rooms that prepare the transition into the next section. The alternation between negative space and interior produces the spatial dynamics of the »percorso« through the museum. The negative spaces that were formed are filled with horizontal or vertical wood or sheet metal elements. The dynamics of this conception are the result of the direct contrast between the massive volume of the buildings and the many-layered »filling«. Stratification is, first of all, brought about by »taking away« building substance, which is subsequently replaced again by an arrangement of new material strata and symbolizes its construction. Scarpa improves and controls the lighting in the Caserma and in the library's reading room. After moving the entrance of the museum from the central axis of the Caserma into the northeast corner, Scarpa organizes the museum by means of a fixed passageway, the »percorso«, which guides visitors through the building and to the exhibits. Here the principle of stratification helps Scarpa to define spaces through surfaces and to link them firmly with specific exhibits.

### The inner courtyard of the Caserma

The inner courtyard of the Caserma is divided into three areas, the former moat, the circulation area with access to the museum, library, Sala Avena and offices, and the centrally located garden. The original entrance of the Caserma is closed down and a stone terrace is placed in front of the opening, which extends the interior outward. A system of paths made of differently structured stone slabs is laid in front of the L-shaped building of the Caserma, guiding visitors toward the building. With the help of the floor covering and the medium-high walls, the paths lead to the museum entrance, library, offices, and the Sala Bogian. A differentiated system of stone slabs is supplemented by two bordered bodies of water, whose level is higher than the walking level (see analysis drawings). Flower beds offer additional texture and create zones opposite the façades. The stone »entrance carpet« dovetails, like rolled-out hemmed lengths of carpet, with the adjoining lawn and gravel areas.

»Scarpa's love for water lasted all his life and is manifested in almost all his projects. In the Castelvecchio this idea is taken up yet one more time: literally in a large pool for fish from which the water flows and beside which Scarpa places a little path on a gentle slope – and, metaphysically, this is located in the museum's interior, on the ground floor, where Scarpa uses the same source of inspiration for the flooring. Here, however, the water is replaced by concrete or by stucco lucido, homogenous and reflecting light from the bases of the sculptures.«[5]

At the same time the fountain and various stone slabs are reintegrated in the overall context as recycled architectural elements. The division of the slabs, their different materials, and the treatment of their surfaces on the various access paths makes the four entrances of the building rhythmic and distinguishes them from each other. Areas formed by slabs of the same size are overlapped by areas that, less present, are formed from the edges of rising elements and the linear relationships on the floor. Individual »swaths« of stone are framed like carpets and lie in a grid made of stone strips. The floor covering represents spaces as zones of movement whose boundaries are emphasized by the strong shaping of the edges of the covering with the support of a few vertical elements, and which form the transition from the courtyard and garden into the building's interior. The areas formed by identical material are subdivided by differentiating the surface treament into increasingly smaller units, which form a carefully planned composition.

The edges of the fragmented concrete walls are defined by rough stone layers or bounded by metal strips. Just as carpets are given borders or hems, elements are bounded, their form surrounded. The floor coverings of the outside area communicate with those of the interior rooms, create the relationship between inside and outside.

### Spaces between interior and exterior

The transitional spaces described previously form new negative spaces and work with all three elements – floor, wall, and ceiling. Scarpa uses the rediscovered Porta del Morbio as a connection between the Caserma and the Reggia, transforming an exterior space that formerly belonged to the interior of the Caserma into a centerpiece of the outside grounds. The hollow space that is created is a connecting link between two tracts, which is lined with different materials. It is also the staging room for the statue of Cangrande.[6] On the floor of the first floor, a stone covering that gives direction develops, visibly »coating« the brick underconstruction. The statue of the smiling Cangrande on horseback soars above on a jib boom. Large-format slabs of stone superimposed on each other lead through the passageway, which ends in front of the Torre del Mastio. The presentation of the statue of Cangrande takes place in the transitional space between interior and exterior, which is furnished with various elements, such as walkways and stone wall panels made of various materials. Walking along the passageway from the Torre del Mastio, after touring the Reggia, one reaches the transitional room of Cangrande once more, one floor higher from a new perspective. A series of vertical concrete slabs of varying sizes accompanies the concrete stairway and leads to the walkway that goes to the upper entrance into the Caserma. The gateway through the »Muro Comunale« in the upper storey is »lined« with concrete slabs that are deposited on the old walls like the sediment of a new era.

Above the negative space for Cangrande, the roof of the Caserma is resolved into individual layers and ends in a beam that is supported by the city wall. The illustrated process of uncovering makes visible imaginary layers of roof structure and makes it easier to cross over into the adjacent buildings. The stepped edges of all surfaces dovetail the elements with their surroundings. A concrete wall of varying height, whose edges are defined by being covered with metal, is placed in front of the stepped exterior wall whose gradual dismantling by Scarpa becomes clear from its gradually decreased thickness, ending with a separated concrete facing and a pillar that stands on it.

In addition to the »vuoto«, the negative space for the statue of Cangrande, which is the pivot and central point of the entire museum passage, the tower on the east side is also differentiated from the Napoleonic barracks. Here, too, Scarpa gradually makes visible, by means of spatial stratification, the individual elements of the building and draws attention to original configurations. He cuts out a section of the massive exterior wall in such a way that a slit down to the ground floor is formed, and builds a new façade – staggered inward – made of wood panels. Thus, a light shaft is created for the reading room of the library, providing improved lighting and a view. The overlapping of the materials makes it possible for the old masonry and new panels to exist simultaneously.

### The façade of the Caserma

The façade that faces the courtyard, which is assembled from fragments of the Gothic palazzo and was inserted in a medieval fortress in lieu of a Napoleonic barracks is supplemented and modified by Scarpa. In the interior he puts a formally independent layer of glass in front of the existing window openings. The way they are divided is reminiscent of the paintings of Mondrian, and they are overlapped by the preexisting stone elements.

Richard Murphy writes as follows about the façade of the Caserma: »What matters most is the idea of the material – the solidity of the building – which at the edges reveals a series of surfaces or layers: It is the progressive increase of layers or strata, as in sedimentary rock. Without doubt the treatment Scarpa reserved for the façade of the Caserma, where he creates thin, overlaid but discontinuous planes, supports this idea. This is particularly evident in the extreme case where the essence of the wall is presented by the cut made by Scarpa.«[7]

### The interior of the Caserma: the exhibition

In the interior Scarpa primarily uses floor stratification to reproportion the rooms. A layer that is offset from the walls that rise through all the storys, which is formed by a stone grid infilled with concrete, lies on the floor of the ground floor like a series of connnected carpets. The existing enfilade is closely connected by means of the floor design and the seemingly continuous ceiling girders. Because they are offset from the wall, the rooms have an inner regular contour formed by the floor covering, and an outer spatial irregular contour formed by the medieval walls that rise through all the storys. A virtual space is formed by the floor design within the existing space. As with the access path in the courtyard, the floor is given rhythm by an irregular structure of stone strips in which the somewhat lower concrete surfaces have been integrated. Double and single linear elements made of stone form the seams in the longitudinal direction of the concrete surfaces.

Scarpa himself comments on the floor design as follows: »The floor is one of the key surfaces in defining the geometry of space. The square geometry of the rooms provides the information for the model. It was necessary to resolve the problem of the seam between the wall which had a vertical luminous surface, and the floor which had a darker, horizontal surface ... I thought of the water surrounding the wall of the castle. That gave me the idea of making a negative seam. The floor of each room was individualized, as if they were a series of platforms.«[8]

The »Sacello«, the only »newly built« room of the museum, is especially differentiated: here, a black-bordered »carpet« of terracotta was installed. The ground floor rooms are plastered, and in the passages between the rooms there are roughly cut stone slabs, former floor slabs, which, as recycled architectural elements, have been transformed into doorcases.

On the top floor of the Caserma, Scarpa develops the sequence of rooms that existed below as a result of the enfilade found there, by means of exhibition walls. These areas are made accessible along the façade that faces the Adige River. The stone traffic area follows the irregular course of the defense wall, while the exhibition areas are defined by a carpet consisting of a regular terracotta surface. The material stratification of the floor is what brings about the clear spatial separation of the individual rooms and once more forms virtual spatial contours in the existing rooms. The exhibit area is clearly separated from the traffic area. The floor covering is designed like a movable carpet and is somewhat higher than the traffic area. Above, the upper spatial boundary is formed by a dropped ceiling made of individual plastered panels whose pattern is reminiscent of tatami mats. The ventilation grilles, in the shape of wooden carabottini,[9] form the centerpiece of the ceilings. The ceiling consists of individual panels with dark frames, which, in contrast to the floor, formulate a surface composed of segments. In the last hall, which was completed later – a connecting space between two tracts for which a new façade was created facing the Adige River (see connecting spaces) – the ceiling is composed of azure panels that tint the entering light blue and are reminiscent of Japanese sliding elements.

After crossing the Caserma, the path to the exit leads down a staircase and is directed by wall clothing in the form of three large panels. The section shows the overlapping of the façade planes, the exterior panels, and interior panels in a drawing.

### Reggia

In the entrance area to the Reggia through the Torre del Mastio the walls are also only partially clad and their original form remains visible. Tall stone slabs that are attached to the walls accompany the ascending staircase. Each of the steps is covered with a stone slab as well. In the exhibition area of the Reggia, which was the first to be renovated, Scarpa again offsets the mostly wooden floors from the walls by means of a stone edging. In an elective didactic renovation historicizing frescoes were removed, while the remains of originally medieval paintings were retained.

The Castelvecchio after Carlo Scarpa's renovation is characterized by an overall reorganization of the complex with various spatial highlights which, in a clearly contemporary stylistic idiom, stand out against the existing architectural features. Stratification is done by the »restacking« or dissecting of preexisting strata, and the adding of panels and surfaces made of stone, stucco, wood, and concrete. Scarpa differentiates floor, wall, and ceiling elements by means of detailed joint design and distancing of the individual elements. Associations with textiles, as in the exterior cladding of the Sacello and the carpetlike floor designs, work together with neoplasticist themes like those of window spacing and of newly integrated areas of color. A part of the archeology of the Castelvecchio is didactically brought out and completed with comments. The fact that the sediments of various periods and uses of the Castelvecchio can be perceived, and the Castelvecchio's function as a venue for staging exhibitions complement each other to form a unified work.

200–207. Carlo Scarpa, Castelvecchio, Verona, 1958–64.

200. Exhibition of Cangrande statue in void created by Scarpa.
201. Section through Reggia.
202–204. Floor Plans, percorso through museum by Avena, 1926.
205. Site plan diagram showing entries and circulation. Key: 1 entrance into Reggia, 2 passage between Caserma and Reggia, 3 secondary access into Caserma, 4 main entrance into museum, 5 entrance to library and Sala Bogian, 6 access to courtyard.
206. Courtyard, waterbasin and fountain.
207. Courtyard, layers of stone »rolled out« as pavement leading to the entry door of the museum.

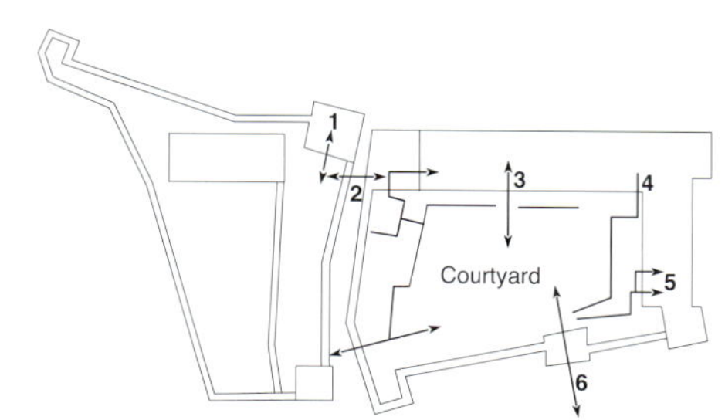
1
2
3
4
Courtyard
5
6

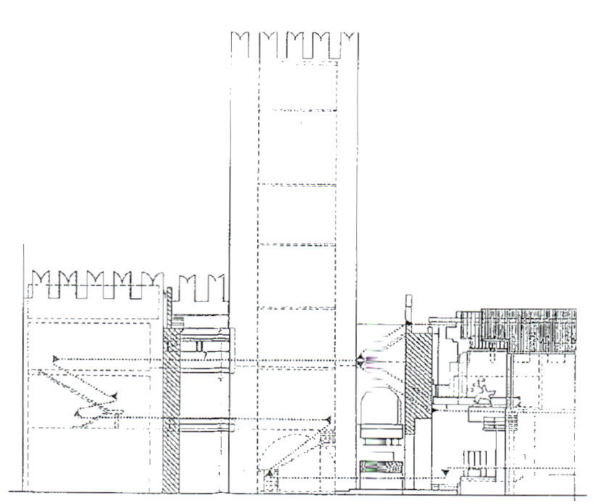

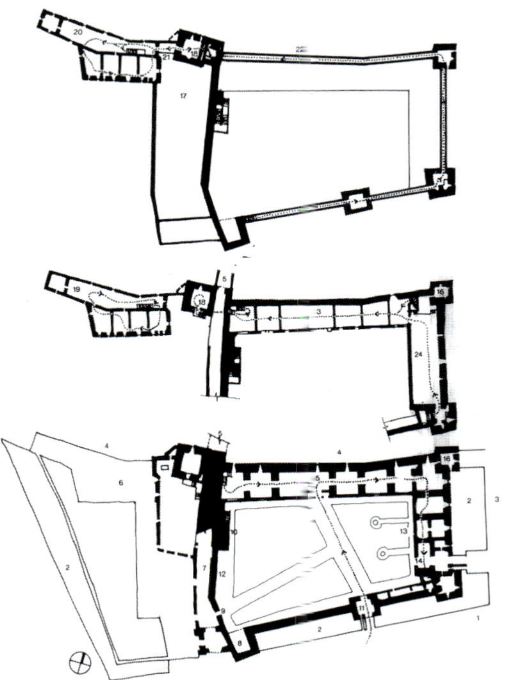

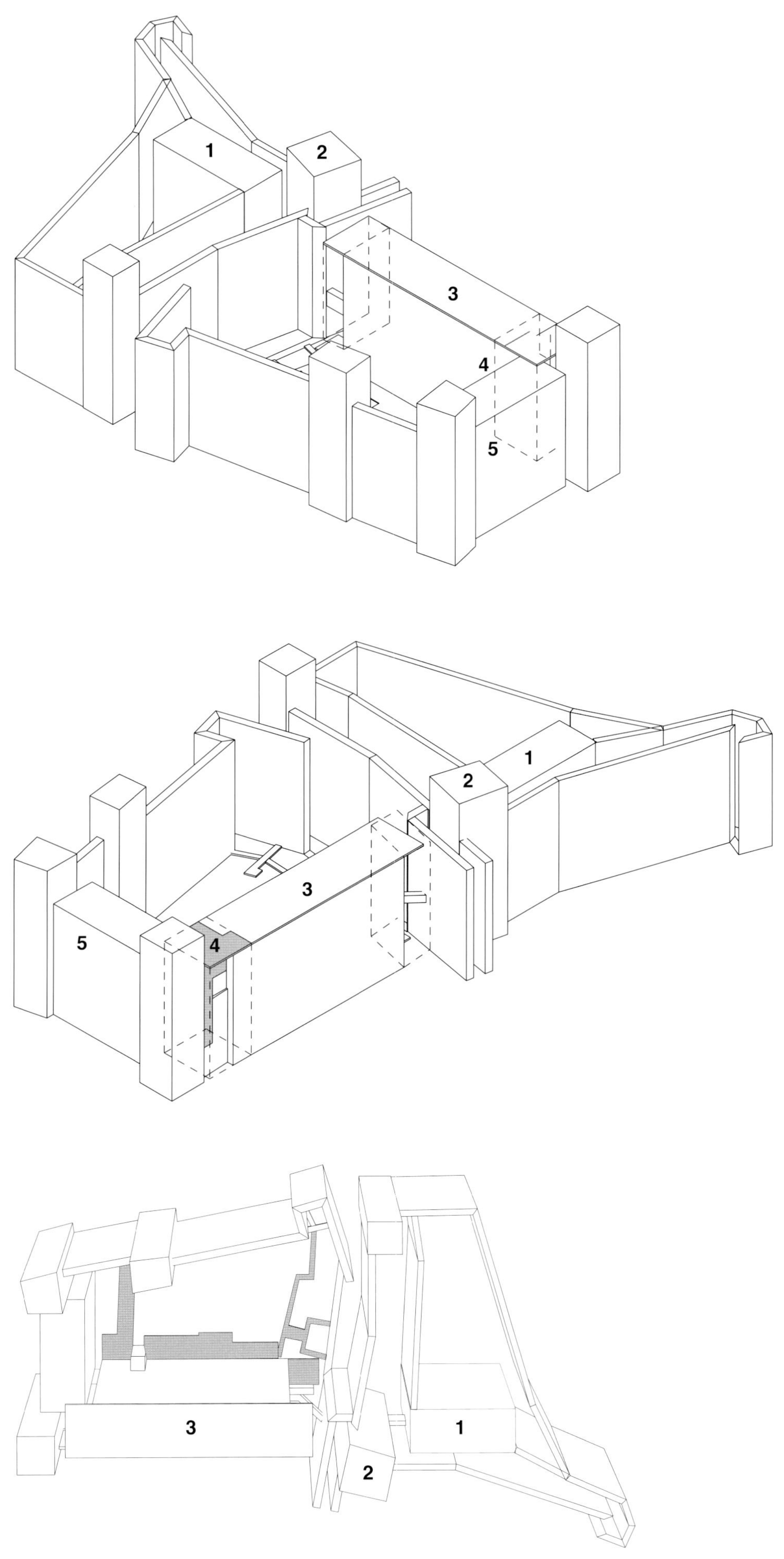


208–211. Carlo Scarpa, Castelvecchio, Verona, 1958–64.

208–210. Locations of layering applied to Castelvecchio. Transition: Caserma Reggia (208), new library area (209), courtyard (210). Key: 1 Reggia, 2 Torre del Mastio, 3 Caserma (Galleria), 4 Sala Avena, 5 Sala Boggian.

211. North façade: wood paneling set back from battlement parapet, metal roof suggesting roof layers.

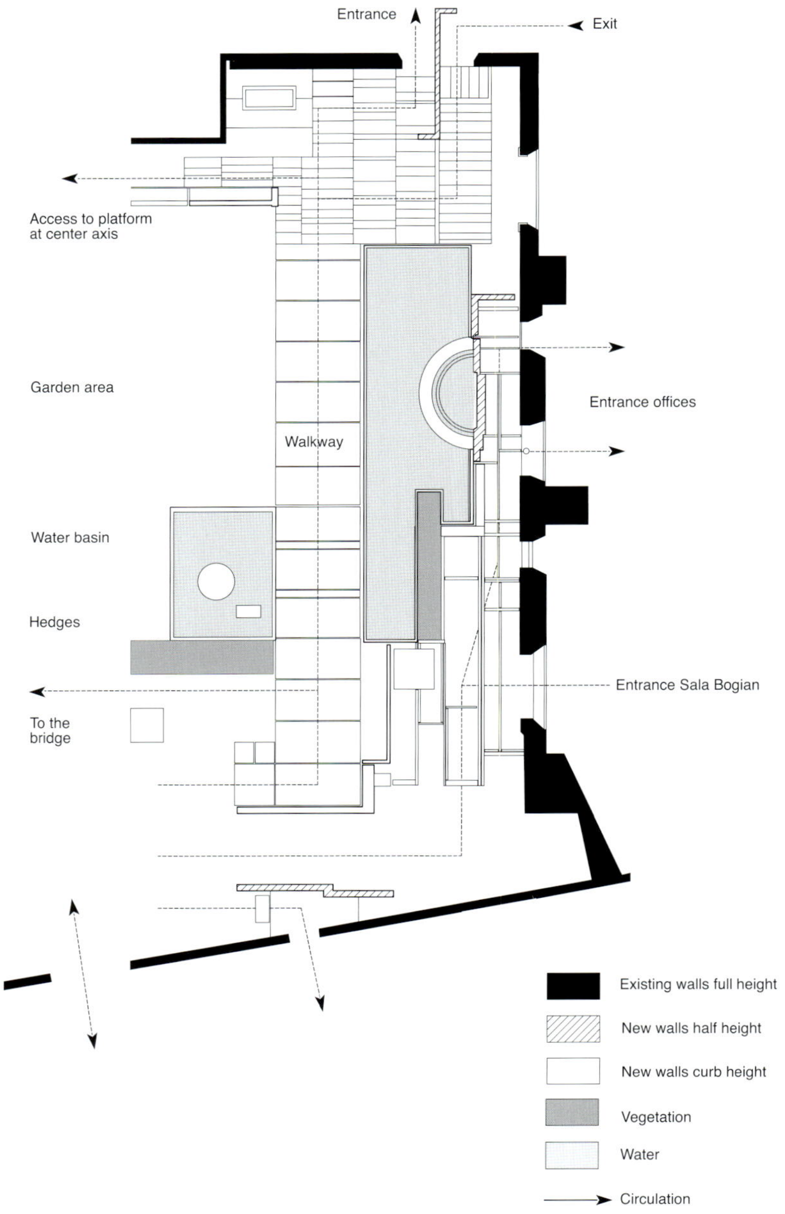

Entrance

Exit

Access to platform at center axis

Garden area

Walkway

Entrance offices

Water basin

Hedges

Entrance Sala Bogian

To the bridge

- Existing walls full height
- New walls half height
- New walls curb height
- Vegetation
- Water
- Circulation

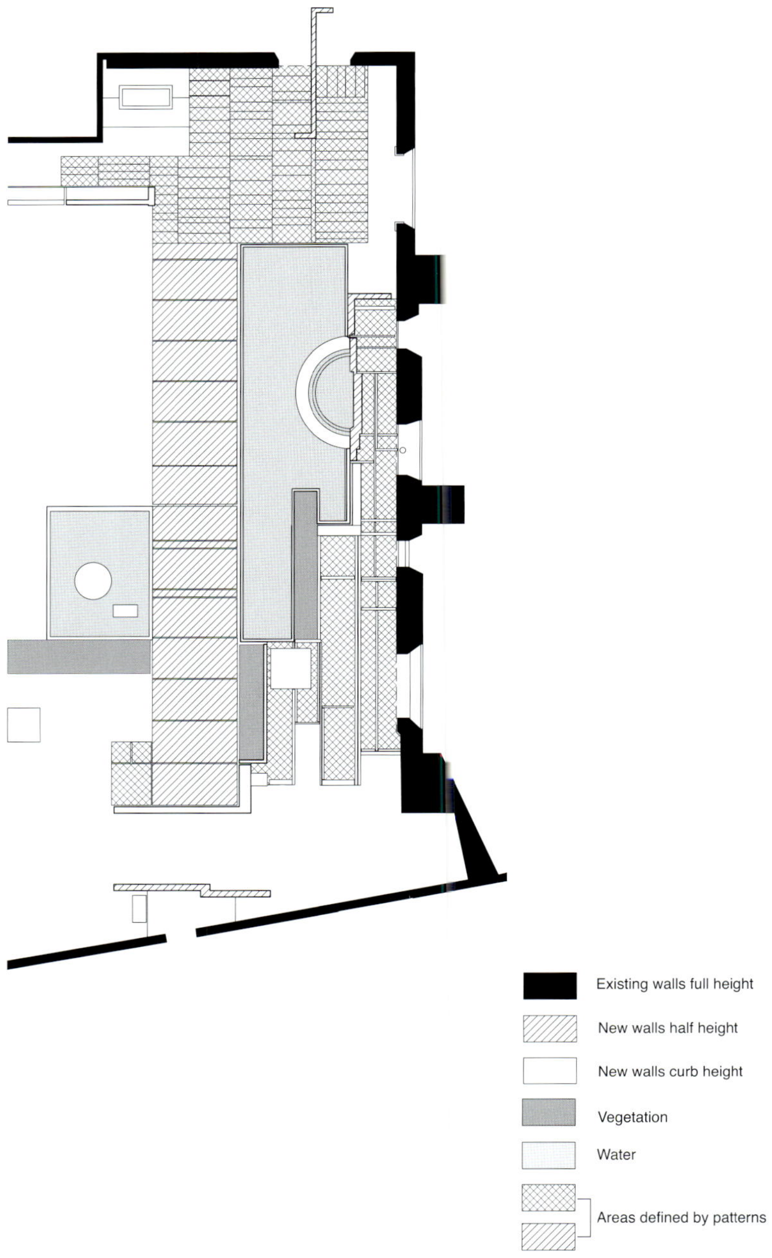

- Existing walls full height
- New walls half height
- New walls curb height
- Vegetation
- Water
- Areas defined by patterns

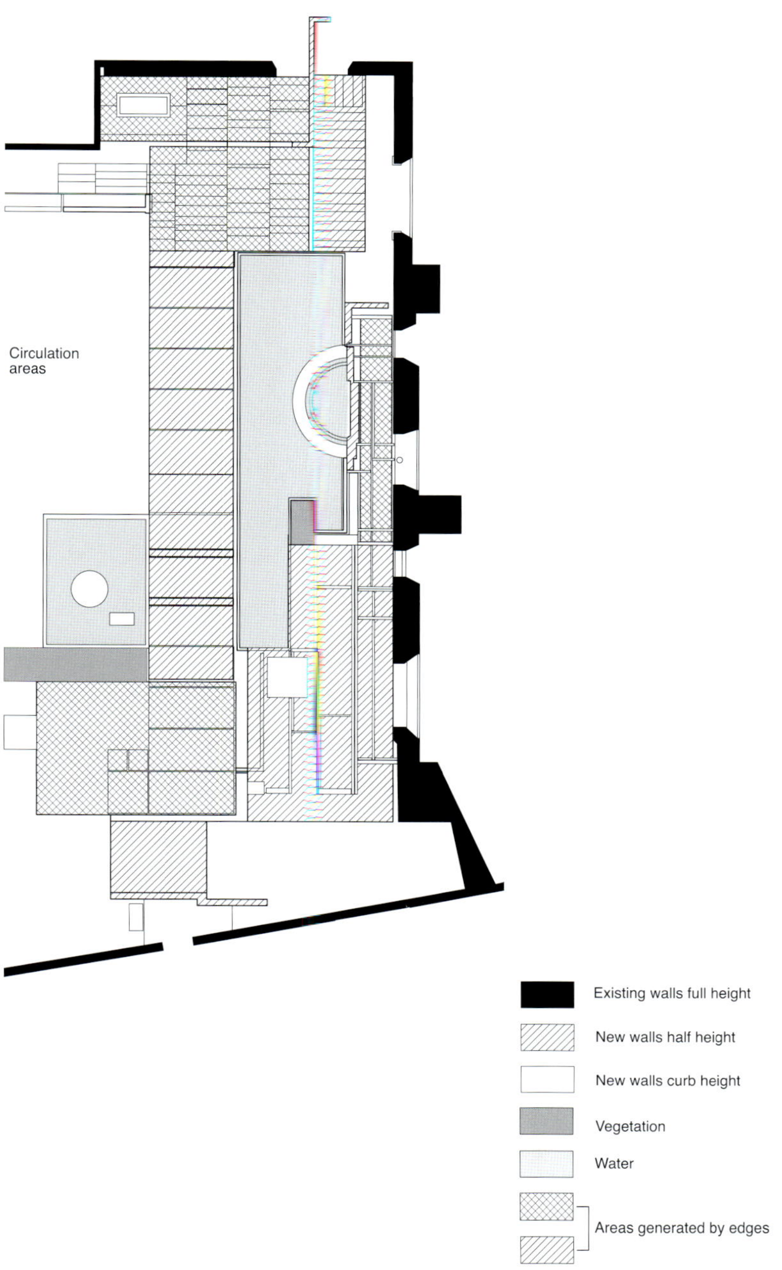

Circulation areas

Existing walls full height
New walls half height
New walls curb height
Vegetation
Water
Areas generated by edges

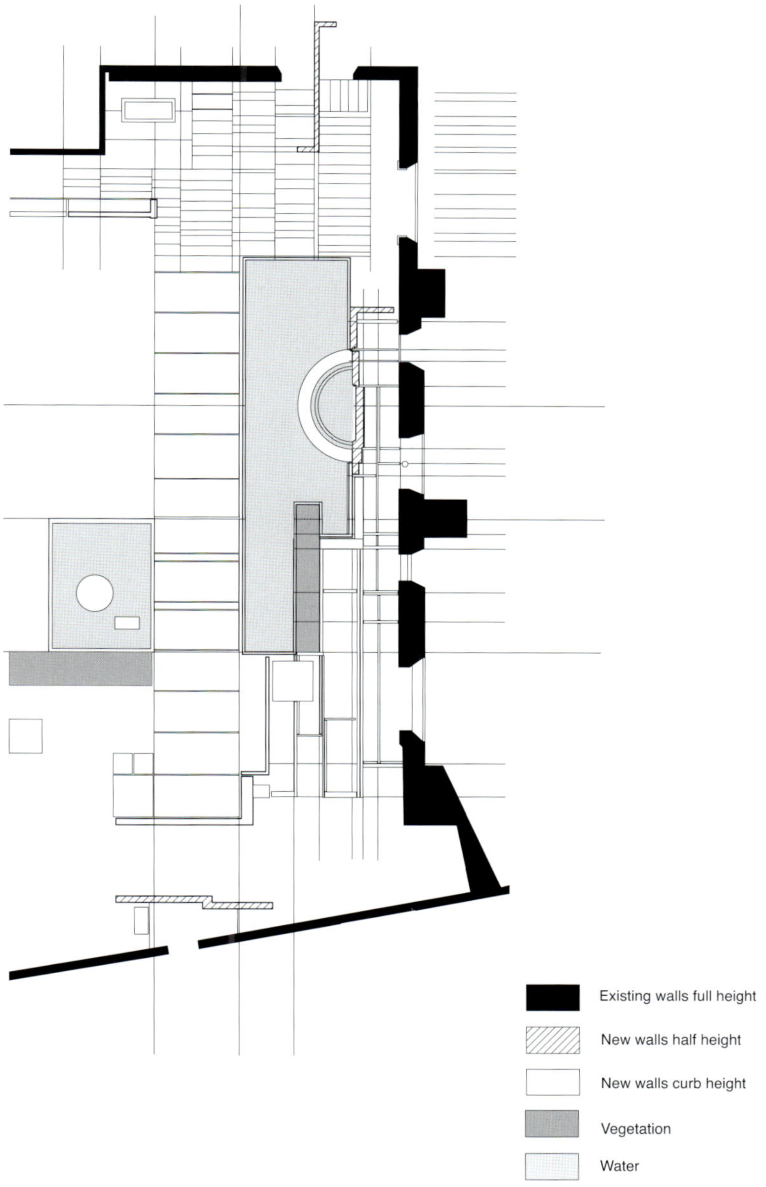

Existing walls full height
New walls half height
New walls curb height
Vegetation
Water

212–220. Carlo Scarpa, Castelvecchio, Verona, 1958–64.

212. Floor plan entry area in courtyard, circulation.
213. Floor plan entry area in courtyard, areas defined by floor pattern.
214. Detail of stone pavement in entry area, different stone patterns and surface treatment.
215. Detail of stone pavement in entry area, edge treatement, height differences.
216. Detail of stone pavement in entry area, stone frame around perimeter and accent strips in elevated pavement area.

217. Floor plan entry area in courtyard, areas defined by elevation changes and edges.
218. Floor plan entry area in courtyard, axis pattern.
219. Library entrance from courtyard, low wall with metal edge.
220. Entrance area, low wall behind fountain with stone edge.

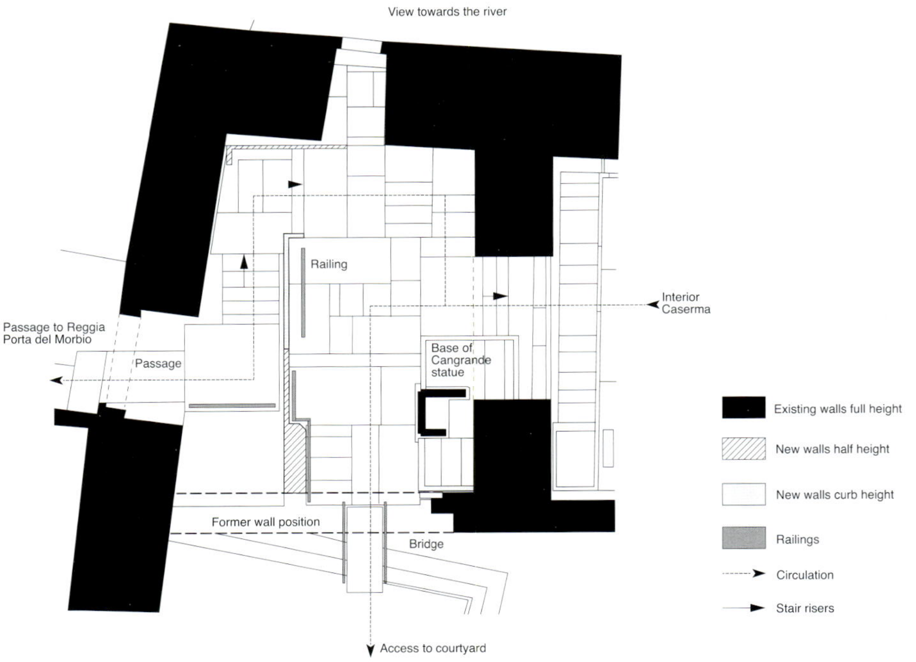

View towards the river

Railing

Interior Caserma

Passage to Reggia Porta del Morbio

Passage

Base of Cangrande statue

Former wall position

Bridge

Access to courtyard

Existing walls full height

New walls half height

New walls curb height

Railings

Circulation

Stair risers

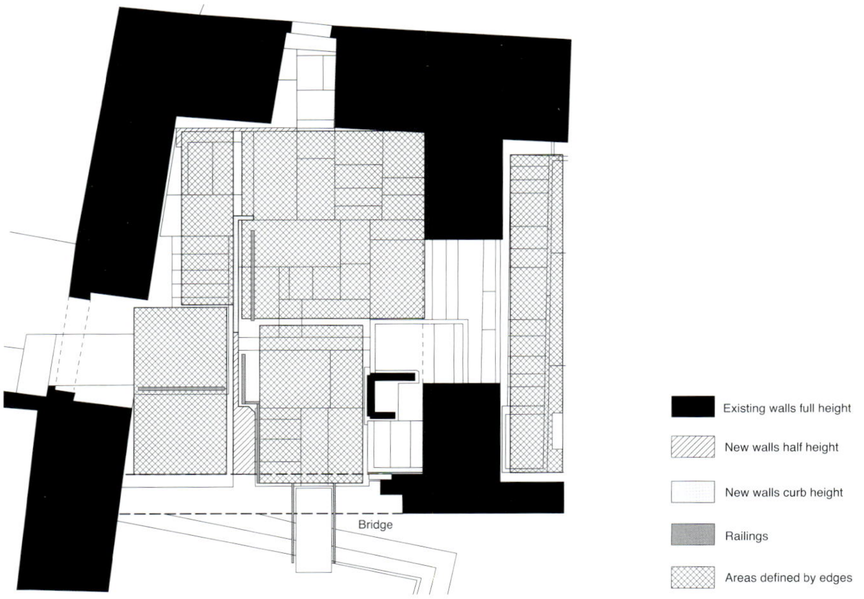

Bridge

Existing walls full height

New walls half height

New walls curb height

Railings

Areas defined by edges

Bridge

Existing walls full height

New walls half height

New walls curb height

Railings

Areas defined by pattern

221–230. Carlo Scarpa, Castelvecchio, Verona, 1958–64.

221. Floor plan Cangrande space, ground floor, circulation and flooring pattern.
222. Floor plan Cangrande space, ground floor, areas defined by floor pattern.
223. Floor plan Cangrande space, ground floor, areas defined by edges and linear elements.
224. Cangrande space, ground floor, seen from above: stone layer cladding floor and parts of existing walls.
225. Cangrande room, stair exposing stone layer.

226. Floor plan Cangrande space, upper floor, circulation and flooring pattern.
227. Floor plan Cangrande space, upper floor, areas defined by floor pattern.
228. Floor plan Cangrande space, upper floor, areas defined by edges and linear elements.
229. Passageway towards Cangrande space: concrete walls inserted into existing space.
230. Cangrande space: concrete wall layers cladding the void created by Scarpa.

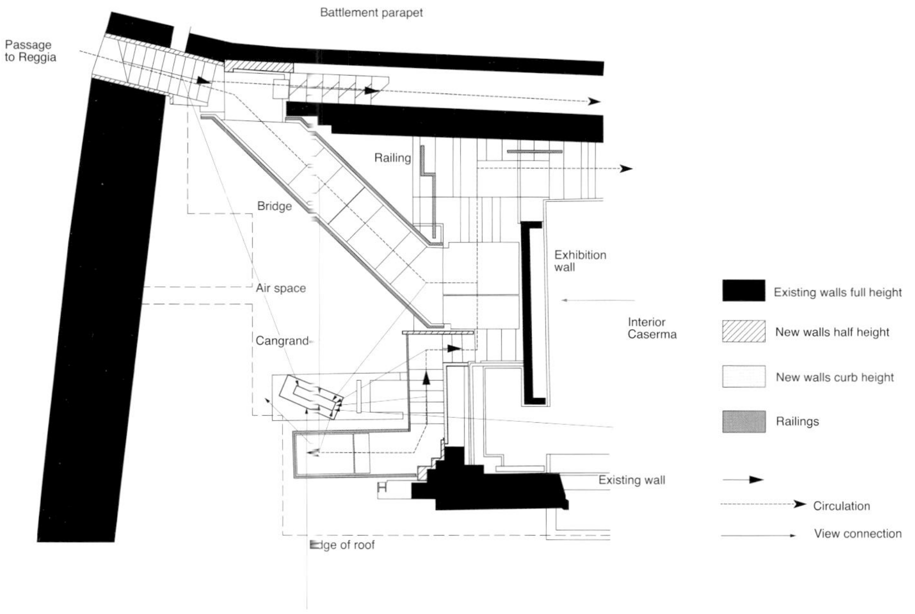

Battlement parapet

Passage to Reggia

Railing

Bridge

Exhibition wall

Air space

Interior Caserma

Cangrand

Existing wall

Edge of roof

Existing walls full height

New walls half height

New walls curb height

Railings

Circulation

View connection

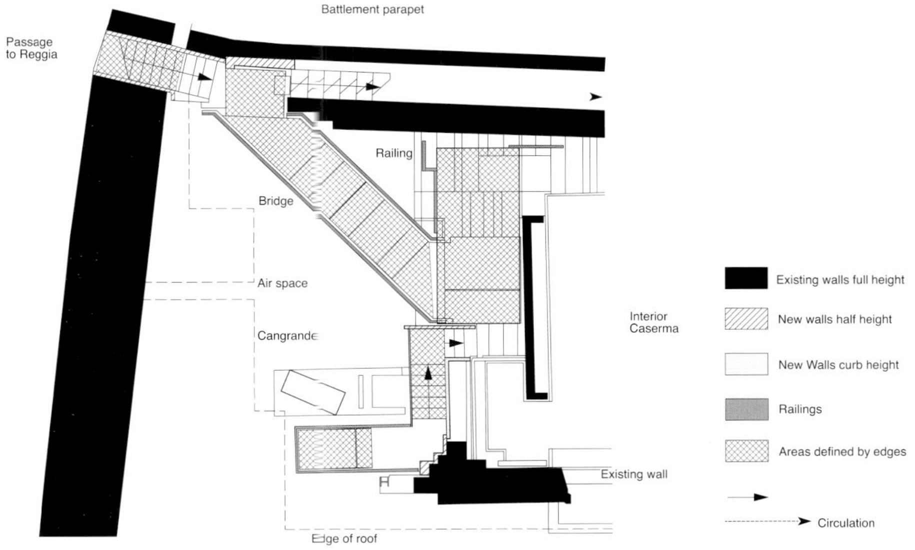

Battlement parapet

Passage to Reggia

Railing

Bridge

Air space

Interior Caserma

Cangrande

Existing wall

Edge of roof

Existing walls full height

New walls half height

New Walls curb height

Railings

Areas defined by edges

Circulation

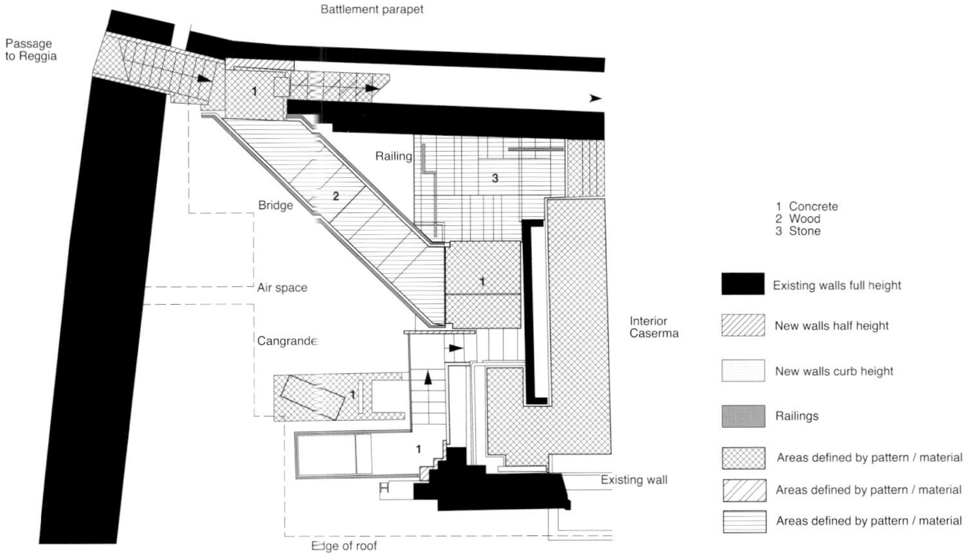

Battlement parapet

Passage to Reggia

Railing

Bridge

Air space

Cangrande

Interior Caserma

Existing wall

Edge of roof

1 Concrete
2 Wood
3 Stone

Existing walls full height

New walls half height

New walls curb height

Railings

Areas defined by pattern / material

Areas defined by pattern / material

Areas defined by pattern / material

231–238. Carlo Scarpa, Castelvecchio, Verona, 1958–64.

231. Cangrande space, additional layer of concrete wrapping exterior walls, edges defined by metal profiles.
232. Cangrande space, detail of concrete step starting a narrow concrete stair to the battlement parapet.
233. Cangrande space, detail of metal framed wood panels hanging off roof underside.
234. Cangrande space, section diagram illustrating layers added and layers subtracted in the Cangrande room.

235. Cangrande space, concrete elements inserted into void created for statue.
236. Cangrande space, undersight of bridge.
237. Library façade, tiles seem peeled off at the edge exposing a thinner layer of the roof intersecting with wood paneling coming up the wall.
238. Library façade, wood paneling in the void created by setting the new façade back.

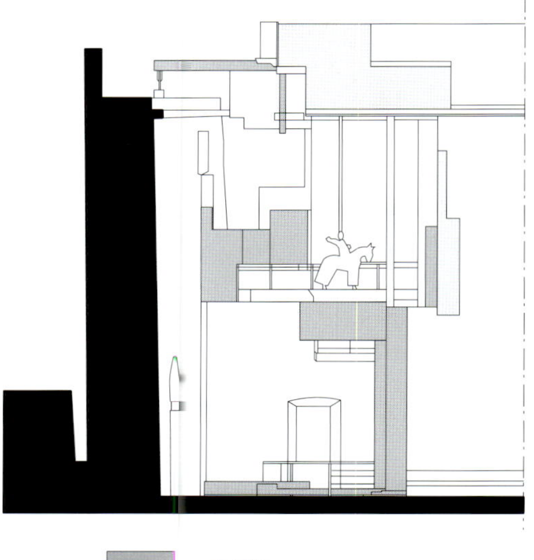

Additions
(addition of concrete or wood layers)

Subtractions (reduction of layers)

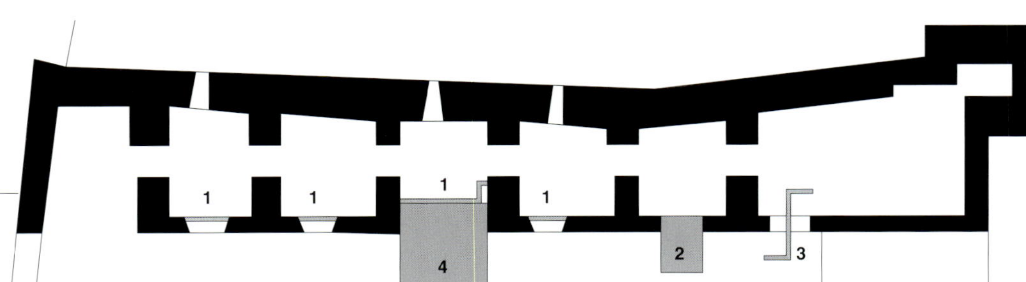


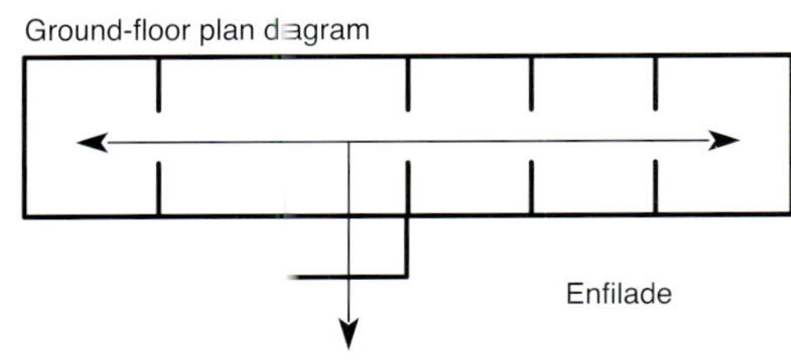


Spatial configuration:
Single spaces connected by circulation

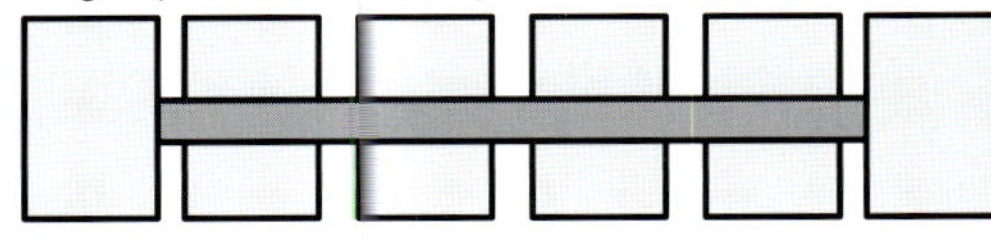

Upper-floor plan diagram

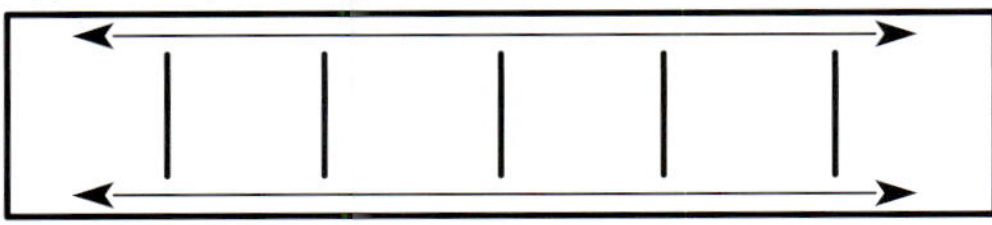

Spatial configuration:
one large space structured by walls

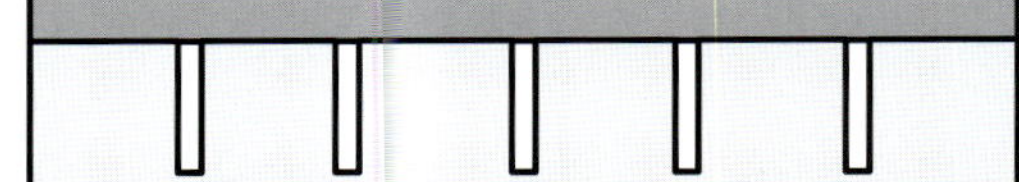

239–246. Carlo Scarpa, Castelvecchio, Verona, 1958–64.

239. Caserma, façade facing courtyard.
240. Caserma, diagram, ground floor. Key: 1 window layers added on interior, 2 Sacello volume added on exterior, 3 wall directing entry and exit circulation, 4 stone carpet added at the central space, façade inset from building edge.
241. Caserma, new window and glazing shown from exterior.
242. Caserma, new window and glazing shown from interior.
243–246. Caserma, diagrams, floor-plan configurations.

260, 261. Carlo Scarpa, Fondazione Querini Stampalia, Venice, 1961–63.

260. View of entrance bridge seen from canal.
261. View of entrance bridge seen from calle.

The walls are either clad with panels that at their seams allow a glimpse of the wall below, or are completely covered with a continuous layer. The stratification of the materials at the ceiling emphasizes elements such as lamps, or structures transitions between the zones. The joint between the floor and wall, and that between wall and ceiling are omnipresent, as are the transitions and seams between differing strata of material. Like the zones of the floor, the colored stucco lustro wall panels form zones of space by means of color choice and size and give each area its specific atmosphere. Different types of ceiling coverings emphasize transitions or areas and contribute to the proportion of the rooms.

## The entrance area

After crossing the bridge, visitors enter a terraced area in front of the museum from which a suspended step goes up to a stone polychrome carpet, a marble mosaic in various colors that are reminiscent of historical church floors. The structure of the area – L-shaped stones and squares to complete them – was used in the Sacello of the Castelvecchio as wall facing. Here it is a regular carpet, whose framing with a single-colored border follows textile formal principles. Semper's demand that surfaces and cladding have borders is taken into consideration here. The ornamentation is geometric, while the composition of colors seems accidental.

As in the Castelvecchio, the material stratification of the floor is used to »adjust« what were formerly irregular room contours. Giuseppe Mazzariol comments on this as follows: »He used a contemporary language – key words, structures, and a modern vocabulary appropriate for 1968 – when he carried out the intervention; but the intention was to recompose a previous reality, and to send it on, to recommend it and entrust it to a future time.«[2] Between its raised border and the walls, which go through all the storeys, the square leaves visible a lower floor stratum, the collecting tank for potential flood waters. When there is a flood, the floor in this room consists of a concrete plane, a layer of water, and a raised concrete slab covered with the marble mosaic. When the water floods in, the usable area seems to be floating on it. »In the Querini the water comes in, winds along the subterranean tunnels, forms a medium between inside and outside, becomes a bright mirror. The water is used as a horizontal screen that gradates levels which are objectively changed by the space.«[3] The raised concrete border of the surrounding pool is lined on the inside with Istrian limestone. All elements are separated from each other. The terminal profiles of the raised borders are reminiscent of the stone ledges of palaces, and the typology of the details brings up associations with images of the city. The walls are clad with beige stucco lustro panels whose seams allow one to see the masonry beneath them. »What is penetrating is the methodological meticulousness that wants to do everything by means of raised additions, separate from preexisting elements which can always be salvaged: for the exterior walls there are airy marmorino linings applied in vertical panels to the walls that are left free to breathe.«[4] The ceiling, too, is paneled with stucco lustro.

Richard Murphy comments on the fact that Scarpa's stratification symbolically refers to the city of Venice: »In my view the stratification of the valuable materials that in the panels themselves are placed in a risky location above the water is like a symbolic reference to the precarious situation of the precious city of Venice as it faces the dangers of the sea.«[5] The use of finishes such as stucco lustro and motifs such as element borders creates a Venetian atmosphere. The passage into the adjoining rooms demonstrates the duality of the old and the new. A preexisting gate is framed in concrete, becoming an architectural relic in its very own original context.

### The walkway to the exhibition hall, the staircase to the water

From the entrance foyer there is access to the exhibition hall by a walkway into the anteroom in which the two watergates also lead. The walkway, which goes from the entrance to the exhibition hall and past it into the adjacent room, is a separate room as well because of a 30 cm high raised border, and is separated from the water entrance. The upper frame of the raised border, which delimits the concrete wall with a stone profile, is accentuated by a joint. Where there are crosswalks, this low concrete wall is connected with the soffit of the door by means of blocklike details. Individual concrete blocks form the steps to the canal. The actual tread surface consists of large stone slabs whose massiveness is visible at the edge. The ceiling takes up the color of the wall panels in the entrance area. At the transition between the ceiling and exterior wall, the light-colored stucco ceiling becomes wooden paneling that surrounds a ceiling light. The wood interlayer is also used over the glass partition between the exhibition hall and the anteroom. In the face walls, the old stone passageways are integrated in concrete panels.

The partition to the large exhibition hall consists of an inserted glass façade with a sculptural radiator cover reminscent of Neo-plasticism. The radiator recess forms a partitioning volume oriented in the direction of the hallway, consisting of a transparent glass skin that is partially overlaid with a layer of stone whose spacing breaks up like a jigsaw puzzle toward the ceiling. The accentuation of the edges by means of brass borders gives the object the aura of a sculpture whose individual parts seem to be in shifting motion. In this transitional area, the strata are made visible, fragmentlike, in a staccato movement toward the symmetrically paneled exhibition hall.

The room in which the concrete walkway ends is also used as an exhibition space, but also functions as a connection to the institution's offices.[6] The longitudinal walls are panelled in beige, and the concrete floor corrects the form of the room into the shape of a rectangle and is offset from the outside façade. Grooves in the floor divide it into four separate areas.

### The exhibition hall

The hall, oriented toward the internal garden, has a beige grey color scheme. The floor, which at the same time forms the base area of the wall, consists of a grid of Istrian limestone whose squares are filled with aggregate concrete. The walls are faced with travertine slabs, whose grain is differently oriented. The surface is divided by a brass rail for hanging pictures, which, like a horizon, focuses the perspective on the garden. The language of the floor is continued in the wall surface by means of recessed light strips. The character of the cladding of the wall is shown in the door, which looks as though it had been punched out, indicating that the cladding is autonomous.

Kenneth Frampton characterizes the treatment of the travertine as follows: »Stone thus appears in two aspects; in the first simply as cladding and in the second as kind of ›wood‹, where it is incised, inlaid and hinged as though it were petrified cabinetwork ... Stone treated as cabinetwork is also evident in the hinged door to the side galery, made out of a single sheet of travertine, that is cut on its front and carved on its retroface. Throughout, brass is the key for this metonymic transposition between stone and wood, since the inlaid picture rail, running around the gallery, recalls a similar use of brass connectors in the bridge handrail.«[7]

The face wall of the room consists of a glass façade whose opening leaves are framed by a wall as high as the base. Two assymetrically placed posts correspond with the series of pillars placed outside. The floor extends into the exterior and incorporates the transition zones between inside and outside into the room. The plastered ceiling is separated from the wall by a joint and was originally divided by a strip in a darker color, which regulated the elongated proportion of the space and provided punctuation against the direction of the garden.[8]

The stratification of material in this room is primarily used in an integrative way, the elements appear in the form of cladding. The garden level is raised to the height of the wall base and can thus be experienced indoors. The color scheme and materials of the room are in the tradition of the Vienna Secession with their contrasting gold edges and the use of precious materials as facings. Motifs such as seams (brass picture rail) reference Semper's theory of cladding, according to which the design of spatial borders springs from motifs of textile clothing. The flooring is separated by means of a continuous strip of Istrian limestone from the travertine facing of the wall. The materials used here do not dirrectly impact on each other, but are separated by joints or connected by means of a seam made from a different material.

### The garden

The garden in the inner court of the Fondazione Querini Stampalia, being completely enclosed, becomes an interior out of doors. A linear watercourse separates the raised lawn from the hall, which moves outside. Two staggered walls form the transition to a small courtyard where the water of the canal ends in a pool. Among the details are a »Venetian« treatment of the edges of the wall ends, which are formed with geometrical stone elements.

### The stairway to the library and to the museum

The stairs to the library consist simultaneously of the preexisting old staircase and the new steps that have been superimposed on them. It is a kind of double floor, made up of a base layer, the old steps, and a new covering layer. There is a distinct space between the new layer and the old substance. The walls are clad with the stucco lustro panels that are already used in the other rooms, while the ceiling is plastered in the same color as the entrance area – orange red. In front of the library entrance the ceiling is recessed for the lighting fixture above the door.

The modification that Scarpa carried out in the Fondazione Querini Stampalia treats the ground floor on the whole as volume that must be clad. Material stratification exists not selectively as in the Castelvecchio, but is compressed and extends over almost the entire surface. Spatial stratification helps create transparency between the rio and the courtyard or garden. References to the city are a construct of memories and references resembling quotations. A metaphor of Venice is brought into the ground floor of a palace in a very concentrated form, as a likeness created with architectonic means. The canal is continued on the walls of the entrance area in miniature form and reproduced in the garden as a river. The costly stuccos of the palazzi become panels soaring above the water. The stone carpet mosaic is an allusion to the sacral and profane floor designs encountered in the city. The bridge, steps, and stairways are part of the city's day-to-day vocabulary.

262–265. Carlo Scarpa, Fondazione Querini Stampalia, Venice, 196[illegible]–63.

262. Ground-floor plan, access and circulation. Key: 1 entrance over new bridge, 2 foyer, 3 access to library, 4 cashier/bookstore, 5 water entrance, 6 small exhibition space, 7 exhibition hall, 8 garden.
263. Ground-floor plan, areas defined by paving materials.

264. Ground-floor plan, areas defined by paving patterns.
265. Ground-floor plan, axis patterns.

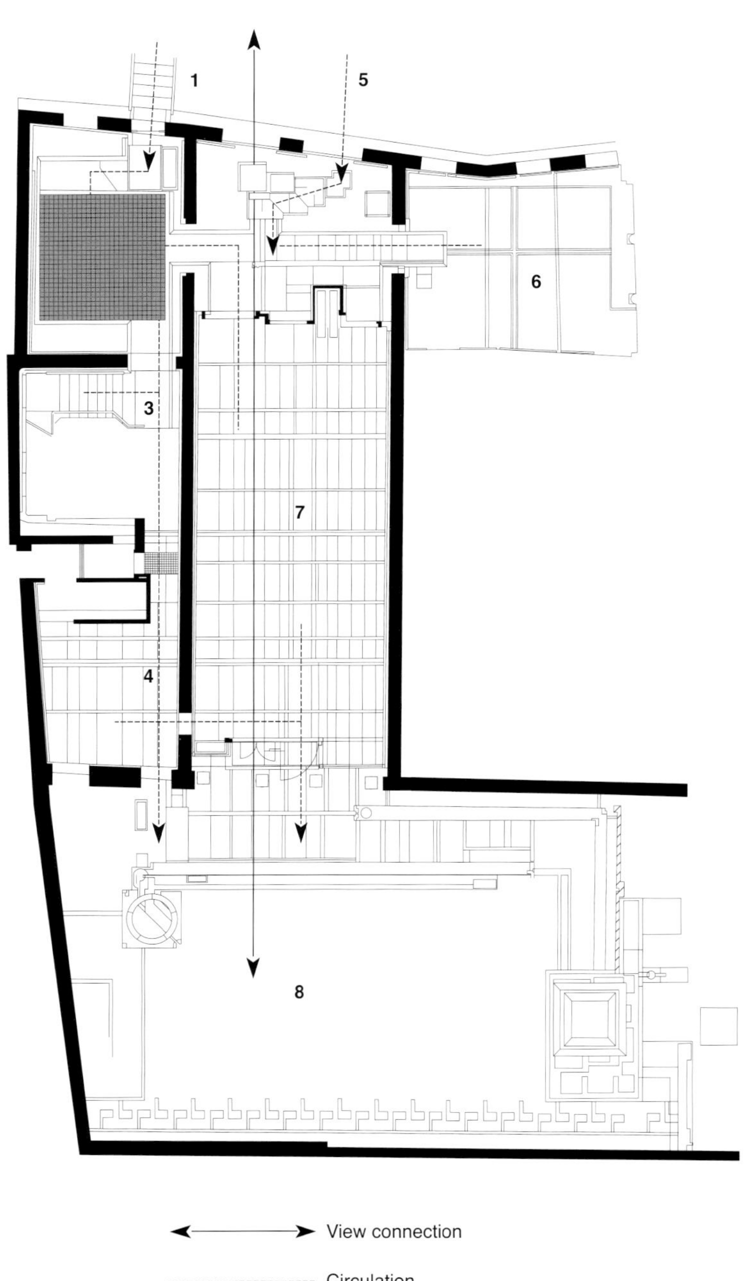


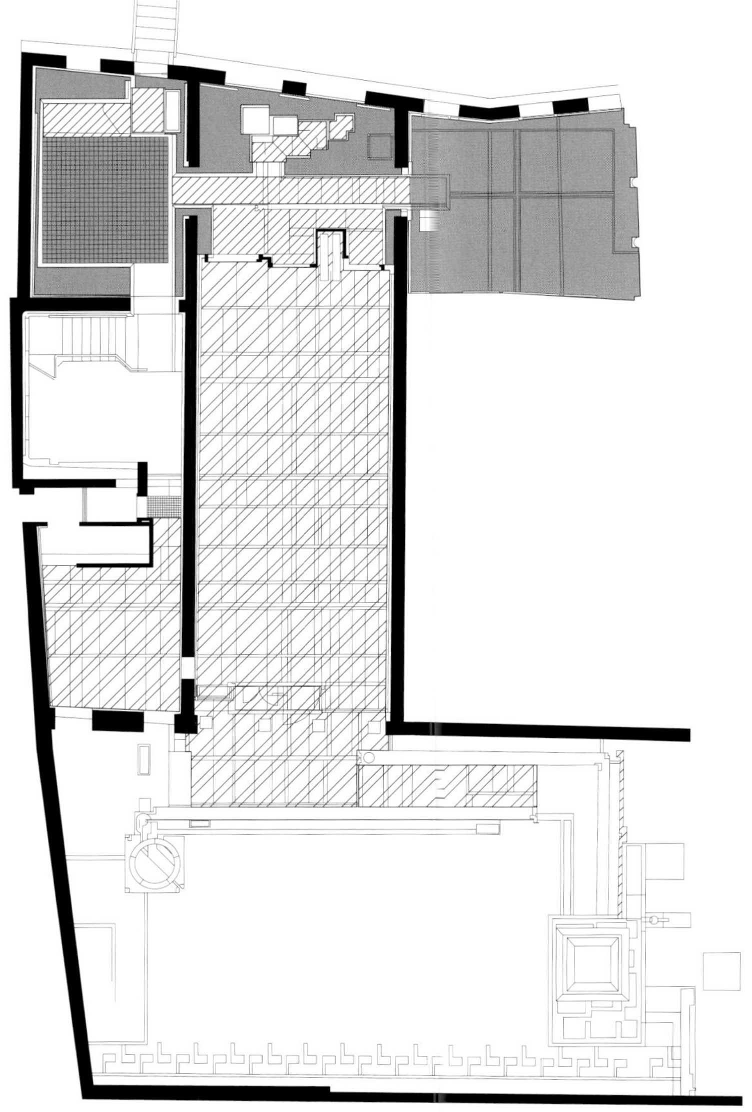

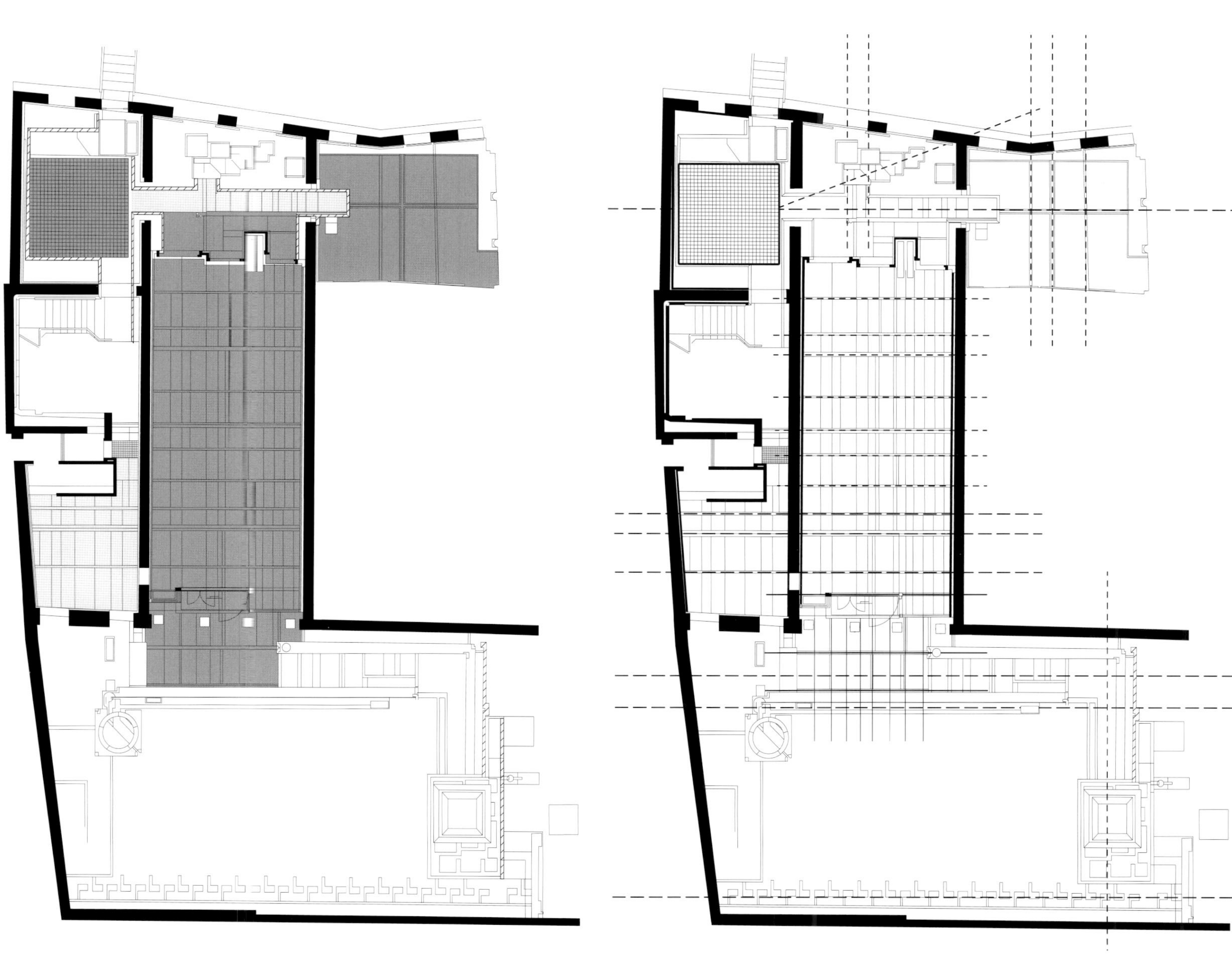

Existing walls full heigh⁻

New walls half height
or less

266–271. Carlo Scarpa, Fondazione Querini Stampalia, Venice, 196[illegible]–63.

266. Entrance area, side view of stucco wall panels, internal »canal« along wall allowing water to enter the space.
267. Axonometric, wall paneling added to existing ground floor.

268. Entrance area, corner detail of stone mosaic pavement and joint at concrete curb.
269. Entrance area, stucco panel detail at metal door.
270. Entrance area, view towards entry door.
271. Entrance area, view into space from entry.

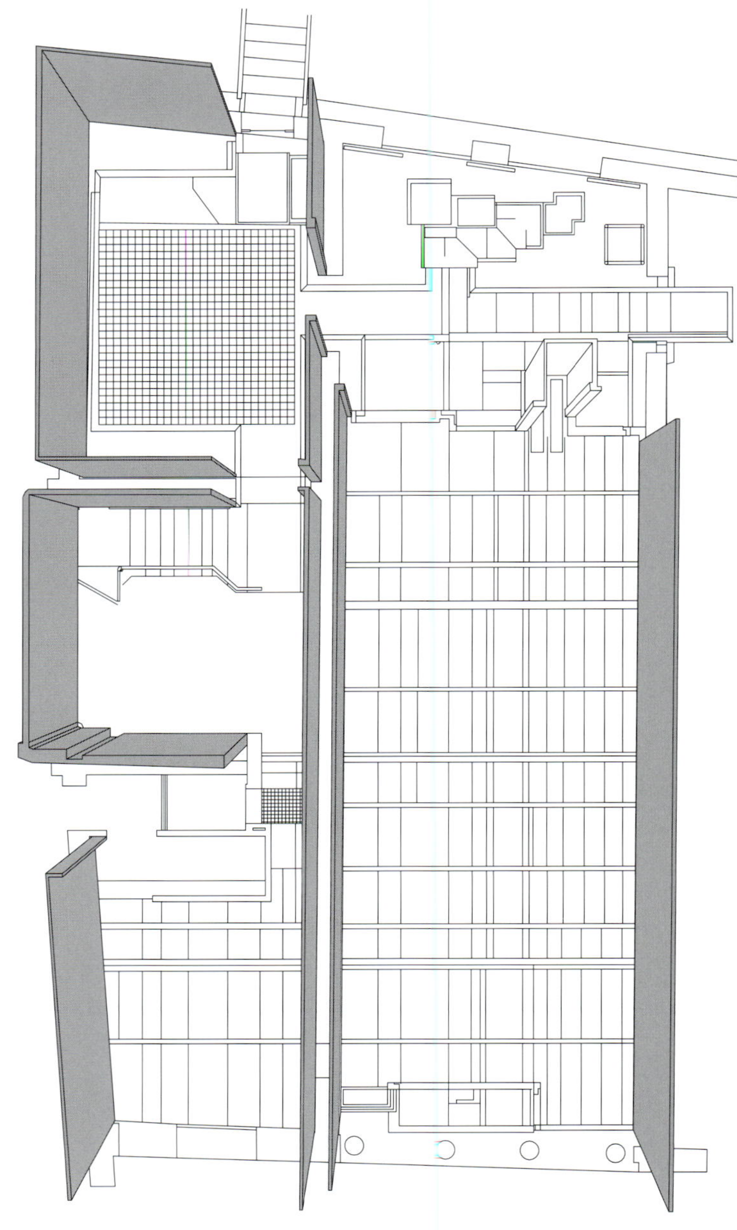

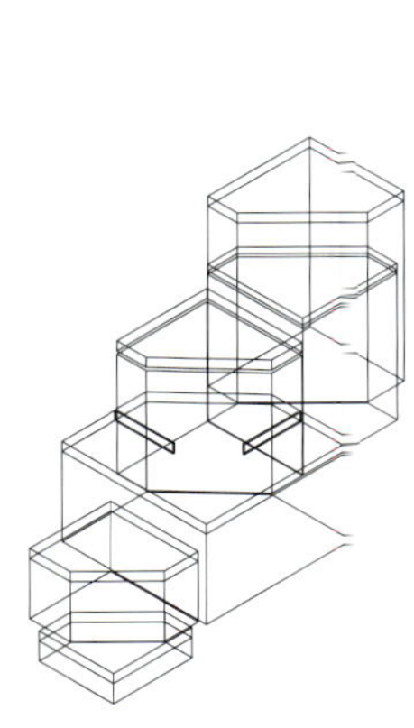

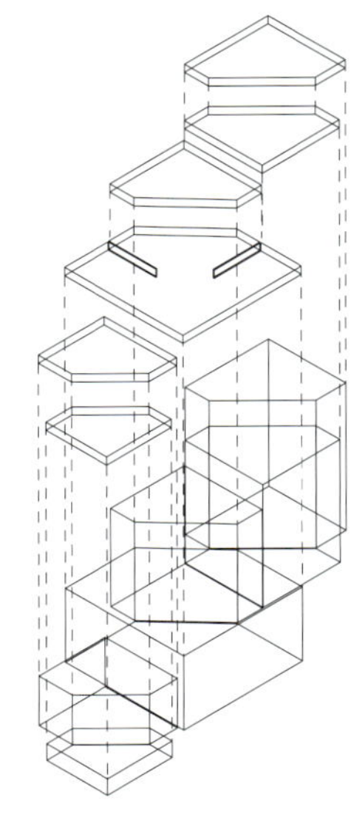

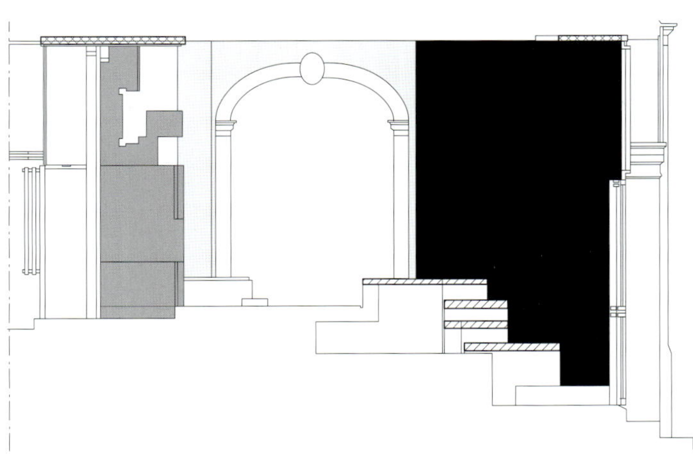

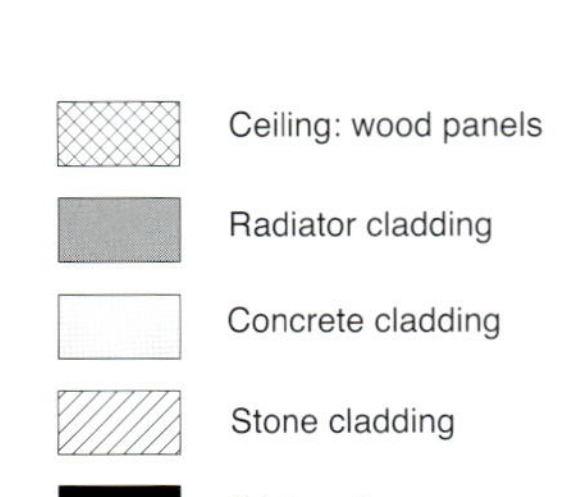
Ceiling: wood panels
Radiator cladding
Concrete cladding
Stone cladding
Brick wall

272–276. Carlo Scarpa, Fondazione Querini Stampalia, Venice, 1961–63.

272. Water entrance, concrete steps with stone treads.
273. Section diagram through hallway at water entrance, materials.
274. Concrete stair with stone treads, diagram.
275. Portal with concrete apron, detail.

276. View of hallway connecting entry area and exhibition hall.

277–288. Carlo Scarpa, Fondazione Querini Stampalia, Venice, 1961–63.

From left to right

277. Hallway, concrete curb, corner detail at brick wall.
278. Hallway, ceiling detail, stucco panel meeting wood panel around light fixture.
279. Hallway, ceiling detail at partition wall.
280. Hallway, transition detail from brick wall to glass wall.
281. Exhibition hall, stone wall cladding with metal strip and translucent glass panels covering light fixtures.
282. Exhibition hall, pavement detail, transition into garden.
283. Exhibition hall, radiator cover from inside.
284. Radiator cover from outside.

285. Small exhibition space.
286. Exhibition hall, view towards garden.
287. Exhibition hall, door cut into wall cladding, closed.
288. Exhibition hall, door cut into wall cladding, open.

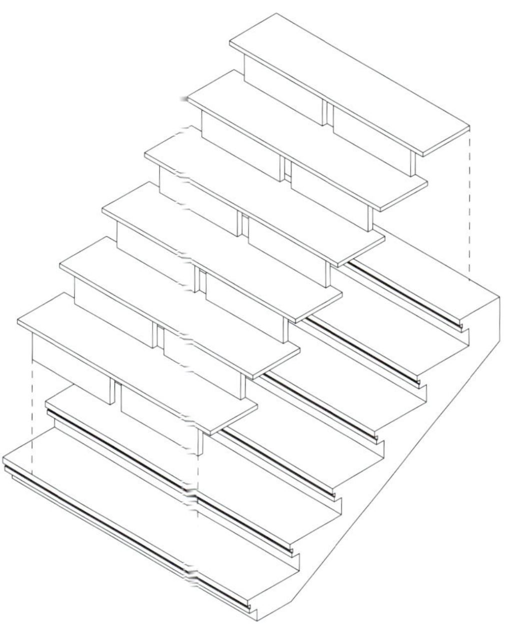

289–295. Carlo Scarpa, Fondazione Querini Stampalia, Venice, 1961–63.

From left to right

289. Staircase to library.
290. Axonometric diagram of stair cladding.
291. Stone cladding of existing stair.
292. Stucco wall panels, detail at steps revealing existing wall surface.
293. Stone pavement added to existing stair, corner detail at landing.

294. Aerial view of garden.
295. Garden, water basin and half height walls.

296, 297. Carlo Scarpa, Fondazione Querini Stampalia, Venice, 1961–63.

296. Garden, water feature, stone element at end of canal.

297. Garden, view of canal.

## 3.3. Banca Popolare, Verona (1970–80)

### History

The Banca Popolare building was built on the Piazza Nogara, a square in the inner city of Verona, not far from the arena. The enlargement of the bank, whose site covers the entire block, meant that a new building was fitted into the gap site between two preexisting buildings. This new building by Carlo Scarpa had to be integrated both in the historic center of Verona and the existing structure of the block. After his sudden death in 1978, construction was completed by Arrigo Rudi among others.[1] Scarpa's last architectural work needed to create a public image for the bank, meet the bank's security needs, and at the same time find its architectonic place in the historical context of the inner city of Verona. The bank is constructed of strata that were not indispensable as a result of the presence of a historical structure, but were designed as the expression of a new modern architectural idiom.

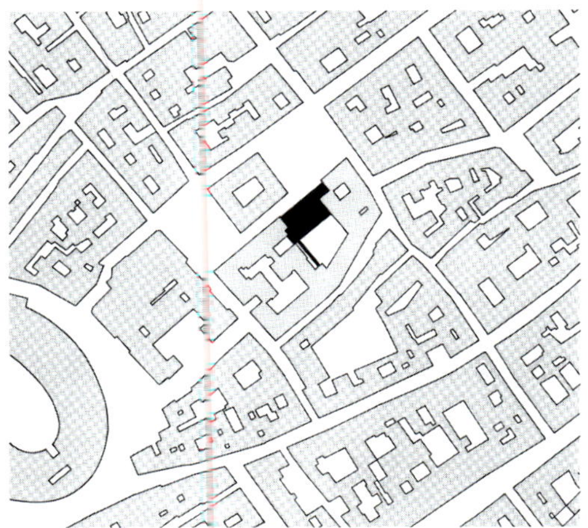

### Stratification

The building basically consists of two façades that close a hollow space within the block. In the inner courtyard the new tract is connected with the building in the rear by an elevated hallway. The volume is articulated three-dimensionally by indents particularly at the transitions to the existing façade and in places that have special functions, such as the stairwell. The mechanical equipment rooms appear on the roof as autonomous volumes. The ground plan is based on a system of coordinates that is inclined by a few degrees wth a different axial grid. The ground floor is lit by deep light shafts. Scarpa demonstrates that the principle of stratification serves not only to integrate individual elements into existing spaces, but is also important as a design principle for creating new façades. Marco Frascari considers the façade of the Banca Popolare to be representative of Italian »façadianism»: »Anyone who looks at the typical characteristics of Italian architecture will soon realize that the use of structural elements for decorative purposes in designing façades is very important. This often reaches a point where a kind of second façade is produced, placed in front of the basic façade like a shield.«[2]

The façade of the Banca Popolare is »placed in front of the building as a freestanding surface. Its elements form a screen-like scenery in the midst of the old city structure of Verona«.[3] Where there are openings, the stratification of materials becomes visible in the transition from inside to outside as in a cutaway model.

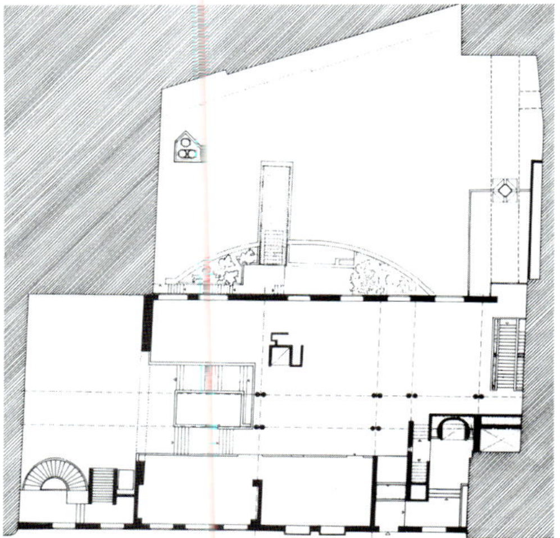

### The façade facing the square

The façade that faces the Piazza Nogara (the city side) has the classic tripartite façade form – base, middle part, and roof, in this case formed by a loggia. The base and middle part are covered by layers of cladding, which in turn are three-dimensionally articulated by ledges, projecting squared-stone masonry, and openings, creating shadow effects. The façade is connected to adjacent façades by slots of fenestration or built-out joints. Variably formed and seemingly irregularly arranged apertures structure the base and the middle part. There is no continuous axial grid, but rather individual systems connected together by a few continuous axes. Cohesion is created by individual systems referring to each other in various places. The elements are related to each other in different ways and form what tend to be geometrical »figures« – openings and three-dimensional elements. The asymmetrical arrangement of axes makes for a creative equilibrium based on the compositional balance of the elements. »The principle of the scales»[4] is founded on the harmony of balancing the individual parts, though this is not a finished process, but involves light, material, and association as part of viewing. By layering various materials over each other, the process of stratification is revealed. Because the distribution of material and relief do not coincide, additional dynamism is produced. If we analyze the materials of the façade, the parts are shown to be clearly differentiated through the choice of their materials. Adjoining the socle of Botticino marble is the medium-coarse plaster surface of the middle area in which the glazing is installed flush in part and in part staggered inward. In the loggia the two-dimensional character of the façade is transformed into the steel framework, which moves to the outside and the glazing, which is located inside. The glazing is behind it. The edge of the roof again picks up the material

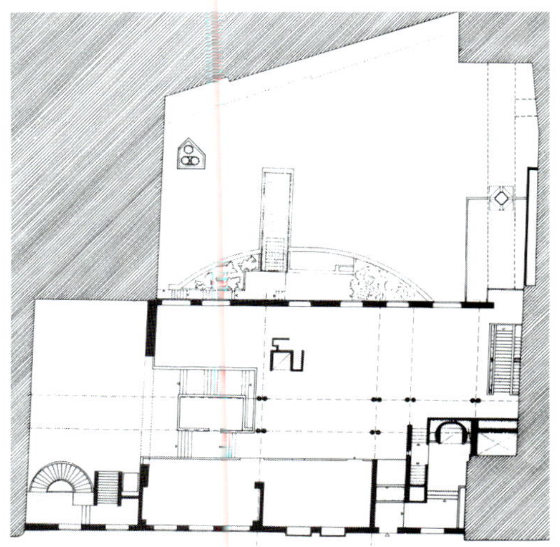

of the base and thus forms the border of the building. If we compare the analysis of the relief with that of the material used, we find slight differences that constitute creative tension. The projecting glass volumes of the middle part are complemented by blocks of concrete. The design systems, which are superimposed on each other, can be experienced simultaneously and nonhierarchically.

The section of the façade makes visible the simultaneous nature of interior and exterior layers of cladding. The superimposition of different geometrical systems of aperture forms distinguishes inside and outside. Layers are applied over a concrete core, the concrete itself does not become visible. Of the concrete construction, only the supporting frame of the loggia appears in the open in the roof, while the loggia's glazing is located on the inside. The sections also show how pronounced is the relief of the façade, depending on the material applied in each case. Scarpa felt that the combined effect of the elements in the overall picture was very important: »The individual element has its power only if it merges perspectively with others.«[5]

## The base

The base, completely faced with Botticino marble, is bounded above by a stepped marble frieze with a sudden jump near the ground floor opening areas almost halfway up. As a result the cladding of the base interlocks with that of the façade's middle area. A series of windows set directly on the base, which lies flush with the exterior shell has a similar effect. The windows, which because of the sudden jump of the base do not adjoin directly, are connected to it again by a

298–302. Carlo Scarpa, Banca Popolare, Verona, 1970–80.

298. Site plan.
299. Floor plan, first floor.
300. Floor plan, top floor.

301. Buildings demolished for new structure.
302. Façade facing Piazza Nogara.

T-shaped ledge. Elements that are set flush with the edge of a layer of material are given a mediating role by having another area superimposed on them. A continuous horizontal division becomes a surface ornament because the areas overlie each other. The door is given a markedly offset frame that is shaped by traces of the stonecutter's tools. The ledge is a way of playing with multiple stepping, resulting in intensive light and shadow effects. The surfaces carved out in the frontmost plane receive the most light and stand out clearly from the shaded negative form of the ledge. The details of the jointing of the stone create the impression that the cladding that is put in front has been additively put together. The material layer of the base is the overarching concept for a surface that is divided into multiple segments by the treatment of the cladding stone, by its division into single slabs, its use as a perforated surface, and the way it has been worked as a relief, as in the ledge. The door in the base is particularly carefully detailed. In the door frame, traces of the dressing of the stone become a symbol and a decorative motif that refers to the process of the building's creation, a reminiscence of the region's crafts.

## The middle zone

The middle zone is plastered, as in the surrounding houses of the old part of Verona. Because of the precise framing of the edges, the layer of plaster is also given the character of what Marco Frascari calls an anterior »screen«,[6] more like a kind of added-on piece of scenery than a textile cladding. The façade is cut at the connecting places to the adjacent buildings. At the cuts the glazing of the loggia is extended downward, though the transition is articulated over the total height of the building. The transition is not created merely by the façade cladding moving away from the adjacent façade; it is also reinforced by the insertion of an additional element – a steel relief. Three strata can be distinguished in the construction: the concrete load-bearing layer, the layer of plaster, and the layer of glass or concrete prisms applied to the façade. Here, glass is given physical materiality and, rather than being two-dimensional, takes on volume. The presence of glass in the various different manifestations of the interior surface, the exterior surface, and the volume causes the same material to be reflective in different ways. The surfaces that lie in the planes of the façade and the glass prisms that break through to the outside reflect the surrounding buildings, while the windows, which are staggered inward, lie in back as dark expanses. The perforations of the layer of plaster do not correspond to the geometrical openings in the load-bearing layer. At the figure-eight windows, the otherwise concealed sequence of strata becomes visible. The fenestration, which is staggered inwards shows that the outermost plane is detached and independent. From inside, there is the effect of the figure-eight element superimposed with a rectangular opening and fenestration, which seems to focus the surroundings as though through a lens. The selected cutouts include the structural surroundings in the design as a view. The division of the glass area is such that rod-shaped elements are overlaid with a punched-out surface. Since, in this new construction, the layers are congruently superimposed on each other, the windows are a way of laying open the mechanics of stratification, showing simultaneous and superimposed layering. The apertures play out, in a number of different ways, the depth and variability of façade stratification.

The upended narrow rectangular apertures have simple framing on the outside, while on the inside the architect picks up on the Byzantine-flavored stepped motifs of the ledges, which surround the aperture like a multiple frame. The large glass area at the transition to the side building is completed in its division by the structural element of the construction, which takes the form of two communicating staggered crosses. Functional details become ornaments: for instance, the linear water channels of the figure-eight windows, which in addition to their functional aspect visually anchor the windows. Aside from the material aspects of the »stratified« façade, there is also an immaterial, associative level. By using motifs such as cornices or window ledges, which are transformed into Scarpa's architectural idiom, he identifies the building with its immediate surroundings.

## The loggia

The classical roof border – a loggia – is formed by the exterior steel construction, which consists of twin columns and a high continuous girder. Cladding – continuous glazing – is found in the interior, seemingly in the same plane as the figure-eight windows. The border of the roof is differentiated in multiple ways; the steel girders, which are superimposed on each other, are divided by a glass mosaic strip and bounded above by a stone cornice that again picks up on the ornamentation of the base molding in an altered form. The association with a cutout from a coffered ceiling in the ancient style merges with one suggesting modified towers of the Venetian Gothic period. The twin columns suggest their classical prototype, with its base, shaft, and capital.

### The courtyard façade

The façade that faces the inner courtyard reflects the same design principles that are used in the façade which is oriented toward the square. At the place where the stairway becomes freestanding on the upper floor, the wall screen of the plaster cladding leaves its structural carrying layer and becomes autonomous. As in the figure-eight windows, the stratification is laid bare. The edges of the detached stratum are framed with stone slabs.

### The interior

The walls and ceilings in the most important rooms are characterized primarily by being coated with stucco lustro or clad with separate panels, as on the ceilings. The elements are separated and emphasized by framing the edges. Two stairs, offset against each other, with their respective side wall panels, clearly show the separation of floor, wall, and ceiling. The layering of material in the surfaces is demonstrated by means of a lighting element integrated in the wall located on the third floor. An opening in an anterior shell leaves open a view of the layer of wall that lies under it. During the day the interior serves as a »light catcher«. Its form – several sectors of a circle – stands out because of the different intensity of light on the surfaces; at night the intervening space is lit. The connecting passage between the bank's old and new tract, which at the same time has to overcome the difference in height between the old and new division into storeys, is paneled entirely with wood.

#### Supports

In the central traffic areas of the ground plan, there are twin columns, whose treatment is reminiscent of classical columns. The concrete shaft is slightly fluted thanks to its mold. At floor level it is covered with a metal shaft, whose one specific rectangular bearing surface is let into the floor like a negative pedestal. The classical tripartite form ends in a »capital area« separated by a gold strip. Just as the foot enters the floor gradually, the capital is separated from the ceiling by a transition. The twin columns are joined by a metal connecting piece, as well as by a joint ceiling panel and a joint metal piece at floor level. The combination of elements creates a type of »load-bearing« torso. This, the last of Scarpa's works, displays his formal repertoire in a considerably more reduced manner than in earlier projects, which were generally smaller in spatial terms. Nevertheless the process of stratification also becomes effective in this new buildng. Separation into floor, wall, and ceiling is made visible on the outside as well by treating the exterior façade two-dimensionally. Inside there is primarily clothing in the form of panels or two-dimensional layers of stucco.

### Summary

With the new building for the Banca Popolare Scarpa shows that the principle of stratification can be used in his new buildings as well. The morphology of stratification is accordingly not limited to modifying preexisting spaces and building up surfaces by means of panels or layers of paint, but is an independent component of his conception of space. This project reflects classical rules of composition, and at the same time Scarpa remains faithful to the Venetian themes of stucco lustro and mosaic as structuring strips. The significance of stratification is not in tectonically representing the building, as in the classical separation of a building into supporting framework and shell. The systems exist side by side nonhierarchically, and what is more important is the interaction of forms, the clarity of architectural archetypes, and the effect of the material used by the architect.

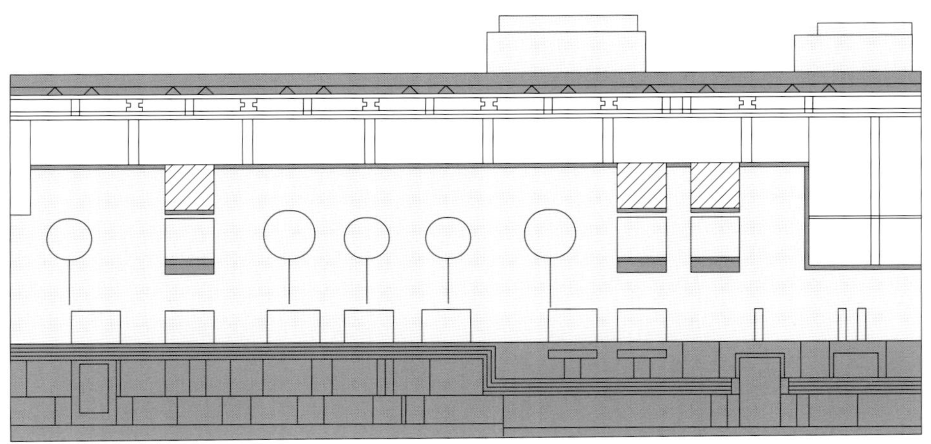

Stucco

Stone, red stone of Verona

Stone, Botticino marble

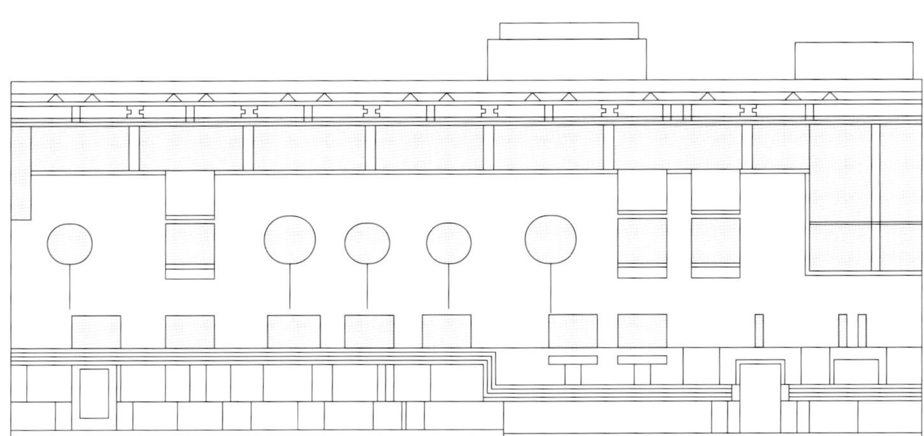

Glass

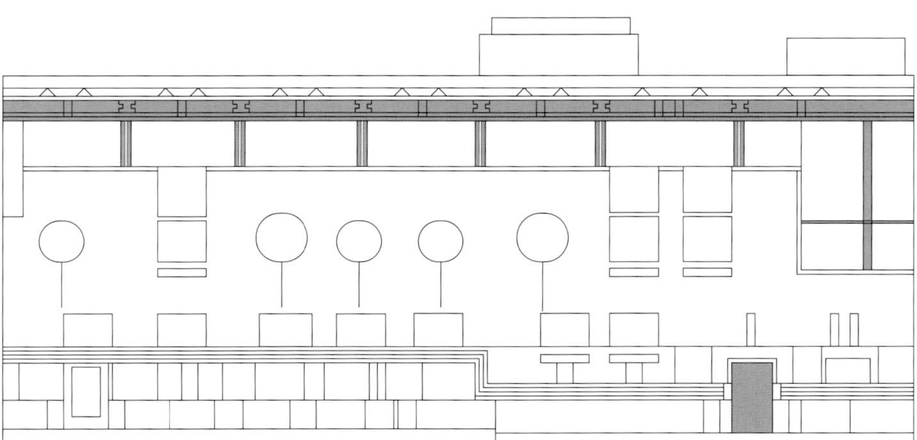

Metal

303–308. Carlo Scarpa, Banca Popolare, Verona, 1970–80.

303. Front façade, layering of materials, stucco and stone.
304. Front façade, layering of materials, glass.
305. Front façade, layering of materials, metal.

306. Courtyard façade, layering of materials, stucco and stone.
307. Courtyard façade, layering of materials, glass.
308. Courtyard façade, layering of materials, metal.

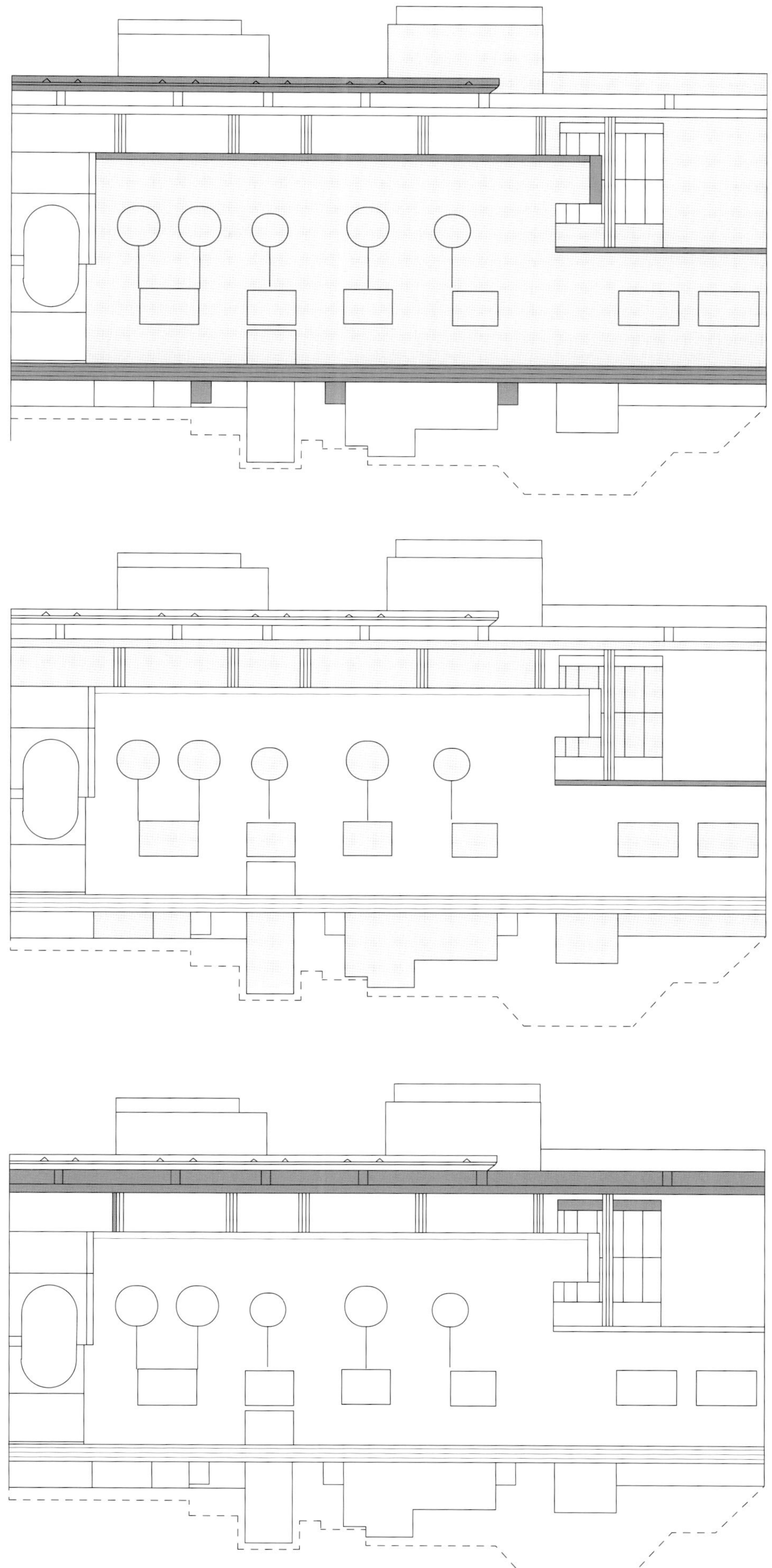

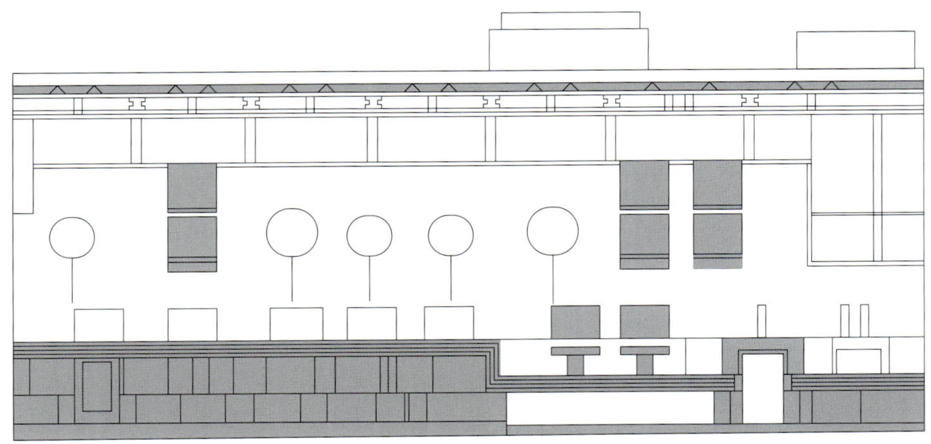

Most protruding elements

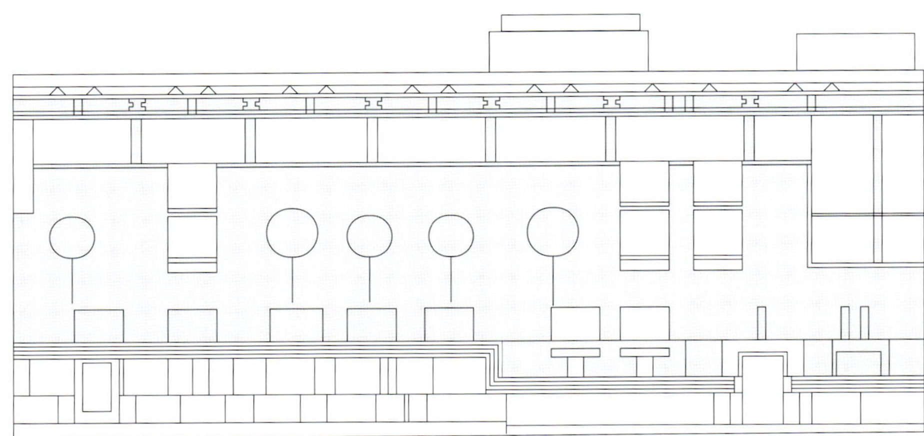

Main surface (wall layer)

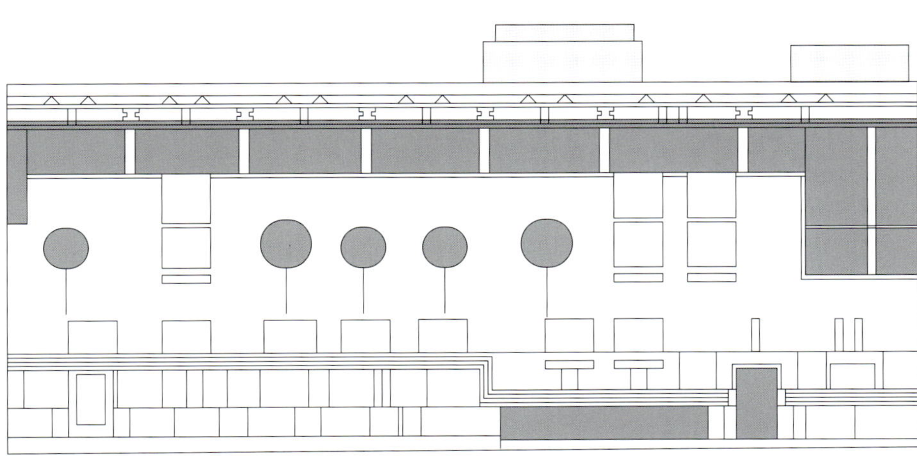

Set back layer

Background layer

309–314. Carlo Scarpa, Banca Popolare, Verona, 1970–80.

309. Front façade, relief of façade, most potruding elements.
310. Front façade, relief of façade, main wall surface.
311. Front façade, relief of façade, set back elements.

312. Courtyard façade, relief of façade, most potruding elements.
313. Courtyard façade, relief of façade, main wall surface.
314. Courtyard façade, relief of façade, set back elements.

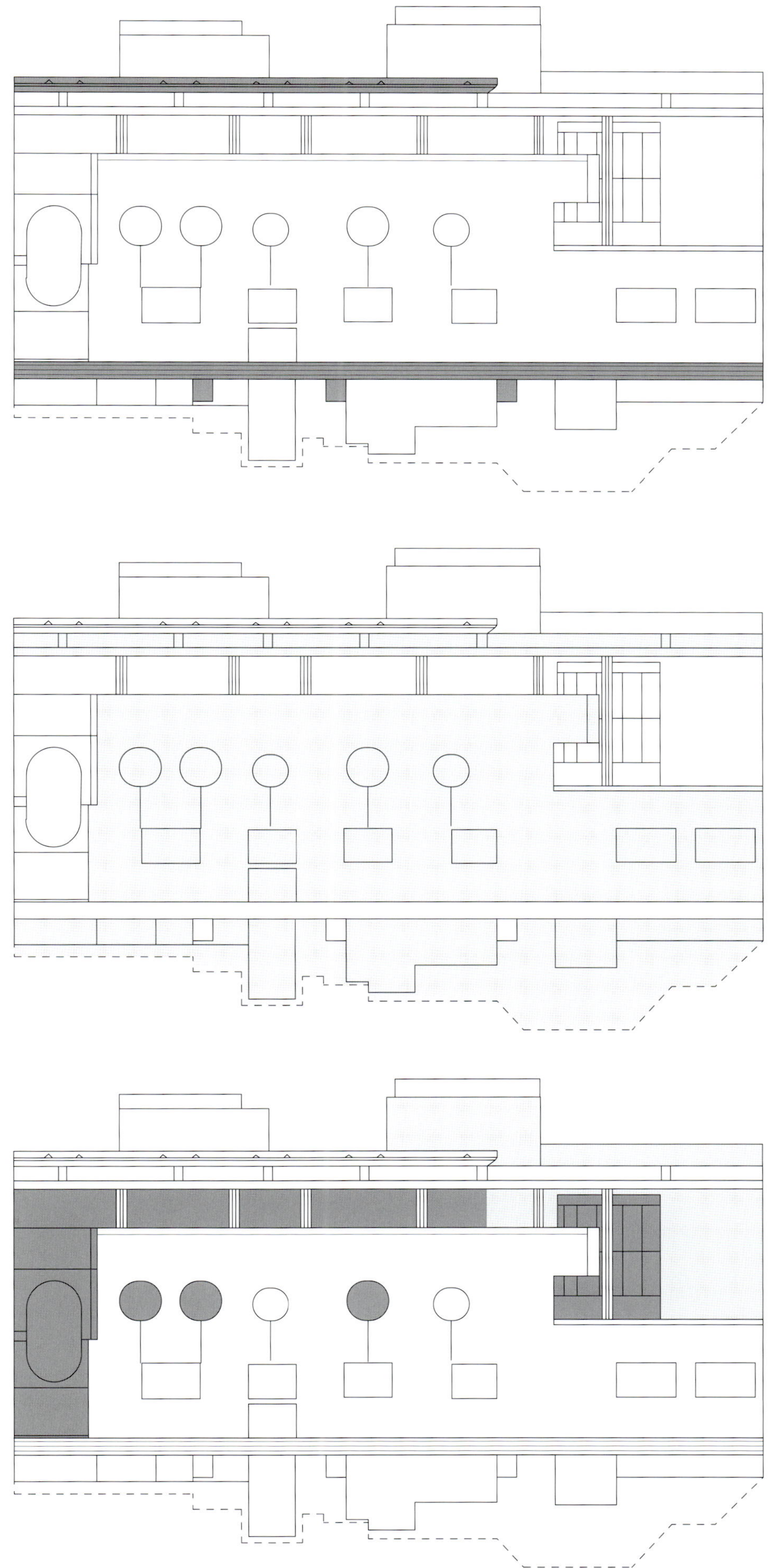

315–321. Carlo Scarpa, Banca Popolare, Verona, 1970–80.

315, 316. Square and courtyard façades, axis patterns.
317. Façade facing square, base zone, stone detail.
318. Joint to adjacent building on the east.
319. Joint to adjacent building on the west.

320. Façade facing square, joint to adjacent building at loggia and eave.
321. Façade facing square, base zone, stone cladding.

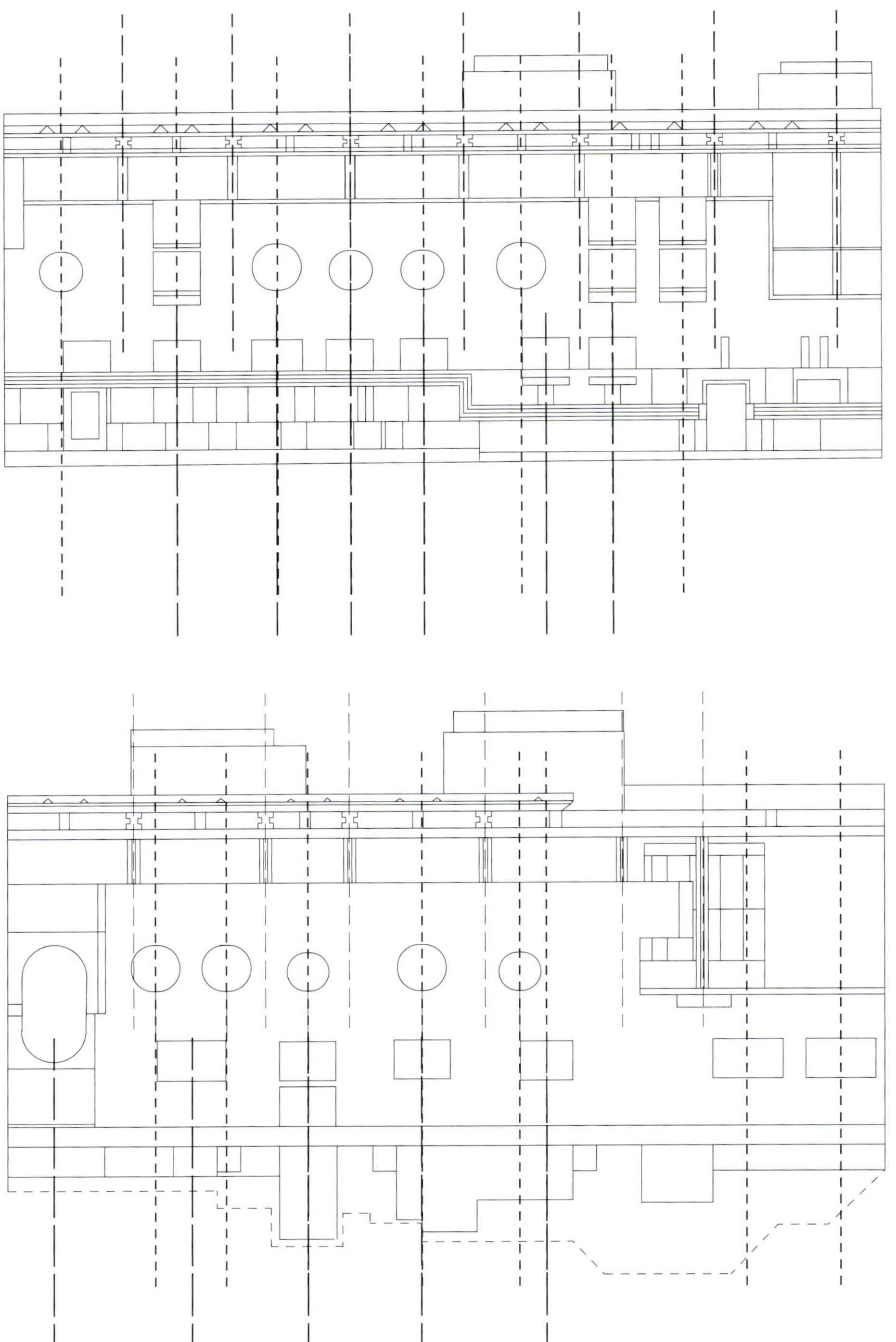

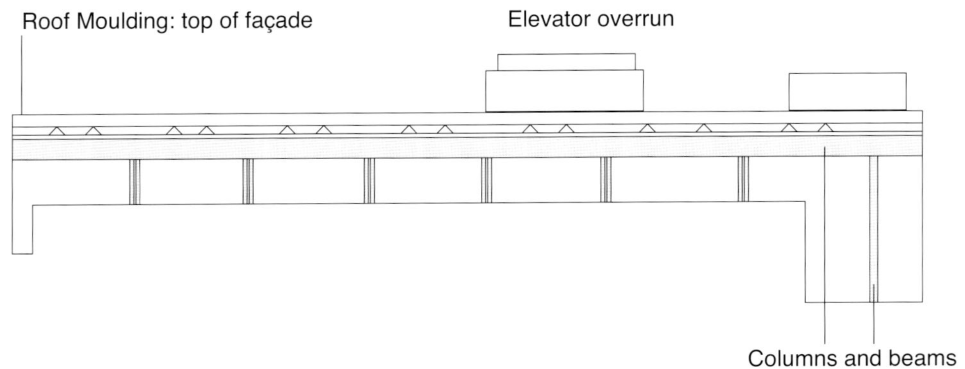


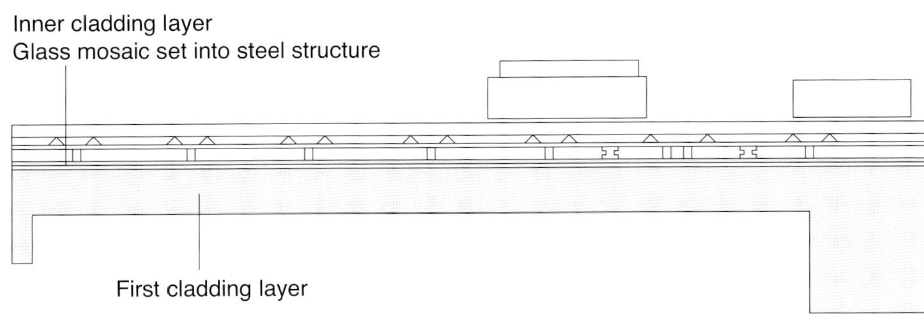


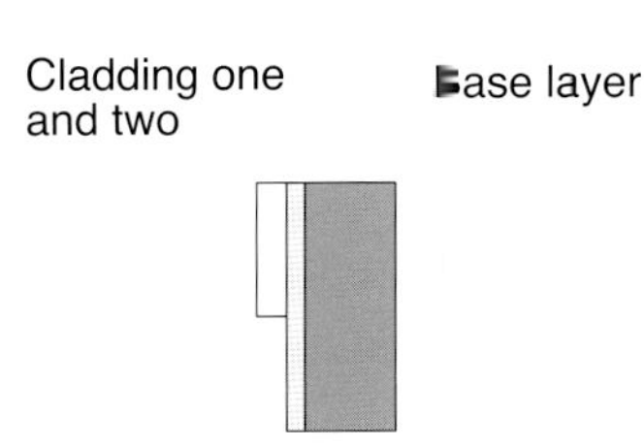


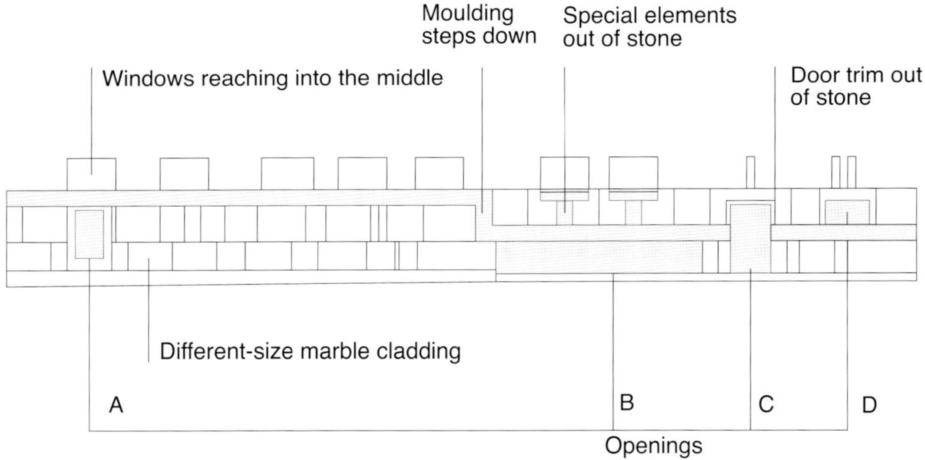


Base layer with openings

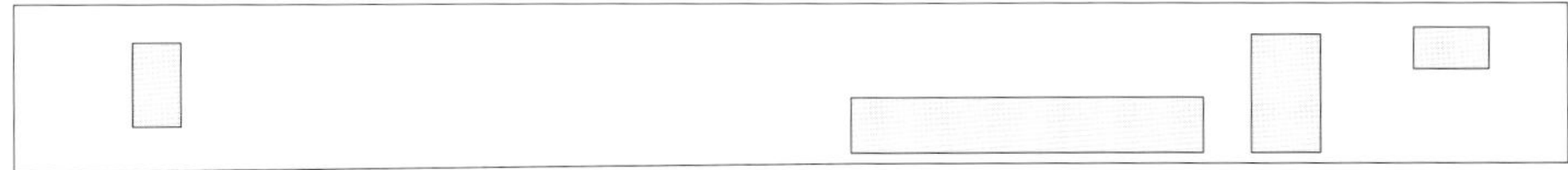

Cladding layer with openings

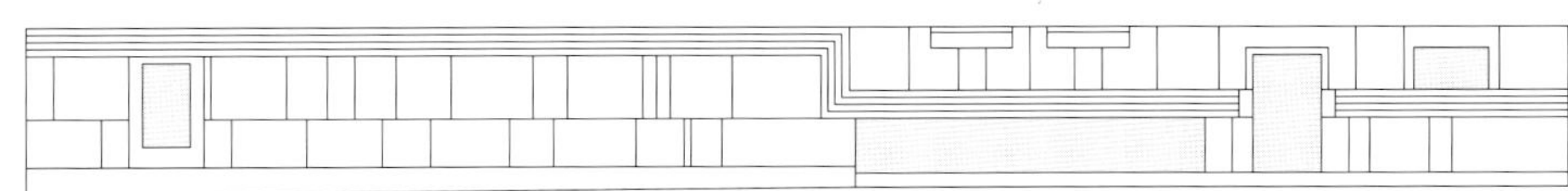

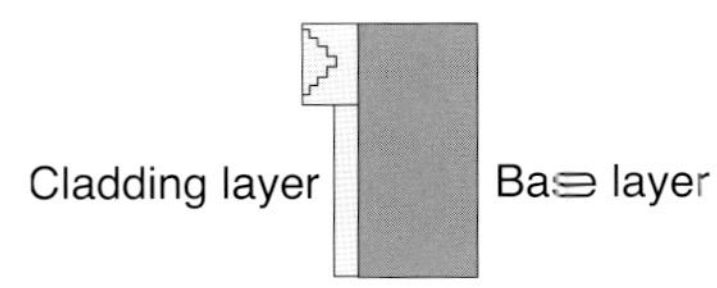

322–330. Carlo Scarpa, Banca Popolare, Verona, 1970–80.

322, 323. Analysis of loggia. Upper portion of façade, layers of material and cladding.
The central wall layer of the façade dissolves in the upper floor into an exposed steel structure. Thin doube columns carry several layers of metal beams faced with glass mosaics. The glazing lays on the inside and appears to align with the glazing of the perforated windows below.
324–326. Analysis of base zone. Lower portion of façade, layers of materials and cladding.
The material layering of stone applied to the lower wall is expressed at the transition into the middle zone of the façade starting at the second floor off the street.

327–330. Analysis of middle zone. Elements, layers of materials and cladding.
The layers are expressed by the position of the glazing, either potruding outward exposing a built wall section, or being flush with the stucco layer or being set on the inside of the wall exposing depth and the layer of stucco and stone frame.

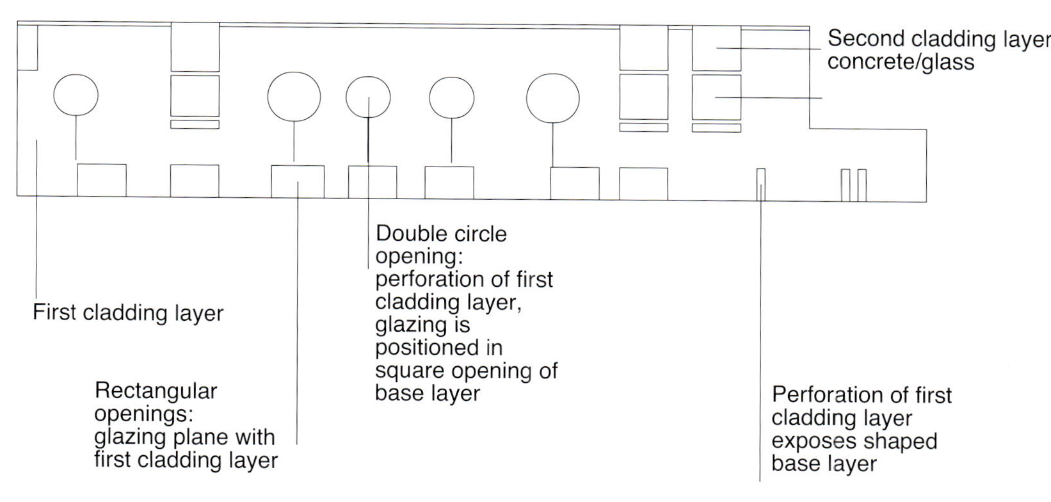


Base layer with perforations

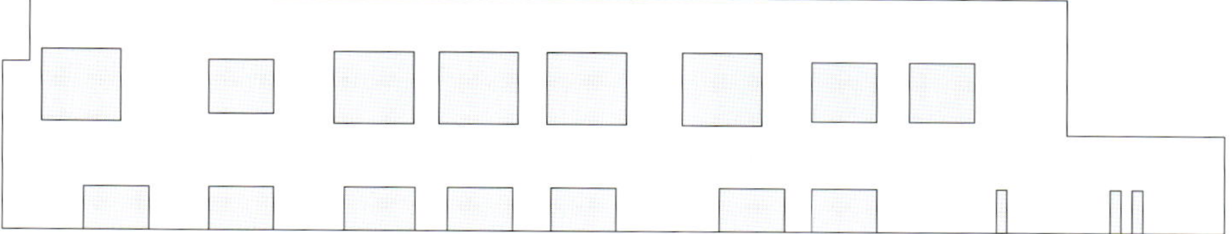

First cladding layer with perforations

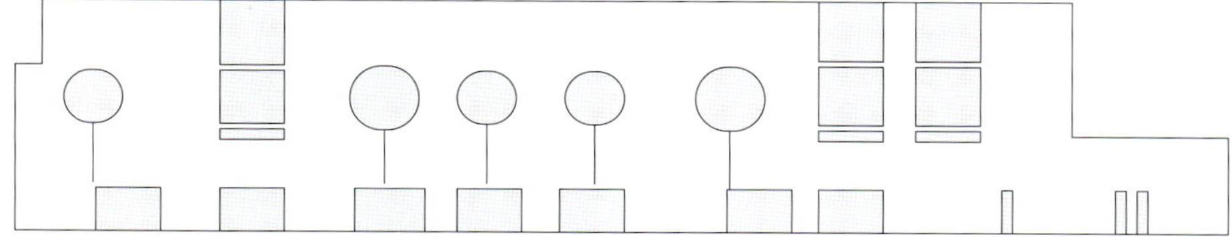

Second cladding layer with perforations

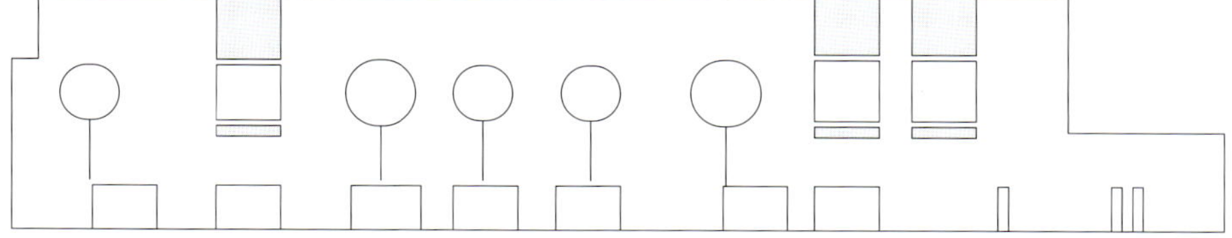

Section

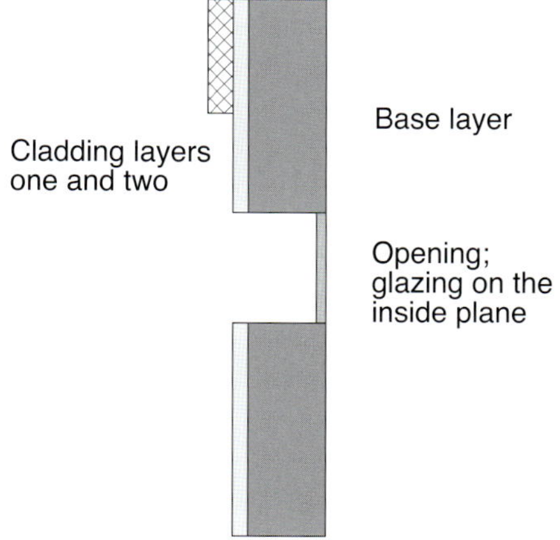

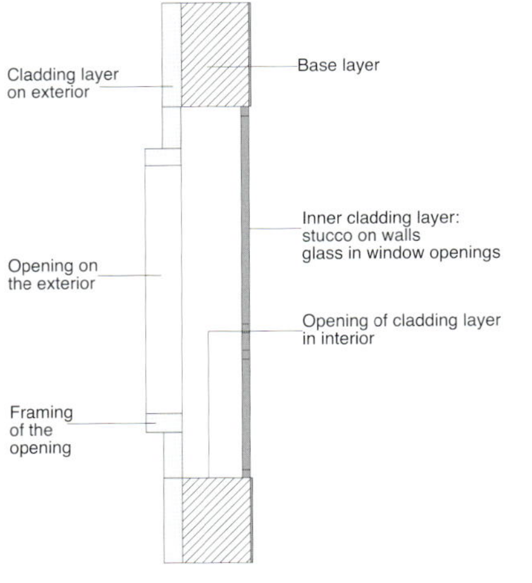


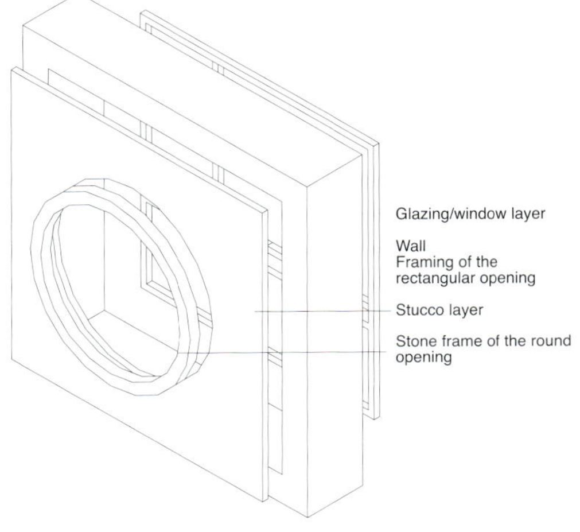

331–338. Carlo Scarpa, Banca Popolare, Verona, 1970–80.

331. Front façade. Detail of extruded glass and stone volume and one figure-eight window.
332. Round perforated window opening seen from inside with square wood frame and rhythmic mullion pattern.
333. Round window. Axonometric of layers.
334. Round window. Section.
335. Front façade. Window detail of round window, with rectangular window below.

336. Façade section. Relief.
337. Façade section. Plane of glazing.
338. Façade section. Stratification of materials.

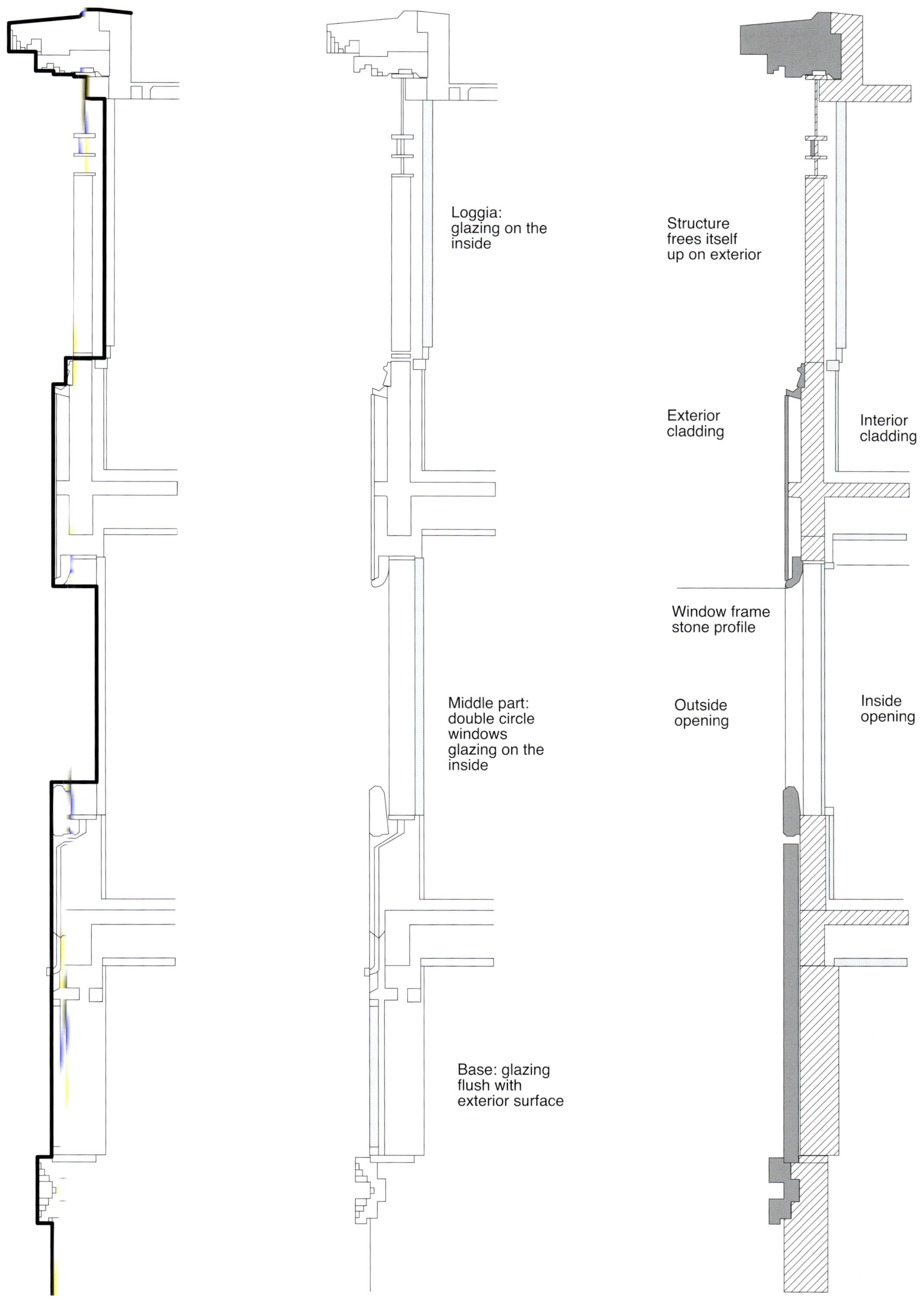
Loggia:
glazing on the
inside
Middle part:
double circle
windows
glazing on the
inside
Base: glazing
flush with
exterior surface
Structure
frees itself
up on exterior
Exterior
cladding
Interior
cladding
Window frame
stone profile
Outside
opening
Inside
opening

339–346. Carlo Scarpa, Banca Popolare, Verona, 1970–80.

339. Façade facing plaza. Loggia detail, double height glazing and exposed structural steel.
340. Façade facing plaza. Loggia detail, double height glazing, mullion and steel structure seen from interior.
341. Façade facing plaza. Rectangular windows with Botticino marble frame and sills.
342. Façade facing plaza. Rectangular window with Botticino marble frame seen from interior.

343. Interior stair. Stucco detail.
344. Interior walls. Double layer exposed in decorative light to accentuate lighting.
345. Courtyard façade. Connecting passage with metal cladding on exterior.
346. Courtyard façade. Connecting passage with wood paneling on interior.

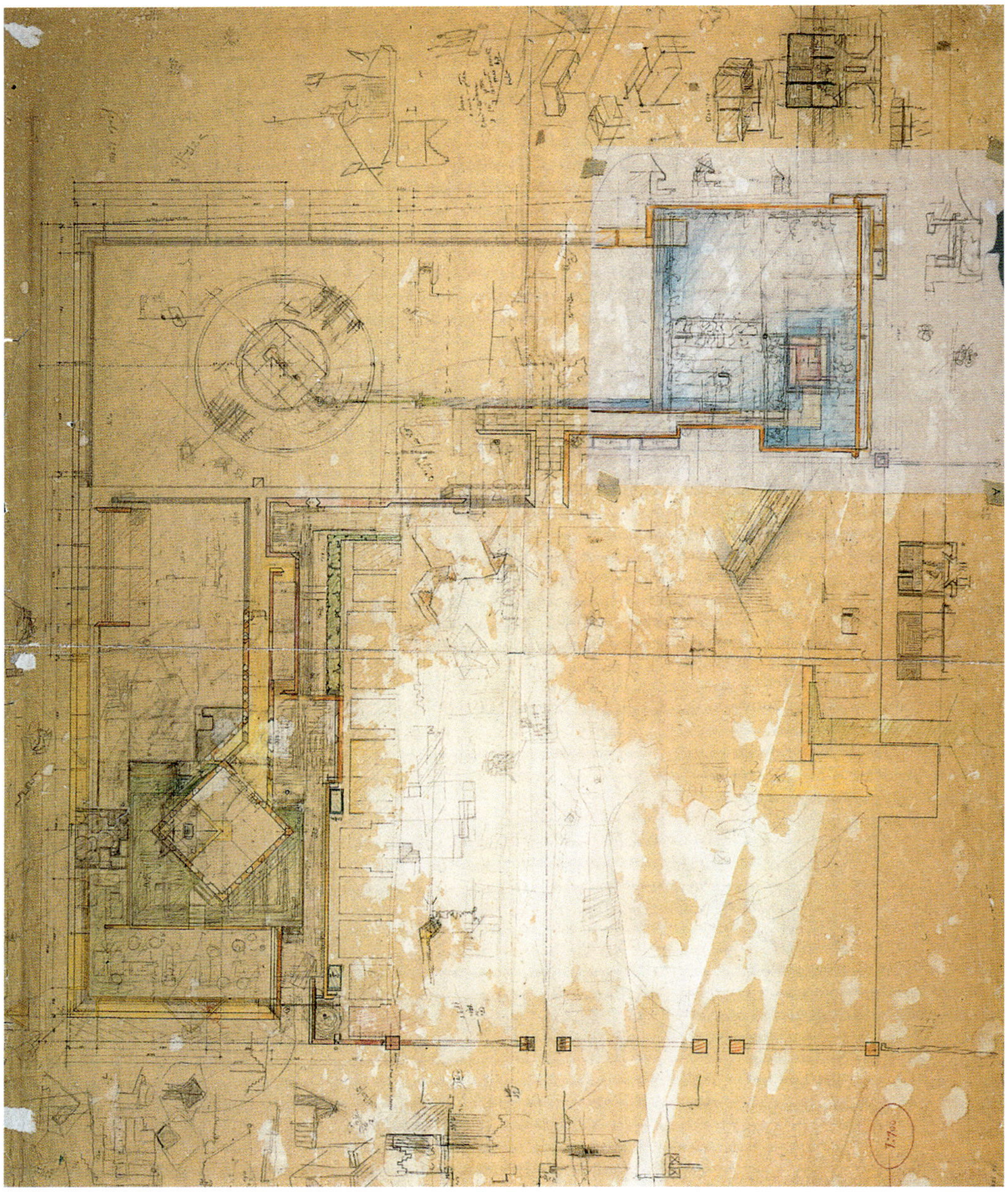

347. Carlo Scarpa, Brion cemetery, San Vito di Altivole, 1970–75. Plan drawing with different detail studies.

## Conclusion

Architecture is the »result of many conversations between an individual and a place – clarified by being filtered through the various strata of the history of the place and the history of the specific individual«.[1]

Stratification is not only an integrative principle for influences that come from various areas of our culture, but is also a way of thinking that spans a number of disciplines and takes into consideration the fact that context is completely changeable.

In examining Scarpa's spheres of influence, a definitive search for the original is irrelevant; it is the great variety of ideas and their subsequent application that go to make up Scarpa's architecture. The proliferation of print media in Scarpa's lifetime, and his turning to American and Japanese models, shows signs of a globalization of information and aesthetics – a phenomenon that is taken for granted today.

Scarpa is modern because he treats architectonic elements in a nonhierarchical way and constructs a unified whole out of them. Working with fragments is also the basis of contemporary creative activity, which demands the capacity to allow these fragments to coexist. Scarpa gives form to the object as well as the space between objects, planes, and spaces. Nonphysical components such as memories and manifested cultural ties are an essential component of the stratified work.

Façades increasingly become vehicles of the whole characteristic profile of a building, which makes the topic of façade stratification one of the most important subjects in present-day architecture discussion. Often the only difference between buildings is the façade stratum covering them. Principles of complex stratification translated into actual design work can lead to stylistically independent but similarly multilayered results. Stratification works with the understanding that spatial volumes consist of floor, wall, and ceiling; of planes that, in contrast to the theory of cladding, do without the hierarchy of a load-bearing material.

Spatial stratification is produced by structural elements whose distance from each other forms a sequence of rooms. The zones can be experienced simultaneously or are at least visible in the form of vistas and their effect is combined, as opposed to that of completely separated suites of rooms.

Material stratification is limited to the treatment of an area organized into planes that may have load-bearing, decorative, illustrative, or symbolic significance. The sequence of the superimposed strata is not laid down by a particular canon of forms, and their motifs may have been combined from a number of sources. It was the Dutch De Stijl movement that used stratification as a development of cladding. They linked the pioneering work of the Secession, who laid bare the cladding of façades, with the philosophy of Frank Lloyd Wright. This resulted in a way of thinking that defines architecture by the additive buildup of its parts and of the materials themselves. The consequence of reducing means of expression to color, form, and finish is that elements are used in their pure form. The planes are increasingly abstracted, and their use in horizontal or vertical orientation becomes formally more and more independent.

»For Scarpa, all materials are alive and pleasuregiving so long as they are worked according to their nature, put in suitable places, with discretion, and near to others which, through contrast or affinity, create a harmonious whole. Scarpa believes in a language of nature and its products, which has to be discovered by the artist, precisely in materials, even in those which are worked and transformed by he himself (such as cement), granted that he recovers their inertia and formlessness through design and reason.«[2]

Scarpa does not eliminate the symbolism of the abstracted forms; he uses the language of the materials consciously and brings out their rhetoric in his forms. The various architectural trends that are used in this analysis of stratification are received by Scarpa in different ways, and the ideas they stand for leave their mark on his work. An examination of spheres of influence shows which mechanisms he adopted and how these combine in his work from individual phenomena into a morphological structure. The movements that were examined are closely related.

The analyses of buildings are to be regarded as exemplary; they show excerpts of Scarpa's works. They are detailed, representative samples of a way of thinking and proceeding that places buildings in the context of their origins. Scarpa can serve as a model today – not so much stylistically as, above all, methodologically. The intensification of architectural motifs that occurs on every scale offers the viewer several simultaneous levels of experience. The superimposition of the different spheres from which Scarpa takes the details to construct his interventions demands that viewers come to terms with the work, look at it repeatedly, and be open to perceiving and interpreting its narrative components.

An examination of his works shows that the phenomenon of stratification is present in modified and new buildings serving different functions. Nevertheless, the effect of his modus operandi can primarily be seen in the way his work fits in with an existing context. In many of his projects, Scarpa stages preexisting rooms and, by his modifications, points to their specific characteristics and qualities. In doing so, he evaluates and interprets what he finds, as in the Castelvecchio project, by removing the 19th-century murals and replacing them with his own architectural idiom. Within the framework of what is possible, he decides what he considers to be worth preserving and capable of a mise-en-scène, and which elements can be eliminated. For his architecture to be able to enter into dialogue with existing circumstances, it must keep its distance from them and at the same time get in touch with them. In the case of the Fondazione Querini, Scarpa's striving for form is strongly emphasized: more than in the Castelvecchio, the rooms bear his personal stamp. Preexisting pillars are integrated in cladding as recycled fragments and are given space by being jointed to the new materials. In this instance the importance of ambience for his architecture becomes evident. Instead of implementing a predefined vision of space, Scarpa works with the atmosphere of the city of Venice and compresses its world of experiences in the smallest of spaces. The Banca Popolare in Verona is a building project whose structural specifications were very flexible. The new building, which replaces two buildings on the same block, consists of two »stratified« façades, one of which must fit into the historical cityscape of Verona. The fact that the courtyard façade is treated according to the same canon of forms as the façade that faces the square shows that the architect did not consider only the immediate visual vicinity.

Scarpa's drawings attest to the integration of strata in his buildings and demonstrate how he differentiates the individual layers that are integrated inside and outside.

An important characteristic of the process of stratification is being flexible enough to integrate characteristics of differing architectural idioms as being of equal value. Architectural motifs can allude to vastly different facts or models; their origin can be ascertained only approximately. Scarpa combined the characteristics of contemporary, historical, and regional sources with his own aesthetic understanding. The intellectual assimilation of his knowledge of architecture theory and his practical skills occur when he translates these directly into his architecture.

Scarpa primarily stages spatial stratification in the existing ambience by designing the floor covering, the wall, or the ceiling. Not only walls, but differentiated horizontal and vertical surfaces form permeable spatial boundaries. More than a physical partition, they express the invisible proportioning of individual spaces. In the designs for exhibitions and museums, the zones are given value by layers of color or panels. They create space and respectful recognition for the exhibits. The constructed aura of the objects settles on the existing surfaces and makes possible the existence of real space, while allowing virtual spaces to be perceived. Instead of following a linear spatial arrangement, visitors move back to the point of departure, as in a circular gallery. In Scarpa's work, the visible stratification of spatial zones arises from the redesigning of preexisting sequences of rooms to whose combined effect he draws our attention. Superimposed planes, vistas, and apertures serve as connecting links. Spatial stratification is brought about by selective application of additional strata of material at crosswalks, stairways, and other important points. By adopting narrative elements, Scarpa creates a metaphorical microclimate of the surrounding city inside his buildings.

The stratification of material ranges from the paneling to the application of paint. Stratification is linked with other phenomena, such as the cladding mentioned above, and the separation of shell and framework. Stratification does not imply a tectonic evaluation of the architectural elements referred to. Accordingly, Scarpa's most important architectural medium is not space, but rather the use of surface and the arrangement of surface elements that result in space. Surfaces are layered over or next to each other; their sequence and stylistic idiom is the vehicle of time-related components. The outermost or uppermost stratum of sediment is often also the most recently applied plane, which momentarily forms the surface of the building. Scarpa's interventions leave open the possibility of a further addition or dismantlement.

Where there is stratification, it is important to look not only at the structure, material, and effect of the stratum itself, but especially the space »between«, the transition from one plane to the next, and the joints within the strata.

Scarpa claims to do justice to both the cultural context and his own cultural urge for self-expression, and adds a narrative component to the arrangement of planes of material. The strata tell something about their context, point visitors to exhibits or architectural elements nearby, and at the same time contain information about the way they were worked. The process by which they were produced is essential. Scarpa's details are created in direct collaboration with the craftspeople[3] and are changed along with the empirical values. Joints and mortises have a didactic background just as much as, for instance, the way sculptures are arranged.[4] The associative level, in which details, materials, or colors refer to built analogies, always remains interpretive and is closely connected with the viewer's own cultural group. The much-described poetic charm of Scarpa's work is related to the associative potential of his motifs and conception. The success of his architecture is due to the fact that his work can be easily interpreted and is ambiguous, leaving room for the viewer's way of understanding it.

Scarpa formulates his design of an interior in terms of the atmosphere he is striving for. He adds to his palette of materials by deliberately using light and water, two elements which thus contribute to his urge for architectonic expression as concrete substances. Scarpa's work itself shows how the aesthetics that influenced him got transformed and developed into an independent formal language. The innumerable factors that inspired him can be only partially reconstructed. The movements and people identified as Scarpa's inspiration show connections among each other: Frank Lloyd Wright for example was interested in Byzantine architecture and was influenced by Japan. The De Stijl movement continued on principles of the Vienna Secession. During the period after the two wars, when he was finding his own way, Scarpa developed a language of his own that reflects existing trends and at the same time bears his personal mark as an architect. Scarpa's ability to combine international and regional modes of expression is a result of a culturally educated and quality-conscious clientele and of a collaboration with skilled craftspeople. Scarpa combines a strict adherence to traditional values with being open to modern trends and new approaches to design, which makes him a solid link in the architectonic development of 20th-century European architecture.

Scarpa's working methods met with a great deal of positive response in the generations of architects that followed. No school ever formed around him, and as a one-of-a-kind figure he attracted one-of-a-kind followers. Nevertheless, particularly in the region of the Veneto, there are current examples of architects who have made a Scarpaesque formal idiom their own. His motifs are utilized particularly in the recycling and restoration of buildings, and many of his details have come into standard use in the design of exhibitions. An understanding of the process of stratification is an opportunity for architects to adopt an up-to-date way of working without quoting Scarpa's work haphazardly.

The aestheticization of stratification can be seen in many contemporary architectures. Visible stratification conveys depth and profundity in more senses than one – actual strength of material, and complexity as regards content. Stratification satisfies technological and normative requirements in façade technology and allows for the ambiguity of thematic elements. It is characteristic of the 20th century that countless impressions and images flood our consciousness, blotting out historical awareness and tradition. The simultaneity of objects, information, and images is omnipresent, and we are applying filters that allow us to extract what is personally relevant to us. In our architectural environment as well, an essential part of the work of urban planners and architects is to fit individual elements into a preexisting network of territories, streets and buildings. This leads to the coexistence of manifestations made in different times. Instead of creating a focus on mimicking historic environments that seem to successfully house and host humans, the principle of layering satisfies challenges practitioners constantly face: overlaying a changing layout onto existing objects. Designed stratification allows to leave a contemporary architectural trace in environments that have been built in historic times. It enables different styles and aesthetics to communicate and coexist. Scarpa's architecture can teach about the applied link between cultural and historic research and contemporary practice. His work unifies professional research, an illustrative aspiration that teaches the viewer and creates beautiful objects and spaces at the same time. The search for a connection between research, education, and practice is and has been one of the most discussed themes in the design profession. While Scarpa was able to apply his research interests successfully to his practical work, he also took advantage of an enlarging amount of information that was accessible worldwide and a steadily increasing radius of travel. With the globalization of economy in the 21st century, architect's work is crossing geographic and cultural borders at even larger scale. Therefore the integrative principle of layering might still be a viable way of approaching the new challenges of producing meaningful architecture in a culturally open context. Strata of new architectures could coexist with the visible testimony of historic times in a similar way that Carlo Scarpa's layers exist within the historic context of Venice. Contemporary building culture could benefit from expressing more of architecture's immaterial and invisible layers. What is often most important in architecture above all is what one does not see, that which lies between the strata, that which can be interpreted in a personal context, or that which arouses amazement and curiosity.

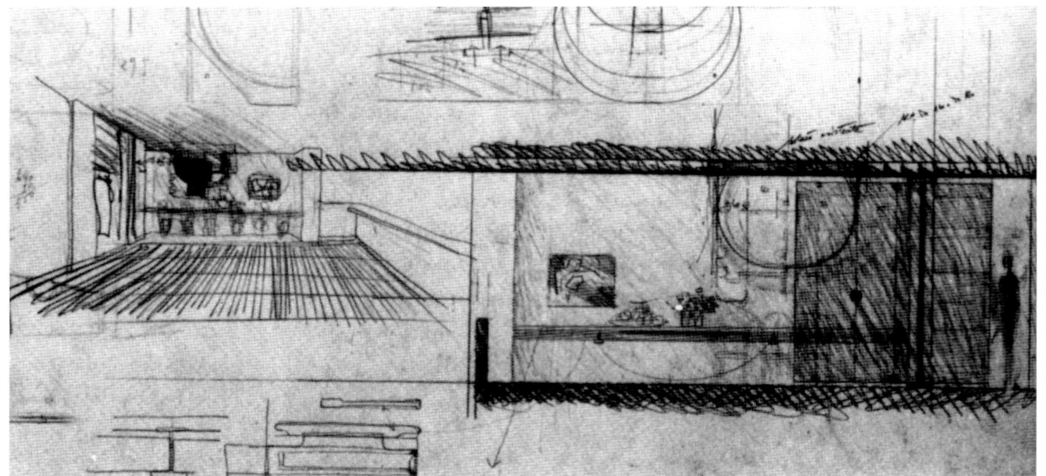

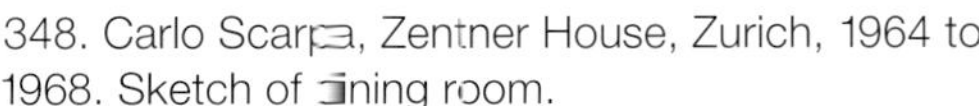

348. Carlo Scarpa, Zentner House, Zurich, 1964 to 1968. Sketch of dining room.

**Afterword**

Carlo Scarpa's highly esteemed architectural legacy goes back to the 1930s and ends unexpectedly in December 1978. Scarpa's work is part of recent architecture history.

One might ask why his work attracts the attention of so many professionals, people who are interested in architecture, and art lovers, and especially how it is relevant in our time. Anne-Catrin Schultz's book *Carlo Scarpa – Layers* examines this question step by step in an extraordinarily well researched study based on the analysis of Scarpa's design methodology and composition strategy.

There are few 20th-century architects whose œuvre is as evasive to explanation and difficult to classify as the work of Carlo Scarpa. Until now none of his critics or analysts, even in Italy, have conducted an in-depth investigation. Instead, he is honored with a certain detachment as one of the great outsiders of his time.

Anne-Catrin Schultz discusses the principle of layering to define space in architecture – beginning with theories at the turn of the 19th century and extending into the 20th century – and applies it specifically to Scarpa's œuvre. The result is an analytical and theoretical foundation that is in keeping with Scarpa's mentality, his immense cultural horizon, and the creative work that grew out of them. A look at how he uses layering allows us to understand and explain his work. Anne-Catrin Schultz comments:

»The process of layering is only one aspect of Scarpa's complex work, which has many more facets than can be examined in this investigation. The three sections of my book attempt to do justice not only to his various influences but also to the impact on his œuvre of his cultural research and integration. The first section of the book discusses influences that have been documented as being formative and important for Scarpa. It looks at them in terms of the phenomenon of layering and draws a relationship between them and Scarpa's projects. The second section analyzes three of his projects to illustrate layering in his built work, and the third section sums up the conclusions, adds to previous assessments and categorization of Scarpa's work, and suggests a position for the principle of layering in contemporary architecture theory. This book investigates one aspect of Scarpa's work that is of interest and significance to contemporary architectural practice, and explains the relevance of his work today.«

In this context we look at Scarpa's personality and the sources of his enormous creativity. The great variety and the curious interplay of architectural elements, the sensitive scale and sophisticated lighting that impress one in his interior and exterior spaces ultimately remain mysteries that are based largely on the complex layering of his personal cultural sedimentation. Scarpa had the visionary ability to isolate these layers as demanded by the tasks he was set, and to integrate them in his architectural modifications or new creations.

This book highlights Scarpa's profound knowledge of Greek, Byzantine, and Islamic art as well as his close ties to the Viennese Secession and to Japanese architecture and landscape design. Carlo Scarpa was first and foremost a Venetian, a son of Marco Polo, but also a custodian of declining Venetian culture. His close ties to his city are documented by his use of local craftsmanship in his work.

I encountered Carlo Scarpa in a special situation, having been hired as a young architect to be in charge of the construction of Casa Zentner in Zurich. This project was to be the only building

Scarpa executed outside of Italy between 1964 and 1966, built directly after the completion of his masterpiece, Castelvecchio. Casa Zentner illustrates the limitations caused by the absence of traditions and techniques of craftsmanship usually available to Scarpa when he was in his accustomed environment.

Venice was and still is an incomparably cosmopolitan milieu. In this regard as well, Scarpa was a true son of his city. As the long-standing artistic director of the Biennale, he was in contact with artists and architects from all over the world. This, too, rejuvenated his work.

From a large number of personal conversations, I had gathered that the architects he held in the highest regard were Frank Lloyd Wright and Josef Hoffmann. He told me that they had a determining influence on him; a strong affinity for Japanese culture was also clearly apparent.

Carlo Scarpa was a poet. He sketched architectural poems, architectural symphonies in many tonalities that unfolded from specific situations and conditions. Highly sensitive as he was, he discovered new points of view daily and constantly gained new insights from the world around him that would later be reflected in his work.

To an observer, his design work appeared to be not only a passion, but also an ordeal that never led to complacency. As he worked, he frequently exclaimed, »Non ce la faccio!« (I can't do it!). His words express the humility of a highly sophisticated architect.

With the help of Anne-Catrin Schultz's comprehensive and methodical analysis of Carlo Scarpa's work, the study of this extraordinary 20th-century genius should lead to deeper understanding. The analysis of the process of layering can serve as a key to new insights and evaluation.

Theo Senn

## Notes

### Preface

[1] Marja-Riitta Norri, »Six Journeys into Architectural Reality«, *The Architectural Review* (London), 1190, April 1996, p. 76.
[2] See also: Rodolpho Machado and Rodolphe El-Khoury, *Monolithic Architecture*, Munich and New York, 1995, p. 17. »This surface may be hard, polished, and higly reflective. It may have a discernible thickness in the texture of the revetment and even greater physical depth in the layering of more or less transparent cladding membranes.«
[3] In addition to the lectures published, the author used tape recordings of lectures available by former collaborators or students.
[4] According to Orietta Lanzarini (Carlo Scarpa. *L'architetto e le arti. Gli anni della Biennale di Venezia* 1948–1972, Venice, 2003), Carlo Scarpa's library is currently located in Treviso, Italy. For this book, the author consulted an inventory list provided by the architect Guido Pietropoli, a former collaborator of Carlo Scarpa (1996).

### Chapter 1.1

[1] *Brockhaus Enzyklopädie*, 19th edition, Mannheim, 1992.
[2] Hans Leo Krämer, *Soziale Schichtung. Einführung in die moderne Theoriediskussion*, Frankfurt a. M., Berlin and Munich, 1983, p. 5.
[3] Cf. Hans Murawski, *Geologisches Wörterbuch*, Stuttgart, 1992, p. 173. »Stratification: the separation of rocks into strata. The term ›stratified rocks‹ is derived from this characteristic. Stratification is created by a change in the sedimentation conditions.«
[4] Willi Ule, *Grundriß der allgemeinen Erdkunde*, Stuttgart, 1931, p. 55.
[5] Wolfgang Viktor Ruttkowski, *Typen und Schichten: Zur Einteilung des Menschen und seiner Produkte*, Bern and Munich, 1978, p. 27.
[6] Ibid.
[7] Rudolf Schwarz, *Die Bebauung der Erde*, Heidelberg, 1949, p. 21.
[8] Carl Gottlieb Boetticher, *Die Tektonik der Hellenen*, Potsdam, 1852, vol. 1, p. XV.
[9] Ibid.
[10] Werner Oechslin: *Stilhülse und Kern*, Zurich and Berlin, 1994.
[11] Eckehard Janofske, *Architektur-Räume. Idee und Gestalt bei Hans Scharoun*, Braunschweig and Wiesbaden 1984, p. 48.
[12] Franco Fonatti, *Giuseppe Terragni. Poet des Razionalismo*, Vienna, 1987.
[13] Pierre von Meiss, *Vom Objekt zum Raum zum Ort. Dimensionen der Architektur*, Berlin, Basel and Boston, 1994, p. 116.
[14] Ibid.
[15] Alfred Breukelmann, »Die Wand, ein Medium?«, *Werk, Bauen+Wohnen*, 4, 1991, p. 26.
[16] Ibid.
[17] Cf. Pierre von Meiss, *Vom Objekt zum Raum zum Ort: Dimensionen der Architektur*, Berlin, Basel and Boston, 1994, p. 199: »Semper's idea corresponds quite well with certain requirements of contemporary construction. The necessities of insulation inevitably lead us to an outside shell of mixed materials. This is why it is a real task for our time to continue developing an architecture of sheathing. The fact that the necessary light and flexible thermal insulation on the outside of the building shows more effect than on the inside will perhaps change the appearance of our buildings. It is only because of the resistance against changing forms that, for the moment, this ›coat‹ continues for the most part to have a conventional appearance.«
[18] The engineer Brian Cody developed the concept of varying spatial conditions for the climate control: zone one consists of an unheated buffer between the first and second façade, in which elevators, service stairs, and traffic areas are located. Zone two consists of the individual offices, and zone three contains the open-plan offices, which are on the inside. Cf. Brian Cody, »Klimakonzept eines Verwaltungsgebäudes«, *AiT Spezial*, July, 1996, p. 43.
[19] Alfred Breukelmann, »Architektur der variablen Häute«, *Arch+*, 104, 1990, p. 54.
[20] Andrea Compagno, *Intelligente Glasfassaden*, Basel, Boston and Berlin, 1996, p. 8.
[21] See also: Pierre von Meiss, *Vom Objekt zum Raum zum Ort. Dimensionen der Architektur*, Berlin, Basel and Boston, 1994, p. 199f.
[22] Mark Wigley, *White Walls, Designer Dresses*, Cambridge, 1995, p. xviii.
[23] Gyorgy Kepes, *Language of Vision. Painting, Photography, Advertising Design*, Chicago, 1964, p. 76: »If one sees two or more figures partly overlapping one another, and each one claims for itself the common overlapped part, then one is confronted with a contradiction of spatial dimensions. To resolve this contradiction, one must assume the presence of a new optical quality. The figures are endowed with transparency; that is, they are able to interpenetrate without an optical destruction of each other. Transparency however implies more than an optical characteristic; it implies a broader spatial order. Transparency means a simultaneous perception of different spatial locations. Space not only recedes but fluctuates in a continuous activity. The position of the transparent figures has equivocal meaning as one sees each figure now as the closer, now as the further one.«
[24] Rudolf Arnheim, *Kunst und Sehen*, Berlin, 1965, p. 86.
[25] Colin Rowe, Robert Slutzky, »Transparency: Literal and Phenomenal«, *The Mathematics of the Ideal Villa and Other Essays*, Cambridge, 1976, p. 174: »We will presume the Palace of the League of Nations as having been built and an observer following the axial approach to its auditorium. Necessarily he is subjected to the polar attraction of its principal entrance which he sees framed within a screen of trees. But these trees, intersecting his vision, also introduce a lateral deflection of interest, so that he becomes successively aware, first, of a relation between the flanking office building and the foreground parterre, and second, of a relation between the crosswalk and the courtyard of the Secretariat. And once within the trees, beneath the low umbrella which they provide, yet a further tension is established: the space, which is inflected towards the General Assembly Building, is defined by, and reads as, a projection of the book stack and library. And finally, with the trees as a volume behind him, the observer at last finds himself standing on a low terrace, confronting the entrance quay but separated from it by a rift of space so complete that it is only by the propulsive power of the walk behind him that he can be enabled to cross it. Within this arc of vision no longer restricted, he is now offered the General Assembly Building in its full extent; but since a newly revealed lack of focus compels his eye to slide along this façade, it is again irrestibly drawn sideways – to the view of gardens and lake beyond. And should the observer turn around from this rift between him and his obvious goal, and should he look back at the trees which he has just abandoned, he will find that the lateral sliding of the space becomes only more determined, emphasized by the trees themselves and the cross alley leading into the slotted indenture alongside the bookstack. While further, if our observer is a man of moderate sophistication, and if the piercing of a volume or screen of trees by a road might have to suggest to him that the intrinsic function of this road is to penetrate similar volumes and screens, then, by inference, the terrace upon which he is standing becomes, not a prelude to the auditorium, as its axial relationship suggests, but a projection of the volumes and planes of the office building with which it is aligned. These stratifications, devices by means of which space becomes constructed, substantial, and articulate, are the essence of that phenomenal transparency which has been noticed as characteristic of the central post-Cubist tradition.«
[26] Colin Rowe and Robert Slutzky, *Transparenz*, Basel and Stuttgart, 1968 (Schriftenreihe der ETH Zürich), p. 27.
[27] Ibid.
[28] Ibid., p. 28.
[29] Ibid., p. 11.
[30] Ibid., p. 48.

### Chapter 1.2

[1] See also Orietta Lanzarini, *Carlo Scarpa l'architetto e le arti. Gli anni della Biennale di Venezia 1948–1972*, Venice, 2003: This text includes a detailed investigation of Scarpa's involvement in the Biennale exhibitions and the resulting connections with artists.
[2] Franco Fonatti and Gustav Peichl (ed.), *Elemente des Bauens bei Carlo Scarpa*, Wiener Akademiereihe, vol. 15, Vienna, 1993, p. 64.
[3] Carlo Scarpa, *»Furniture«*, address delivered at the Academy of Fine Arts, Vienna, November 16, 1976, in: Francesco Dal Co and Giuseppe Mazzariol, *Carlo Scarpa. The complete works*, Milan and New York, 1985.
[4] Karljosef Schattner, »Carlo Scarpa«, *Baumeister*, 10, 1981. »Dieses Sezieren, dieses Arbeiten mit ›Skalpell‹, begegnet einem bei all seinen Bauten. Wenn er eine Mauer aufbricht, um sie mit einer Brücke zu durchstoßen, werden Elemente in Form von Betonscheiben dazwischengestellt, um jede Vermischung zu vermeiden.«
[5] Inge Habig and Kurt Jauslin, *Der Auftritt des Ästhetischen. Zur Theorie der architektonischen Ordnung*, Frankfurt a. M., 1990, p. 25.
[6] Ibid.

[7] Otto Friedrich Bollnow, *Mensch und Raum*, Stuttgart, Berlin and Cologne, 1994, p. 17.
[8] Hermann Czech, *Zur Abwechslung. Ausgewählte Schriften zur Architektur*, Vienna, 1978, p. 78.
[9] Ibid.
[10] Ibid.
[11] Marco Frascari, »The body and architecture in the drawings of Carlo Scarpa«, *Res*, 14 (autumn), 1987, p. 125.
[12] Pier Carlo Santini, »Ricordando Carlo Scarpa«, *Ottagono*, December 1979. »Voglio vedere le cose, non mi fido che di questo. Le metto qui davanti a me sulla carta, per poterle vedere. Voglio vedere e per questo disegno. Posso vedere una immagine solo se la disegno.« (Translation: Boris Podrecca, »La presunta particolarità – Carlo Scarpa aus Wiener Sicht«, *Bauforum*, 106, 1985, p. 10).
[13] Martín Domínguez, »Entrevista a Carlo Scarpa«, *Quaderns*, 158, 1983, p. 76.
[14] Richard Murphy, *Carlo Scarpa & Castelvecchio*, Venice, 1991, p. 14. Original text: »In primo luogo c'è l'idea di materia – la solidità dell'edificio – che ai margini si rivela in una serie di piani o lamine: è l'accrescimento progressivo di strati sottili, o depositi, come nelle rocce sedimentarie. Indubbiamente il trattamento che Scarpa riserva alla facciata della caserma napoleonica, dove si prefigge di creare dei piani sottili giustapposti ma discontinui, convalida questa idea. Ciò è particolarmente evidente all'estremità, dove l'essenza del muro è esposta tramite il taglio praticato da Scarpa. Qui le implicite stratificazioni sono chiaramente visibili dove terminano, ognuna chiaramente distinta dalle altre.«
[15] The inventory list of the library was critically re-evaluated by the author. The list was provided by architect Guido Pietropoli, a former collaborator of Carlo Scarpa (1996).
[16] Works on French architecture theory at the turn of the 20th century appear to have been part of Scarpa's library for example: Eugène Emmanuel Viollet-le Duc, *Entretiens sur l'architecture*, Paris, 1863; Eugène Emmanuel Viollet-le Duc, *Dictionnaire raisonné de l'architec-ture française du XI au XVI siècle*, Paris, 1854.
[17] Manfredo Tafuri, *History of Italian Architecture 1944–1985*, Cambridge, MA, 1989 (original Turin, Einaudi, 1982), p. 114.
[18] Bruno Zevi, *Saper vedere l'architettura*, Turin, 1993 (original 1948), p. 18. Original text: »Il gusto di una ornamentazione che preferisce giocare sull'intersezione di materiali diversi (per esempio, pareti di stucco vicino a pareti di legno, cemento armato giustapposto a pietra naturale e vetro), il nuovo senso del colore, una nuova inspirazione alla gioia che segue la severa freddezza della teorica funzionalista, sono determinati da un migliore approfondimento psicologico.«
[19] Ada Francesca Marcianò, *Carlo Scarpa*, Zurich, 1989, p. 198.
[20] Manlio Brusatin, »Carlo Scarpa architetto Veneziano«, *Controspazio* March–April, 1972, p. 5. Original text: »D'ora in avanti Scarpa preferiva rivolgersi verso l'artigianato qualificato, svolgendo un paziente lavoro di contemplazione della fatica umana nei forni dei vetrai.«
[21] Ada Francesca Marcianò, *Carlo Scarpa*, Zurich, 1989, 2nd edition, p. 198.
[22] Giuseppe Mazzariol and Giuseppe Barbieri, »Vita di Carlo Scarpa«, in: Francesco Dal Co, Giuseppe Mazzariol, *Carlo Scarpa. Opera completa 1906 to 1978*, Milan, 1984, p. 13. Original text: »Nelle lampade e nei vasi murrini, e nel rito antico delle mani e delle bocche e del fuoco Carlo Scarpa apprendeva l'intreccio inesplicabile che lega alla provvisorietà la bellezza, rendendole entrambe necessarie e viziose: e questo attraverso l'alta coscienza della non realizzabilità di ogni progetto.«
[23] Manlio Brusatin, »Carlo Scarpa architetto veneziano«, *Controspazio*, 3/4, 1972, p. 6. Original text: »Nel ritiro e nella tranquillità della bottega Carlo Scarpa ritroverà il suo giusto posto di lavoro, traducendo i segreti della fabbrilità come convinzione morale: la consapevolezza del mestiere, la pazienza, la misura del definire, la passione nel tastare le cose; il piacere e lo stimolo artigianale nasce dalla convinzione di sapere e di poter fare poche cose e benfatte.«
[24] Andrea de Eccher and Giulia Del Zotto, *L'opera di Carlo Scarpa*, Milan, 1994, p. 131.
[25] Giuseppe Mazzariol, »Opere di Carlo Scarpa«, *L´Architettura Cronache e Storia*, 3, 1955, p. 342. Original text: »Scarpa intese i valori luminosi dell'interno che i guasti settecenteschi e ottocenteschi avevano profondamente alterato: arretrando la vetrata dell'ingresso rispetto alla linea delle colonne architravate, liberando la scala sul canale per mezzo di un cubo cristallo che sostituiva le porte a battenti, permise alla luce di vibrare lungo le pareti di cotto con modulazioi pastose, animando il portico a terreno di una variabilità di toni che l'acqua mutevole del canale governa secondo le ore della stagione. La luminosità è condizionata dalla temperie cromatica dei pannelli-parete che esercitano una funzione di assorbimento e ricreano, con mezzi lunguistici nuovi, l'effetto originario di questi percorsi spaziali. Era allora di moda il restauro istologico; Scarpa per primo propose il ripristino organico di un'architettura antica a Venezia, volle farla rivivere nella sua interezza senza ricorre a protesi grottesche e funerarie.«
[26] Sabine Forsthuber, *Moderne Raumkunst – Wiener Ausstellungsbauten von 1898 bis 1914*, Vienna 1991, p. 8.
[27] See also: Maria Antonietta Crippa, *Carlo Scarpa – il pensiero il disegno dei progetti*, Milan, 1984, p. 80. »Da questa analisi potrebbe derivare una valutazione dell'uso che i architetti ed artisti moderni hanno fatto dello strumento espositivo per diffondere i loro messaggi.«
[28] Percorso (It.) means a tour through the museum.
[29] Bianca Albertini and Sandro Bagnoli, *Scarpa Ausstellungen und Museen*, Tübingen and Berlin, 1992, p. 190.
[30] Ibid., p. 254.
[31] Carlo Scarpa in all probability knew Hoffmann's work through the magazine *Moderne Bauformen*, No.8, 1930, which was in his library. He met Hoffmann in Venice in 1934, the year in which the Austrian Pavilion was completed. See also: Orietta Lanzarini, *Carlo Scarpa. L'architetto e le arti – Gli anni della Biennale di Venezia 1948–1972*, Venice, 2003, p. 27 and p. 63.
[32] Bianca Albertini and Sandro Bagnoli, *Scarpa. Ausstellungen und Museen*, Tübingen and Berlin, 1992, p. 190.
[33] Ibid., p. 256.
[34] Ibid., p. 193.
[35] Ibid.

**Chapter 1.3**

[1] See also: Hanno Walter Kruft, *Geschichte der Architekturtheorie*, Munich, 1985, p. 316.
[2] Quatremère de Quincy, *Jupiter Olympien: ou l'art de la sculpture antique considéré sous un nouveau point de vue; ouvrage qui comprend un essai sur le goût de la sculpture polychrome*, Paris, 1814. Translation of the title: The Olympic Jupiter: or the art of ancient sculbture considered from a new point of view; a work that includes an essay about the taste for polychrome sculpture.
[3] Robin Middleton, »Perfezione e colore: la policromia nell'architettura francese del XVIII e XIX secolo«, *Rassegna*, 23, 1985, p. 57.
[4] Hanno Walter Kruft, *Geschichte der Architekturtheorie*, Munich, 1985, p. 316.
[5] Quatremère de Quincy, *Dictionnaire Historique d'Architecture*, vol.II, Paris 1932, p. 9.
[6] Quatremère de Quincy, *Dictionnaire Historique d'Architecture*, Paris 1932, under the entry for »Façade«.
[7] Quatremère de Quincy, *Dictionnaire Historique d'Architecture*, vol. II, Paris, 1932, p. 9.
[8] Quatremère de Quincy, *Dictionnaire Historique d'Architecture*, vol. II, Paris 1932, under the entry for »Construction«.
[9] See also: R. D. Middleton, »Hittorff's polychrome campaign«, in: *The Beaux-Arts and nineteenth-century French architecture*, Cambridge, 1982, p. 175: »He thought to apply colour, inside and outside, to buildings. And in support of this programme he undertook detailed and thorough investigations into the use of colour in classical antiquity. For if it could be shown that the hallowed architecture of ancient Greece itself was coloured with paint, no other precedent for his present performance would be required, no further explanation needed.«
[10] Hanno Walter Kruft, *Geschichte der Architekturtheorie*, Munich, 1985, p. 317.
[11] Robin Middleton and David Watkin, *Klassizismus und Historismus*, vol. 2, Stuttgart, 1987, p. 284.
[12] Hanno Walter Kruft, *Geschichte der Architekturtheorie*, Munich, 1985, p. 327.
[13] Ibid., p. 328
[14] Auguste Choisy, *Histoire d'Architecture*, 1899, vol.I, p. 285. Original text: »L'usage de recouvrir la pierre d'une enveloppe de poterie parait une tradition des temps où l'insuffisance de l'outillage rendait pénible la taille d'un parement régulier.«
[15] Auguste Choisy, *Histoire d'Architecture*, 1899, vol.I, p. 295. Original text: »La peinture architecturale – ainsi che l'a prouvé Hittorff les monuments grecs étaient peints.«
[16] Robin Middleton and David Watkin, *Klassizismus und Historismus*, vol. 2, Stuttgart, 1987, p. 228.
[17] Hanno Walter Kruft, *Geschichte der Architekturtheorie*, Munich, 1985, p. 318.
[18] Karl Hammer, *Jakob Ignaz Hittorff. Ein Pariser Baumeister*, Stuttgart, 1968, p. 125.
[19] Franz Kugler, *Über die Polychromie der griechischen Architektur und Skulptur und ihre Grenzen*, Berlin, 1835, p. 38.

[20] Ibid., p. 46.
[21] Ibid., p. 10.
[22] Karl Boetticher, *Die Tektonik der Hellenen*, vol.1, Potsdam, 1852, p. XIV.
[23] Ibid., p. XIV.
[24] Ibid., p. 8.
[25] Heinrich Hübsch, *Die Architektur und ihr Verhältnis zur heutigen Malerei und Skulptur*, Berlin, 1985, first edition: Tübingen 1847, p. 33.
[26] Ibid., p. 41.
[27] Heinrich Wölfflin and Josef Gantner (ed.), *Kleine Schriften (1886–1933)*, Basel, 1946, p. 24.
[28] Gottfried Semper, »Vorläufige Bemerkungen über bemalte Architektur und Plastik bei den Alten«, in: Hans and Manfred Semper (eds.), *Kleine Schriften*, Mittenwald, 1979, p. 219.
[29] Gottfried Semper, *Der Stil in den tektonischen Künsten*, vol.1, Mittenwald, 1977, p. 228.
[30] Gottfried Semper, »Vorläufige Bemerkungen über bemalte Architektur und Plastik bei den Alten«, in: Hans and Manfred Semper (eds.) *Gottfried Semper. Kleine Schriften*, Mittenwald, 1979, p. 219.
[31] Ibid., p. 224.
[32] Ákos Moravánszky, *Die Erneuerung der Baukunst – Wege zur Moderne in Mitteleuropa 1900 bis 1940*, Salzburg and Vienna 1988, p. 65.
[33] Ibid., p. 46.
[34] Gottfried Semper, *Der Stil in den tektonischen Künsten*, vol.1, Mittenwald, 1977, p. 228.
[35] Hans Prinzhorn, *Gottfried Sempers aesthetische Anschauungen*, diss., Stuttgart, 1909, p. 16.
[36] Gottfried Semper, *Der Stil in den Tektonischen Künsten*, vol.1, Munich, 1878, p. 227.
[38] Ibid., p. 185.
[39] Ibid., p. 390.
[40] Ibid., p. 206.
[41] Ibid., p. 281.
[42] Gottfried Semper, »Die vier Elemente der Baukunst«, in: Heinz Quitsch, *Gottfried Semper. Praktische Ästhetik und politischer Kampf*, Braunschweig and Wiesbaden, 1981, p. 54.
[43] Ibid.
[44] Ibid.
[45] Ibid.
[46] Ibid., p. 57.
[47] Gottfried Semper, »Die vier Elemente der Baukunst«, in: Heinz Quitsch, *Gottfried Semper. Praktische Ästhetik und politischer Kampf*, Braunschweig and Wiesbaden 1981, p. 58.
[48] A more detailed study of »cladding/clothing« (Bekleidung) in architecture in the literal sense of the German word is found in Karin Harather, *Haus-Kleider. Zum Phänomen der Bekleidung in der Architektur*, Vienna, Cologne and Weimar, 1995.
[49] Kenneth Frampton, »Carlo Scarpa und die Verherrlichung des Gelenks«, in: *Grundlagen der Architektur: Studien zur Kultur des Tektonischen*, Munich, 1993, p. 368.
[50] Orietta Lanzarini reaches the same conclusion that Carlo Scarpa probably did not read Gottfried Semper's works in the original, but absorbed Semper's ideas indirectly. See: Orietta Lanzarini, *Cario Scarpa l'architetto e le arti – Gli anni della Biennale di Venezia 1948–1972*, Venice, 2003, p. 19.
[51] Gottfried Semper, *Der Stil in den Tektonischen Künsten*, vol. 2, Munich, 1878, p. 211.
[52] Gottfried Semper, *Der Stil in den Tektonischen Künsten*, vol.1, Munich, 1878, p. XXVII.
[53] Ibid.
[54] Ibid., p. 61.
[55] Ibid., p. 53.
[56] Ibid., p. 169.
[57] Boris Podrecca, »La presunta particolarità«, in: Francesco Dal Co and Giuseppe Mazzariol, *Carlo Scarpa: opera completa 1906–1978*, Milan, 1984, p. 243. Original text: »Anche la parete, il grande tema nell'opera di Carlo Scarpa, segue il principio classico della trasfigurazione loosiana del parcour narratif. E allora quale definizione può meglio adattarsi a questo anteporsi delle pareti di Scarpa che le massime desute da Gottfried Semper per fini museali e che in certo qual modo alludono all'origine dell'architettura legata all'arte della tessitura.«
[58] Kenneth Frampton considers Scarpa's work from the perspective of the joint: Kenneth Frampton, »Carlo Scarpa und die Verherrlichung des Gelenks«, in: *Grundlagen der Architektur. Studien zur Kultur des Tektonischen*, Munich, 1993, p. 368.

### Chapter 2.1

[1] Giovanni Fanelli and Roberto Gargiani, *Il principio del rivestimento. Prolegomena a una storia dell'architettura contemporanea*, Roma and Bari, 1994, p. 13. Original text: »Nel passagio tra Otto- e Novecento essa diviene centrale nella riflessione teorica della cultura architettonica internazionale sul rivestimento. ›Bekleidung‹ o ›Verkleidung‹, rivelare o mascherare sono concetti di una problematica resa ancora più attuale, cogente e drammatica, nel mutato orizzonte tecnico o tecnologico che non contempla più soltanto la situazione tradizionale di una struttura continua muraria che risolve l'involucro alla quale il rivestimento aggiunge un grado di qualità materica e di finitezza, ma vede anche l'affermarsi ineluttabile della struttura a telaio in ferro e in calcestruzzo armato che esaspera la diversità di natura e di funzione del rivestimento e della costruzione, rendendo irresolubile, rispetto al traguardo della verità, il loro rapporto se informato alla volontà di conservare ancora l'mmagine dell'architettura lapidea.«
[2] Josef Gantner, inaugural lecture at the University of Zurich 30 April 1927, in: Josef Gantner, *Revision der Kunstgeschichte*, Vienna, 1932, p. 80.
[3] Ibid., p. 89.
[4] Friedrich Achleitner, »Zu Otto Wagners Dialektik des Schönen«, in: Gustav Peichl, *Die Kunst des Otto Wagner*, Vienna, 1984, p. 13.
[5] Ákos Moravánszky, *Die Erneuerung der Baukunst: Wege zur Moderne in Mitteleuropa 1900–1940*, Salzburg and Vienna, 1988, p. 46.
[6] Otto Wagner, *Die Erneuerung der Baukunst*, Vienna, 1979, reprint of the 4th edition 1914, pp. 61, 131.
[7] Ibid., p. 59.
[8] Peter Haiko, in the preface of the book: Otto Wagner, *Einige Skizzen, Projekte und ausgeführte Bauwerke von Otto Wagner*, complete, reprint of the four original volumes of 1889, 1897, 1922, Tübingen, 1987, p. 6.
[9] Otto Wagner, *Die Erneuerung der Baukunst*, Vienna, 1979, reprint of the 4th edition 1914, p. 33.
[10] Friedrich Achleitner, »Zu Otto Wagners Dialektik des Schönen«, in: Gustav Peichl, *Die Kunst des Otto Wagner*, Vienna, 1984, p. 14.
[11] Ákos Moravánszky, »Byzantinismus in der Baukunst Otto Wagners als Motiv seiner Wirkung östlich von Wien«, in: Gustav Peichl, *Die Kunst des Otto Wagner*, Vienna, 1984, p. 14.
[12] Otto Wagner, *Die Erneuerung der Baukunst*, Vienna 1979, reprint of the 4th edition 1914, p. 41.
[13] Ibid., p. 34: »Keine Epoche, kein Stil hat hiervon eine Ausnahme gemacht. Recht anschaulich wird diese Tatsache durch ein Zusammenhalten von Kostümbildern mit den gleichzeitigen Werken der Baukunst, oder noch besser durch die Betrachtung von Gemälden, welche beides vereint zeigen.«
[14] Otto Wagner, »Moderne Architektur«, Vienna 1895, 4th edition 1914, in: Sigfried Giedion, *Raum, Zeit und Architektur*, Munich and Zurich, 1992, p. 217 (original edition: *Time, Space. and Architecture*, Cambridge, MA, 1941).
[15] Otto Wagner, *Die Baukunst unserer Zeit*, Vienna 1914, p. 41.
[16] Ákos Moravánszky, *Die Architektur der Jahrhundertwende und ihre Beziehungen zur Wiener Architektur der Zeit*, diss., Vienna, 1983, p. 36.
[17] Friedrich Achleitner, »Zu Otto Wagners Dialektik des Schönen«, in: Gustav Peichl, *Die Kunst des Otto Wagner*, Vienna, 1984, p. 14.
[18] Otto Wagner, *Die Erneuerung der Baukunst*, Vienna, 1979, reprint of the 4th edition 1914, p. 67.
[19] Wolfgang Pehnt, »Verwerfungen im Untergrund«, in: Gustav Peichl, *Die Kunst des Otto Wagner*, Vienna 1984, p. 14.
[20] Friedrich Achleitner, »Zu Otto Wagners Dialektik des Schönen«, in: Gustav Peichl, *Die Kunst des Otto Wagner*, Vienna, 1984, p. 14.
[21] Otto Wagner, *Die Erneuerung der Baukunst*, Vienna, 1979, reprint of the 4th edition 1914, p. 60.
[22] Heinz Geretsegger and Max Peintner, *Otto Wagner (1841–1918). Unbegrenzte Groszstadt Beginn der Modernen Architektur*, Salzburg, 1976, p. 30.
[23] See also Ákos Moravánszky, *Die Erneuerung der Baukunst – Wege zur Moderne in Mitteleuropa 1900 bis 1940*, Salzburg and Vienna, 1988, p. 103.
[24] Ibid.
[25] Ibid., p. 191.
[26] Daniele Baroni and Andtionio D'Auria, *Josef Hoffmann und die Wiener Werkstätte*, Stuttgart, 1981, p. 48.
[27] Ibid., p.38.
[28] Ibid., p.126.
[29] William R. Curtis, *Modern Architecture since 1900*, Oxford, 1982, S.34 (about Palais Stoclet).
[30] Eduard F. Sekler, *Josef Hoffmann: Das architektonische Werk. Monografie und Werkverzeichnis*, Salzburg and Vienna, 1982, p. 85.
[31] See also: Rossana Bossaglia, *L'Art Deco*, Roma and Bari, 1997, p. 69. Original text: »È all'insegna di questo secessionismo che, nella seconda metà degli anni Dieci, avviene il graduale passaggio all'architettura déco della cui prima fase l'hoffmannismo costituirà la chiave di lettura e di cui protagonisti principali sono identificabili in Piacentini, Fichera, Greppi, Valle, Torres. La lezione hoffmanniana, tradotta in chiave semplificata, è ravvisabile nell'opera di Provino Valle la cui villa Leoncini a Udine (1911–12) può essere assunta a prototipo di quell'hoffman-

nismo diffuso che troverà ampio spazio nella piccola edilizia privata ...«

32 In: Peter Noever, *Die unbekannte Stadt*, Berlin and Vienna, 1989, p. 22.: »Im Grunde bin ich ein Byzantiner, und im Grunde hat auch Josef Hoffmann etwas von einem orientalischen Charakter, und zwar in dem Sinn, wie ein Europäer sich zum Orientalischen hinwendet.«

33 See also: Sabine Forsthuber, *Moderne Raumkunst: Wiener Ausstellungsbauten von 1898 bis 1914*, Vienna, 1991, p. 146.

34 Eduard F. Sekler, *Josef Hoffmann. Das architektonische Werk. Monografie und Werkverzeichnis*, Salzburg and Vienna, 1982, p. 52.

35 Ibid.

36 Adolf Loos, »Ornament und Verbrechen«, in: *Trotzdem*, Vienna, 1988.

37 Gottfried Semper, »Wissenschaft, Industrie und Kunst«, essay 1852, in: *Wissenschaft, Industrie und Kunst und andere Schriften über Architektur, Kunsthandwerk und Kunstunterricht*, p. 97.

38 Quoted from Adrian von Buttlar, »Jenseits von Stil-Architektur«, in: *Gründerzeit – Adolf Loos. Jahrhundertwende. Rückblick und Ausblick im Spiegel der Wiener Architektur unter Einbeziehung der Gründerzeitarchitektur*, exhibition catalogue, Karlsruhe, 1987, p. 39.

39 Adolf Loos, »Das Prinzip der Bekleidung«, in: *Ins Leere gesprochen*, Vienna, 1987, original edition: Zurich, 1921, p. 139.

40 Ibid., p.141.

41 Ibid.

42 Ibid.

43 Ákos Moravánszky, *Die Erneuerung der Baukunst – Wege zur Moderne in Mitteleuropa 1900 bis 1940*, Salzburg and Vienna, 1988, p. 75.

44 Adolf Loos, *Die Potemkinsche Stadt*, Vienna, 1983, p. 56.

45 Ibid.

46 Ibid., p.56.

47 Ibid.

48 Adolf Loos, »Das Prinzip der Bekleidung«, in: *Ins Leere gesprochen*, Vienna, 1987, original edition: Zurich, 1921, p. 139.

49 Publication of Loos's works in Italy: Giulia Veronesi, photograph series in: *L'Architettura – Cronache e Storia*, published in the issues from 1962 to 1971.

50 Josef Rückwert, »Adolf Loos: Das neue Sehen«, in: *Ornament ist kein Verbrechen: Architektur als Kunst*, Cologne, 1983, p. 118.

51 Richard Murphy, *Querini Stampalia Foundation: Carlo Scarpa*, London, 1993, p. 11.

52 Josef Durms in: *Gründerzeit – Adolf Loos. Jahrhundertwende*, exhibition catalogue, Karlsruhe, 1987, p. 276.

53 Ibid., p.64.

54 Arnold Schönberg, »Zum 60. Geburtstag«, in: Adam Opel (ed.), *Kontroversen: Adolf Loos im Spiegel der Zeitgenossen*, Vienna, 1985, p. 149.

55 K. Lhota, »Architekt Adolf Loos spricht. Ausschnitte aus Aufzeichnungen«, *Architekt SIA Praha*, 32 (1933), no. 8, pp.137–143, quoted from D. Worbs, *Der Raumplan*, diss., 1982, p. 56 fn. 3.

56 Johannes Spalt, »Wohnungseinrichtungen«, in: *Adolf Loos*, exhibition catalogue, Vienna, 1989, Graphische Sammlung Albertina, p. 60.

57 Manlio Brusatin, »Carlo Scarpa architetto veneziano«, in: *Controspazio*, 3/4, 1972, p. 7: »In molti particolari degli arreddi e delle nuove sistemazioni ci appare un latente interesse per Adolf Loos.«

58 Johannes Spalt, »Wohnungseinrichtungen«, in: *Adolf Loos*, exhibition catalogue, Vienna, 1989, Graphische Sammlung Albertina, p. 60.

59 Scarpa integrates pictures in travertine panels at the exhibition in the Museo Correr.

60 Hermann Czech, »Der Umbau«, in: *Adolf Loos*, exhibition catalogue, Vienna 1989, p. 160.

**Chapter 2.2**

1 Frank Lloyd Wright, »Preface«, in: *Ausgeführte Bauten und Entwürfe von Frank Lloyd Wright*, Tübingen, 1986, reprint of the portfolio edition, published in 1910, p. 13.

2 Vincent Scully, »Preface«, in: *Ausgeführte Bauten und Entwürfe von Frank Lloyd Wright*, Tübingen, 1986, reprint of the portfolio edition, published in 1910, p. 13.

3 Inventory list of Scarpa's library, (currently located in Treviso) provided by the architect Guido Pietropoli, a former collaborator of Carlo Scarpa (1996). (See: Orietta Lanzarini, *Carlo Scarpa. L'architetto e le arti. Gli anni della Biennale di Venezia* 1948–1972, Venice, 2003.)

4 Francesco Dal Co, »Genie ist Fleiss: L'architettura di Carlo Scarpa«, in: *Francesco Dal Co, Giuseppe Mazzariol, Carlo Scarpa 1906–1978*, exhibition catalogue, Venice 1984, p. 46. Original text: »Ma l'incontro con Wright, inevitabile per molteplici ragioni, non è motivato solo da considerazioni formali. La curiosità intellettuale è la molla che determina la cinematica anche del linguaggio wrightiano. Le forme dell'architetto americano intendono suscitare e controllare suggestioni derivate da tradizioni culturali di diversa matrice, destinate, a loro volta, a sedimentarsi in esperimenti composti. Come Scarpa, Wright è un collezionista di immagini e un tenace osservatore. Ambedue, pur operando in ambienti tanto differenti e con finalità per certi versi opposte, attribuiscono nel proprio lavoro notevole importanza al problema della tradizione, dando al contempo libera espressione ad ipotesi compositive conscie dell'avvenuta dissacrazione di ogni normativa stilistica.«

5 Crippa, Maria Antonietta, *Carlo Scarpa – Il pensiero il disegno i progetti*, Milan, 1984; p. 34: »Influenze Wrightiane sono già presenti nei primi allestimenti delle Biennale Veneziane, come si vedrà più avanti. Ma tale rapporto fu esplorato con particolare insistenza nella progettazione di nuovi edifici fra 1947 e il '60. Segnalando nel 19478 la trasformazione in corso, i progetti per un edificio di abitazioni a Padova, con struttura portante a vista e balcone aggettanti, e per la banca cattolica di Tarvisio con ampie fasce orizzontali: nel 1949 il progetto di massima per un edificio su quattro piani a Feltre, dalle grandi terrazze in legno composte e gradonate; nel 1950 il disegno di villa Guarnieri, composta in tre volumi orizzontali attorno una zona di passaggio (tema presente anche nel Padiglione Venezuela alla Biennale) e con un'articolazione in facciata di elementi orizzontali e verticali ed un primo accenno nella decorazione al motivo di gradonature, poi ornamento costante di ogni architettura.«

6 Giovanni Fanelli and Roberto Gargiani, *Il principio del rivestimento*, Rome and Bari, 1994, p. 29: Scarpa's disappointment was being described by several former collaborators.

7 See chapter: »Organic Space of Our Time«, in: Bruno Zevi, *Architecture as Space: How to Look at Architecture*, New York, 1993 (original edition: 1974).

8 Frank Lloyd Wright in the preface to: *Ausgeführte Bauten und Entwürfe*, Berlin, 1910, here in the slightly altered form of the introduction to an exhibition in the Palazzo Strozzi in Florence 1951, quoted from: Edgar Kaufmann and Ben Raeburn, *Frank Lloyd Wright Schriften und Bauten*, Munich and Vienna, 1963, p. 105.

9 Frank Lloyd Wright, »Prairie und Architektur« (in *Modern Architecture*, 1931), in: Edgar Kaufmann and Ben Raeburn *Frank Lloyd Wright: Schriften und Bauten*, Munich and Vienna, 1963, p. 259.

10 Frank Lloyd Wright, »Moderne Architektur«, in: Edgar Kaufmann and Ben Raeburn, *Frank Lloyd Wright: Schriften und Bauten*, Munich and Vienna, 1963, p. 194.

11 Frank Lloyd Wright, »Die Kunst und die Fertigkeit der Maschine«, lecture, March 6, 1902 to the Arts and Crafts Society and March 20 to the Western Society of Engineers, in: Wolfgang Braatz (ed.), *Frank Lloyd Wright. Humane Architektur*, Berlin 1969, p. 86.

12 Frank Lloyd Wright, »Ein Testament 1957«, in: Edgar Kaufmann and Ben Raeburn, *Frank Lloyd Wright: Schriften und Bauten*, Munich and Vienna, 1963, p. 251.

13 Frank Lloyd Wright, »Das Kaiserliche Hotel«, (*Architecture and Modern Life*, 1937), in: Frank Lloyd Wright and Wolfgang Braatz (ed.), »Humane Architektur«, Berlin 1969, p. 97.

14 Frank Lloyd Wright, »Ein Testament 1957«, in: Edgar Kaufmann and Ben Raeburn, *Frank Lloyd Wright: Schriften und Bauten*, Munich and Vienna, 1963, p. 242.

15 Frank Lloyd Wright, *Ausgeführte Bauten und Entwürfe*, Tübingen, 1986, reprint of the Wasmuth portfolio edition, published in 1910, p. 14.

16 Ibid., p. 18.

17 Edward R. Ford, *Das Detail in der Architektur der Moderne* (introduction), Basel, Berlin and Boston, 1994, p. 3.

18 See Giovanni Fanelli and Roberto Gargiani, *Il principio del rivestimento*, Rome and Bari, 1994, p. 28.

19 Frank Lloyd Wright, »Talk to the Taliesin Fellowship«, quoted from: Bruce Brooks Pfeiffer (text), Peter Gössel and Gabriele Leuthäuser (eds.), *Frank Lloyd Wright*, Cologne, 1991, p. 25.

20 Frank Lloyd Wright, »Ein Testament 1957«, in: Edgar Kaufmann and Ben Raeburn, *Frank Lloyd Wright: Schriften und Bauten*, Munich and Vienna, 1963, p. 251.

21 Frank Lloyd Wright, »Prairie und Architektur« (in Modern Architecture 1931), in: Edgar Kaufmann and Ben Raeburn, *Frank Lloyd Wright: Schriften und Bauten*, Munich and Vienna, 1963, p. 41.

22 Frank Lloyd Wright, *Ein Testament*, Munich, 1959, p. 157.

23 Frank Lloyd Wright in a talk to the junior chapter of the American Institute of Architects, New York City, 1952, tape transcript corrected by Frank Lloyd

Wright, quoted from: Edgar Kaufmann and Ben Raeburn, *Frank Lloyd Wright: Schriften und Bauten*, Munich and Vienna, 1963, p. 231.
[24] Cf. Otto Antonia Graf: *Die Kunst des Quadrats. Zum Werke von Frank Lloyd Wright I*, Vienna, 1983
[25] Frank Lloyd Wright, »Ein Testament 1957«, in: Edgar Kaufmann and Ben Raeburn, *Frank Lloyd Wright: Schriften und Bauten*, Munich and Vienna, 1963, p. 259.
[26] Ibid., p. 259.
[27] Maria Antonietta Crippa, *Carlo Scarpa. Il pensiero il disegno i progetti*, Milan, 1984, p. 34. Original text: »La Villa Zoppas a Conegliano fu progettata in tre fasi diversificate, nel corso delle quali Scarpa passò da una planimetria molto aperta, allungata, ancora memore del rapporto interno-esterno di Mies van der Rohe, ad un impianto più compatto, legato in primo momento allo studio di forme romboidali wrightiane, sciolto da meccaniche ripetizioni ma strettamente fedele nella proposta finale alle indicazioni dell'architetto americano. Lo spazio era articolato attorno all'ingresso, fulcro dell'insieme e punto di conessione di piani ortogonali e in diagonale in pianta ed alzato. Ben definiti sono nel progetto i dati decorativi alla Wright: dai pilastri a sezione circolare ripetuti in ogni punto di snodo della pianta, alle sagome a specchiature emergenti in alzato sugli spigoli della parte alta centrale, al disegno di grandi aperture circolari nella recinzione in muro pieno, alla penetrazione dell'elemento naturale in grandi vasche dell'atrio.«
[28] Neil Levine, *The Architecture of Frank Lloyd Wright*, Princeton, 1996, p. 33.
[29] Maria Antonietta Crippa, *Carlo Scarpa. Il pensiero il disegno i progetti*, Milan, 1984, p. 36: »A dar ragione della forma scelta possono essere opportunamente fornite motivazioni d'ambiente: occorreva infatti staccarsi dalle ortogonali casuali del perimetro del lotto. Inoltre la continuità mossa e senza rigidezze delle varie parti del giardino avrebbe dato respiro ad uno spazio sordo, senza qualità. Tuttavia l'origine della forma base va ricercata in Wright, che aveva già progettato molte abitazioni su moduli geometrici elementari come il quadrato, l'esagono o il triangolo e nel 1938 aveva sperimentato per la prima volta il cerchio come forma base planimetrica.«
[30] Ibid., p. 38: »L'intenzionalità di Scarpa a Udine rimase legata al tema geometrico wrightiano.«
[31] Edward R. Ford, *Das Detail in der Architektur der Moderne*, Basel, Berlin and Boston, 1994, p. 49.
[32] Neil Levine, *The Architecture of Frank Lloyd Wright*, Princeton, 1996, p. 17: »The division of the Winslow House into a series of horizontal layers marked by the changes in material and expressing differences in function was a direct translation into domestic terms of Sullivan's design of the tall office building.«
[33] Giovanni Fanelli and Roberto Gargiani, *Il principio del rivestimento*, Rome and Bari, 1994, p. 28. Original text: »Molto spesso adotta il rivestimento in forme che sono totale mascheramento delle strutture e che obediscono alla legge della stratificazione dal basso verso l'alto, a indicare sempre un radicamento tettonico della parete al suolo, mai dichiarando la natura di strato applicato o appeso del rivestimento. Quelle che sembrano strutture di laterizio o di pietra sono di solito rivestimento. E sino alla fine degli anni Dieci la costruzione in legno – si risolve nella continuità di una superficie di rivestimento a intonaco che produce l'effetto visivo di murature traditionali o di calcestruzzo.«
[34] Daniel Treiber, *Frank Lloyd Wright*, Basel, Boston and Berlin 1988, p. 73.
[35] Otto Antonia Graf, *Die Kunst des Quadrats: Zum Werk von Frank Lloyd Wright*, vol. 1, Vienna, 1983, p. 146.
[36] Frank Lloyd Wright, *Ein Testament*, Munich, 1959, p. 58.
[37] Ibid., p.107.
[38] »Frank Lloyd Wright«, *Architectural Record*; January, August 1928, July 1929, quoted from: Edgar Kaufmann and Ben Raeburn, *Frank Lloyd Wright: Schriften und Bauten*, Munich and Vienna, 1963, p. 48.
[39] Frank Lloyd Wright, »Die Kunst und Fertigkeit der Maschine«, quoted from: Edgar Kaufmann and Ben Raeburn, *Frank Lloyd Wright: Schriften und Bauten*, Munich and Vienna, 1963, p. 48.
[40] Frank Lloyd Wright, *Das natürliche Haus*, Munich, 1961, p. 20.

**Chapter 2.3**

[1] Frank Lloyd Wright, *An Autobiography*, London 1932, p. 221.
[2] André Corboz, »Moderne Architektur und japanische Tradition«, in: Tomoya Masuda and Henri Stierlin (ed.), *Japan*, Lausanne, 1995, p. 3.
[3] Walter Gropius, »Architecture in Japan«, in: Walter Gropius, Kenzo Tange, Yasuhiro Ishimoto and Herbert Bayer, *Katsura. Tradition and Creation in Japanese Architecture*, New Haven, 1960, p. 1.
[4] Ibid., p. 2.
[5] Kenzo Tange, »Tradition and Creation in Japanese architecture«, in: Walter Gropius, Kenzo Tange, Yasuhiro Ishimoto and Herbert Bayer, *Katsura. Tradition and Creation in Japanese Architecture*, New Haven, 1960, p. 1.
[6] Arata Isozaki, Osamu Sato and Yasuhiro Ishimoto, *Katsura. Der Kaiserpalast in Kyoto*, Stuttgart and Zurich, 1993 (original edition: 1967), p. 12.
[7] Yasuhiro Ishimoto, »Der Katsura-Palast. Raum und Form«; in: Arata Isozaki, Osamu Sato, Yasuhiro Ishimoto, *Katsura. Der Kaiserpalast in Kyoto*, Stuttgart and Zurich 1993 (original edition: 1967), p. 265.
[8] Marc Treib and Ron Herman, *A Guide to the Gardens of Kyoto*, Tokyo, 1980, p. 5.
[9] Carlo Scarpa, »Interview with Barbara Radice«, *Modo*, 16, 1979. Original text: »Si, sono molto influenzato dal Giappone, non solo perchè, anche prima di esserci stato, ammiravo la loro essenzialità e soprattutto il loro sovrano buon gusto. Quello che noi chiamiamo buon gusto loro lo hanno ovunque. È un gusto non sofisticato, povero, non proprio contadinesco ma quasi. Guardavano anche molto alla Cina, ma nelle loro virtù personali i giapponesi sono essenziali e di una pulizia incredibile.«
[10] The list of Scarpa's library (provided by architect Guido Pietropoli, a former collaborator of Carlo Scarpa in 1996) contains the following titles: Werner Blaser, *Tempel und Teehaus in Japan*, Lausanne, 1955; Norman F. Jr. Carver, *Form and Space of Japanese Architecture*, Tokyo, 1966; Walter Gropius, Kenzo Tange, Yasuhiro Ishimoto, and Herbert Bayer, *Katsura. Tradition and Creation in Japanese Architecture*, New Haven, 1960; Jiro Harada, *The Gardens of Japan*, London, 1928; Richie Donald and Nil N. Atsuko, *Forme Giapponesi*, Milan, 1963; Tsuda Noritake, *ABC of Japanese Art*, Tokyo, 1937; Tetsuro Yoshida, *Der japanische Garten*, Tübingen, 1957; Yé Firme, *Giappone*, Milan, 1961.
[11] Tetsuro Yoshida, *Japanische Architektur*, Tübingen, 1952, p. 159.
[12] Ibid.
[13] Martin Möhring, Uwe Abraham, »Aspekte des japanischen Raums«, in: Helmut Striffler, *Japan – Tradition und Moderne*, Darmstadt, 1988, seminar report, p. 59.
[14] Ching-Yu Chang, »Japanese spatial conception 5«, *The Japan Architect*, 8, 1984, p. 62.
[15] See also: Tetsuro Yoshida, *Japanische Architektur*, Tübingen, 1952, p. 19.
[16] Cf. Tetsuro Yoshida, *Japanische Architektur*, Tübingen, 1952, p. 20: »Einer der wichtigsten Charakterzüge der japanischen Architektur ist die unsymmetrische Gestaltung des Innern wie auch des Äußeren. Auch in der Anordnung der Räume legte man keinen Wert auf Symmetrie, während dies in der chinesischen und westlichen Architektur von großer Bedeutung ist.«
[17] Arata Isozaki and Osamu Sato, *Katsura. Der Kaiserpalast in Kyoto*, Stuttgart and Zurich, 1993, (original edition: 1967), p. 12.
[18] Ashihara Yoshinobu, *The Hidden Order*, Tokyo and New York, 1989, p. 68.
[19] Arata Isozaki and Osamu Sato, *Katsura. Der Kaiserpalast in Kyoto*, Stuttgart and Zurich, 1993, (original edition: 1967), p.18.
[20] Tetsuro Yoshida, *Das japanische Wohnhaus*, Tübingen, 1969, p. 74.
[21] Ching-Yu Chang, »Japanese spatial conception«, *The Japan Architect*, 8, 1984, p. 61.
[22] Edward S. Morse, *Das Haus im Alten Japan: Leben und Bauen mit natürlichen Materialien*, Hamburg, 1983, (original edition: *Japanese Homes and their Surroundings*, 1886), p. 10.
[23] Tetsuro Yoshida, *Das japanische Wohnhaus*, Tübingen, 1969, p. 74.
[24] Eleanor von Edberg-Consten, *Grundsätze des Wohnens im westlichen und östlichen Raum: Baustil und Bautechnik in Amerika und Japan*, Cologne and Opladen, 1964; p. 26.
[25] Kenzo Tange, »Tradition and Creation in Japanese Architecture«, in: Walter Gropius, Kenzo Tange, Yasuhiro Ishimoto, and Herbert Bayer, *Katsura. Tradition and Creation in Japanese Architecture*, New Haven, 1960, p.22.
[26] Tetsuro Yoshida, *Das japanische Wohnhaus*, Tübingen, 1969, p. 70.
[27] Barrie B. Greenbie, *Space and Spirit in Modern Japan*, New Haven and London, 1988, p. 23.
[28] Eleanor von Edberg-Consten, *Grundsätze des Wohnens im westlichen und östlichen Raum: Baustil und Bautechnik in Amerika und Japan*, Cologne and Opladen 1964, p. 20.
[29] Tetsuro Yoshida, *Das japanische Wohnhaus*, Tübingen, 1969, p. 90.
[30] Ibid., p.104.
[31] Ibid.
[32] Ibid., p.146.
[33] Edward S. Morse, *Das Haus im Alten Japan. Leben und Bauen mit natürlichen Materialien*, Ham-

burg, 1983 (original edition: *Japanese Homes and their Surroundings*, 1886), p. 88.
[34] Werner Blaser, *Orient/Occident: Einfluß auf Design und Architektur*, Düsseldorf, 1991: He studies the influences of the Orient in more detail. He, too, includes Scarpa's Brion cemetery in his investigations.
[35] Tanizaki Jun'ichiro, *Lob des Schattens: Entwurf einer japanischen Ästhetik*, Zurich, 1988, p. 34 ff.
[36] Francesco Dal Co, Giuseppe Mazzariol, *Carlo Scarpa – Opera completa 1906–1978*, Milan, 1984, p. 220. Original text: »Quando si guarda alle opere di Carlo Scarpa è possibile cogliere in esse un gusto non dissimile al particolare riscontrabile in ogni angolo dell'edificio e del giardinetto della casa urbana agitata di Kyoto. Dalla combinazione di forme geometriche osservabile nei particolari dei suoi edifici, si può trarre l'impressione che ci sia una qualche lontana corrispondenza con Frank Lloyd Wright: ma questo è naturale, dato che egli rispettava e ammirava l'architetto americano. Egli però asseriva che il gusto di Wright non poteva essere definito orientale. Si può pensare che questa sua affermazione si basasse su osservazioni dell'architettura giapponese effetuate in occasione di un viaggio a Kyoto. Probabilmente egli pensava che fosse la sua opera quella che fra le due aveva legami più stretti con l'Oriente. Ciò che per me, nelle opere di Carlo Scarpa, somiglia alla cura premurosa tipica della casa cittadina di Kyoto è inanzitutto la puntuale sensibilità con cui egli sa combinare i materiali. Fra le case urbane giapponesi quelle che risentono dell'influenza delle sukiya (padiglione per la cerimonia del tè) presentano una combinazione di materiali delle specie più diverse. Contemporaneamente,con la sapiente introduzione nel loro insieme di frammenti stilistici di origine diversa, creano un senso di armoniosa fusione. Proprio questa a me sembra sia la tecnica che si ritrova in tutta l'opera di Carlo Scarpa, dagli inizi agli ultimi lavori.«
[37] Sergio Los believes »interpretive architecture« began with Carlo Scarpa, in: Sergio Los, *Carlo Scarpa*, Hatje Architekturführer, Stuttgart, 1995.
[38] Yasuhiro Ishimoto, »Der Katsura-Palast – Raum und Form«, in: Arata Isozaki and Osamu Sato, *Katsura. Der Kaiserpalast in Kyoto*, Stuttgart and Zurich, 1993, p. 18.

**Chapter 2.4**

[1] Scarpa's library contains several important publications about the De Stijl movement, beside a 1951 exhibition catalogue of the Stedelijk Museum in Amsterdam about De Stijl, the standard work by Jaffé (H. L. C. Jaffé, *De Stijl 1917–1931*, Amsterdam, 1986), Giulia Veronesi's book about J. J. Peter Oud, and a book about Rietveld's Schröder House and others.
[2] Piet Mondrian, »Die Verwirklichung der neuen Gestaltung in weiter Zukunft und in der heutigen Architektur«, in: Hagen Bächler and Herbert Letsch, *De Stijl. Schriften und Manifeste zu einem theoretischen Konzept ästhetischer Umweltgestaltung*, Leipzig and Weimar, 1984, p. 148.
[3] Hendrik Petrus Berlage and Bernhard Kohlenbach (ed.), »Gedanken über Stil in der Baukunst«, lecture given in Krefeld on 22 and 23.January 1904, in: *Über Architektur und Stil: Aufsätze und Vorträge 1894–1928*, Basel, Berlin and Boston, 1991, p. 65.
[4] Ibid., p. 77.
[5] Ibid., p. 62.
[6] Ibid., p. 62.
[7] J. J. P. Oud, »Über die zukünftige Baukunst und ihre architektonischen Möglichkeiten«, in: Hagen Bächler and Herbert Letsch, *De Stijl. Schriften und Manifeste zu einem theoretischen Konzept ästhetischer Umweltgestaltung*, Leipzig and Weimar, 1984, p. 243.
[8] Ibid.
[9] Roland Günther, »Balance. De Stijl und die Tradition niederländischer Stadtkultur«, *Daidalos*, 15 (March), 1995, p. 82.
[10] Ibid.
[11] Ibid.
[12] Ibid.
[13] Ibid.
[14] Theo van Doesburg, *Grundbegriffe der neuen gestaltenden Kunst*, Neue Bauhausbücher, Mainz and Berlin, 1966, (first edition 1925), p. 7.
[15] Yves Alain Bois, »Zur Definition des ›De Stijl‹«, *Werk, Bauen+Wohnen*, 7/8, 1983, p. 48.
[16] Ibid.
[17] At the beginning of his career, Scarpa painted and contemplated becoming a professional painter. see also: Francesco Dal Co, Giuseppe Mazzariol, *Carlo Scarpa – Opera completa 1906–1978*, Milan, 1984.
[18] Ákos Moravánsky, *Die Erneuerung der Baukunst: Wege zur Moderne in Mitteleuropa 1900–1940*, Salzburg and Vienna, 1988, p. 199.
[19] »De Stijl 1917–1922 Rechenschaftsbericht«, in: Hagen Bächler and Herbert Letsch, *De Stijl. Schriften und Manifeste zu einem theoretischen Konzept ästhetischer Umweltgestaltung*, Leipzig and Weimar, 1984, p. 60.
[20] Carlo Scarpa, *Un'ora con Carlo Scarpa*, Rai film, ca. 1975 (video copy owned by the author).
[21] Theo van Doesburg, »Die neue Architektur und ihre Folgen«, in: Hagen Bächler and Herbert Letsch, *De Stijl. Schriften und Manifeste zu einem theoretischen Konzept ästhetischer Umweltgestaltung*, Leipzig and Weimar, 1984, p.189.
[22] Ibid.
[23] Cf. Bruno Zevi, *Poetica dell'architettura neoplastica – Il linguaggio della scomposizione quadridimensionale*, Turin, 1974, p. 182. Original text: »Mies non ha più bisogno, come van Doesburg e Rietveld, di partire dalla scatola edilizia sconnettendone gli angoli, differenziandone le pareti e tagliandole in rettangoli piú o meno aggettanti e variamente colorati, travaglio in fondo epidermico che lascia inalterato il ritmo spaziale. Per Mies la scatola non esiste: l'ha distrutta Wright, quindi è inutile accanirsi a disgregarla. Egli prende le mosse da uno spazio continuo, ininterrotto fra esterno e interno, in nessun caso irretito entro quattro mura, e ne incanala le influenze mediante divisori che, prolungandosi oltre le lastre del pavimento e del tetto, stabiliscono un colloquio incessante tra edificio aperto e ambiente circostante.«
[24] Hagen Bächler and Herbert Letsch in: *De Stijl. Schriften und Manifeste zu einem theoretischen Konzept ästhetischer Umweltgestaltung*, Leipzig and Weimar, 1984, p. 26.
[25] Carsten-Peter Warncke, *Das Ideal als Kunst – De Stijl 1917–1931*, Cologne, 1990, p. 137.
[26] Walter Eugen Ehrmann, *Moderne Architektur und konstruktivistisches Bild, unter besonderer Berücksichtigung der De-Stijl-Bewegung*, diss., Karlsruhe, 1972, p. 76, Schröder House: »Von der Kernform des Hauses ausgehend bildet das Schröder Haus hauptsächlich Raum mittels der drei Balkone (zusammengefügt aus einfachen waagerechten und senkrechten Einzelplatten, verschieden langen, vertikal angeordneten Stahlstützen und ausschließlich horizontalen, dünnen Geländerstangen), die eine sowohl äußerst simple als auch sehr präzise und differenziert abgestufte Raumschicht bilden. Außerhalb dieser Schichten besonders aktiven Raumes zeigt sich stiller, flächiger, fast als Fond, der größere, massivere Teil der Architektur, zusammengesetzt aus Plattenelementen verschiedener Dimensionen und Formen, in die die Fenster, weniger oder stärker unterteilt, eingeschnitten oder zurückspringend eingesetzt sind. Da die einzelnen Flächenplatten sich überwiegend im Vertikalen unterschiedlich optisch überschneiden, entsteht ein etwas baukastenhaft wirkendes Gefüge von addiert oder montiert erscheinenden Schichtungen.«
[27] For more comments on Scarpa's exhibition designs see chapter 2.4.
[28] Paul Overy, *De Stijl*, London, 1991, p .25.
[29] Yves Alain Bois, »Zur Definition des ›De Stijl‹«, *Werk, Bauen+Wohnen*, 7/8, 1983, p. 48.
[30] Cf. Bruno Zevi, *Poetica dell'architettura neoplastica. Il linguaggio della scomposizione quadridimensionale*, Turin, 1974, p. 134: »Con l'aiuto dei colori (ornamentazione) si decora un ambiente, senza rapporto organico con la costruzione. Il colore serve soltanto a nascondere la costruzione (Berlage ha perfino indicato, nelle sue opere, il posto dove applicare l'ornato in architettura). Non c'è un rapporto sostanziale tra costruzione e pittura: esistono l'una vicino all'altra, invece l'una per l'altra, e perciò non evocano alcun effetto sinottico.«
[31] Aldo Camini and Theo van Doesburg, »Farben in Raum und Zeit«, in: Ákos Morawánsky, *Die Erneuerung der Baukunst. Wege zur Moderne in Mitteleuropa 1900–1940*, Salzburg and Vienna, 1988, p. 199.
[32] Theo van Doesburg, *Über europäische Architektur. Gesammelte Aufsätze aus Het Bouwbedrijf 1924–1931*, Basel, Berlin and Boston, 1992, p. 163.
[33] S. Umberto Barbieri, in collaboration with H. Engel and J. De Heer, »Architecture and Colour«, *Dutch Art + Architecture Today*, 19, 1986, p. 33f.
[34] ibid.: The author's German translation for this term is »malerische Polychromie«.
[35] ibid.: The author's German translation for this term is »strukturelle Polychromie«.
[36] Vincent Scully, »Tra Wright e Louis Kahn«, in: Francesco Dal Co and Giuseppe Mazzariol, *Carlo Scarpa – Opera completa 1906–1978*, Milan, 1984, p. 267. Original text: »Scarpa in effetti addomestica De Stijl, nel marmo italiano – il peso stesso, lo spessore palmabile, la chiara fredda durezza, tenute in soggezione, afferrate di nuovo, ma con una testimonianza profonda autentica.«
[37] From Bruno Zevi, *Poetica dell'architettura neoplastica. Il linguaggio della scomposizione quadridimensionale*, Turin, 1974, p. 134: »Si è effetivamente abusato nell'uso decorativo dei colori in architettura. Ma il colore è indispensabile all'uomo come la luce. Nell'architettura moderna, le superfici chiedono di

essere animate, cioè di essere composte con ausilio del colore puro, il colore dello spazio. Anche prescindendo da ogni rivestimento cromatico, l'impiego conveniente dei materiali moderni e sottoposto alle stesse leggi dei colori nello spazio e nel tempo.«

[38] Ibid., p. 138.

[39] Axel Feuß, »Farbige Innenräume des Art Deco«, *Die Mappe*, 11, 1989, p. 5.

[40] Yves Alain Bois, Zur Definition des »De Stijl«, *Werk, Bauen+Wohnen*, 7/8, 1983, p. 48.

[41] Ákos Moravánsky, *Die Erneuerung der Baukunst. Wege zur Moderne in Mitteleuropa 1900–1940*, Salzburg and Vienna, 1988, p. 196.

[42] Maria Antonietta Crippa, *Carlo Scarpa – Il pensiero il disegno i progetti*, Milan, 1984, p. 157. Original text: »Dal pittore olandese infatti, dal suo linguaggio programmaticamente spoglio di componenti soggettive e comunque figurative per una iconoclastica puritana nella quale convergevano posizioni teosofiche e socialisteggianti, dalla sua ricerca di ritmi ed armonie in tessiture geometriche aperte, ove era eliminato ogni accenno alle forme curve, egli trasse la possibilità di strutturare senza leggi fissse ogni elemento piano dell'architettura sulla base di pochi dati compositivi. Dagli architetti neoplastici, sia da quelli ancora sensibili all'influsso di Wright e Berlage come Van 't Hoff, Wils, Oud, sia da quelli più formalisti, come Lissitzky, Richter e soprattutto Rietveld, apprese ad organizzare nello spazio valori formali di superficie col fine di mantenere aperta e animata da ritmiche corrispondenze la volumetria complessiva. Da questi riprese anche l'uso del colore come elemento essenziale del comporre, ma si staccò da una valorizzazione programmatica dei colori primari per legarsi alla colorazione naturale dei materiali della tradizione costruttiva veneta e, negli intonaci e negli stucchi, ad una gramma coloristica ampia, variata, spesso preziosa. Sopratutto nel ripristino di antichi edifici, in particolare come si vedrà – a Castelvecchio in Verona, Scarpa utilizzò possibilità figurative neoplastiche, trasformando la compattezza e chiususura degli antichi volumi in continuità spaziali tra esterno ed interno tramite assi visivi, aperture di finestre e più sottili e complesse strutturazioni geometriche dell'insieme spesso non immediatamente percepibili.«

[43] Conversation with Luigi Scarpa, (former secretary of the Biennale) in October 1993 in Venice.

[44] Cf. *De Stijl*, exhibition catalogue, Dortmund, 1964.

[45] Hagen Bächler and Herbert Letsch, *De Stijl. Schriften und Manifeste zu einem theoretischen Konzept ästhetischer Umweltgestaltung*, Leipzig and Weimar, 1984, p. 25.

[46] Ibid., p. 50.

[47] Ibid.

[48] Piet Mondrian, »Die neue Gestaltung in der Malerei«, in: Hagen Bächler and Herbert Letsch, *De Stijl. Schriften und Manifeste zu einem theoretischen Konzept ästhetischer Umweltgestaltung*, Leipzig and Weimar, 1984, p. 65.

[49] Theo van Doesburg, *Über europäische Architektur. Gesammelte Aufsätze aus Het Bowbedrijf, 1924–1931*, Basel, Berlin and Boston, 1992, p. 163.

[50] Ibid.

[51] Theo van Doesburg, »Von der neuen Ästhetik zur materiellen Verwirklichung« (lecture given in Leipzig, Weimar, and Berlin), in: Hagen Bächler and Herbert Letsch, *De Stijl. Schriften und Manifeste zu einem theoretischen Konzept ästhetischer Umweltgestaltung*, Leipzig and Weimar, 1984, p. 189.

[52] Kenneth Frampton, »Carlo Scarpa und die Verherrlichung des Gelenks«, in: *Grundlagen der Architektur: Studien zur Kultur des Tektonischen*, Munich and Stuttgart, 1993, p. 341: »Scarpas typische Verkleidungsart kommt besonders zum Tragen bei den Travertinwänden der großen Halle, in welcher, abgesehen von dem traditionellen Rückgriff auf den Stein, die Vorstellung eines metonymen Austauschs zwischen Holz und Mauerwerk, d. h. zwischen dem Holz der Brückenbahn und des Geländers und dem Travertin an der Wand des Ausstellungsbereiches, erweckt wird. Der Stein wird unter zwei Erscheinungsformen wahrgenommen, zunächst als einfache Verkleidung, dann als eine Art Holz, eingeschnitten, eingelegt und durch ein Gelenk verbunden, als handle es sich um eine in den Stein übertragene Tischlerarbeit.«

## Chapter 2.5

[1] Giuseppe Mazzariol and Giuseppe Barbieri, »Vita di Carlo Scarpa«, in: *Carlo Scarpa 1906–1978 opera completa*, exhibition catalogue, Milan, 1984, p. 9.

[2] Marco Frascari, »Carlo Scarpa in Magna Graecia – The Abatellis Palace in Palermo«, *AA Files*, Nr. 9, 1985, p. 3.

[3] Eduardo Detti, »Scarpa e la città«, in: Philipp Duboy, *Dilemma del futuro di Firenze*, Milan, 1993, p. 174. Original text: »Carlo Scarpa aveva il ›senso del luogo‹. Anche se le sue opere e i suoi progetti riguardavano in prevalenza Venezia e il Veneto, dev'essere forse attenuato quell'attributo di ›venezianità‹ che, anche se non vuol essere considerato una mera caratteristicha stilistica, ha l'effetto di farlo aparire un personaggio anomale, quasi indefinibile.«

[4] Dietmar Steiner writes about ›stratification‹ in a city (Vienna): »Architektur in Wien ist ständig konfrontiert – im geistigen wie im praktischen Sinne – mit dem Vorhandenen, dem es eine neue Schicht auferlegen muß. Symbolisch vorweggenommen ist diese architektonische Haltung schon bei der Wiener Stephanskirche. Um die regelmäßigen Gottesdienste nicht unterbrechen zu müssen, wurde der spätromanische Bau von den gotischen Baumeistern sukzessive ummantelt. So stülpt sich der heutige Dom wie eine neue Haut über seinen ›abgestorbenen‹ Vorgänger. Auch die jeweilige Einheitlichkeit und Geschlossenheit vieler historischer Kirchen Wiens ist nur scheinbar. Sie sind Schicht um Schicht umgestaltet worden; gotische Kirchen wurden barockisiert, um später wieder neogotisiert zu werden. Eine 600jährige Baugeschichte ist nicht selten anzutreffen. Romanik, Gotik, Barock, Rokoko, Neugotik – bis hin zu den beileibe nicht immer zimperlichen Restaurierungen der letzten Jahrhundertwende – hinterließen ihre Spuren und präsentieren sich heute als gewohntes, homogenes Bild.«, in: *Architektur in Wien*, Vienna, 1990, p. 37.

[5] Sergio Bettini, *Venezia – Nascita di una città*, Milan, 1988, p. 97. Original text: »Il documento tuttavia è importante anche perché attesta il modo di fare caratteristico dei costruttori veneziani del Medioevo: quello di radoprare, di inserire negli edifici nuovi quanto si riusciva a trasportare sulla Laguna, e quanto valeva di salvare dei vecchi, demoliti o che si demolivano. Il materiale di recupero consisteva soprattutto di relitti marmorei, specie se scolpiti: insomma, colonne, capitelli, architravi, cornicioni ecc.; ma anche forse non elaborato, come par di capire da un altro passo del testamento che ho citato dinanzi.«

[6] Vittorio Magnago Lampugnani, »Introduction«, in: *Carlo Scarpa Architektur*, Stuttgart, 1986, p. 15.

[7] Ennio Concina, *Storia dell'Architettura di Venezia dal VII al XX secolo*, Milan, 1995, p. 133.

[8] Peter Lauritzen and Alexander Zielcke, *Venezianische Paläste*, Munich, 1980, p. 46.

[9] Boris Podrecca, »La presunta particolarità – Carlo Scarpa aus Wiener Sicht«, *Bauforum*, 106, 1984, p. 10.

[10] Carlo L. Ragghianti, »La crosera de Piazza di Carlo Scarpa«, *Zodiac*, 4, 1960, p. 133. Original text: »Ma l'inspirazione di Scarpa si è nutrita anche di un ambiente che ha nel sangue e che non è la brada natura, e di strutture e di forme risalenti alla più originale storia architettonica veneziana.«

[11] Pier Carlo Santini, »Construire con l'acqua«, *Ottagono*, June, 1984, p. 40. Original text: »L'acqua non è più, ora, uno specchio riflettente, o non è tanto e soltanto questo. Non è più un sottile velo cristallino o uno strato di poco spessore. Nello stagno con l'edicola, che avrebbe dovuto avere in fondo d'argilla naturale, è un liquido opaco, che contiene microorganismi, insetti, piante acquatiche, ninfee. Il tempo e le stagioni vi si riverberano, e vi lasciano visibili segni. Ma il tempo, il sentimento del tempo è uno dei contenuti più vibranti a San Vito, e non si può non avvertire lo scorrere implacabile e fatale.«

[12] Ibid., p. 30. Original text: »L'acqua alta è un fenomeno naturale a cui Venezia è abituato da secoli, e poichè si può prevedere quando arriva ... Nella Querini Stampalia Carlo Scarpa ritenne assurdo cercare di opporsi all'acqua alta; che quando arriva tocca sbocco negli interni, canalizzata e fatta defluire in sedi appositamente architettate. L'acqua invade un sito già predisposto dall'architetto, come le sacche di lato al Po; e tutte le funzionali della biblioteca possono continuare svolgersi.«

[13] Italo Furlan, *Venezia e Bisanzio*, exhibition catalogue, Milan, 1974, p. 26. Original text: »I gusto nativo dei Venetici era dunque ovviamente per il colore: colore vivo, scorrevole, aperto all'esperienza, al tempo: tempo della natura, e tempo dell'uomo. Cioè sentimento, il quale intenziona anche quel che diciamo natura, e in essa cerca e trova risposta. Qui in queste isole, essi trovarono una natura priva di plasticità – non monti o colline o masse d'alberi – solo acqua ed aria: elementi puri, immateriali, di colore. E la forma di questa città, tutta costruita dall'uomo, a cominciare dallo stesso terreno su cui si imposta, essi la sognarono fiorire tra l'acqua e l'aria: innestarsi sulla linea inafferabile, quasi indistinguibile, dove l'aria e l'acqua si toccano: le quali sono illiminate, come dimensioni: sono puri valori qualitativi, che non possono essere formati, cioè dominati e composti, che nell'ordine del tempo.«

[14] Henry Plummer, »Poetics of Light«, *A+U Architecture and Urbanism*, December, 1987 (extra edition), p. 29: Chiaroscuro: »Perhaps the most enduring and elementary technique of light-handling is the modeling of a surface to grate light and etch shadows. Surface reliefs collect light along the terrain rather

than inside the subcutaneous body of matter. Yet the topography which forms a site for tonal play is able to entangle and harbor light deeply within the textural pores of a substance, filling hollows with pooled shadow and skimming peaks with lambent rays, so that the surface builds up a liquescent residue of light. Such a light is wedded to a substance, settling and steeping into the physical anatomy. Chiaroscuro encodes this visible dialogue between the spatial properties of a surface and the character of incident radiation. Facets lying perpendicular to oncoming light blaze up according to their angles, while deeply cut hollows receiving little light or completely absorbing captured rays empty into cold black vacuums.«

[15] Henry Plummer, »Poetics of Light«, *A+U Architecture and Urbanism*, Dec. 1987 (extra edition), p. 23.

[16] Carlo Scarpa, *Un'ora con Carlo Scarpa*, Rai film, c. 1975, video film.

[17] Italo Furlan, *Venezia e Bisanzio*, exhibition catalogue, Milan, 1974, p. 25.

[18] Ibid., p. 81. Original text: »Frattempo appare anche chiaro, che la facciata di San Marco è della Piazza, la parete più importante, più densa di espressione, e quella che riassume il valore. Tutta la piazza è superficie, colore e ritmo; ma sulla facciata di San Marco s'accentrano il colore pù intenso e più articolato, e il ritmo più alto e più risolutivo. Le fitte colonne marmoree dello zoccolo tingono i pilastri tra porta e porta, e spiegano alla grande luce marina una deliberata dovizia di materie preziose. Sopra, si stendono marmi e mosaici, coprendo l'intera superficie. È una grandiosa ›tabula‹, un dossale intarsiato di marmi, di tessere multicolori d'oro.«

[19] Gottfried Semper, *Der Stil in den technischen und tektonischen Künsten oder praktische Ästhetik*, Munich, 1878, vol. 1, p. 10.

[20] Peter Lauritzen, Alexander Zielcke, *Venezianische Paläste*, Munich, 1980, p. 40.

[21] From an April 1996 conversation with the plasterer Eugenio de Luigi in Venice.

[22] Henry Plummer, »Poetics of Light«, *A+U Architecture and Urbanism*, December, 1987 (extra edition), p. 23.

[23] Italo Furlan, *Venezia e Bisanzio*, exhibition catalogue, Milan, 1974, p. 26. Original text: »... l'architettura veneziana dovette farsi così leggera e diafana; tradursi in valori di colore, di luce di ritmo; dissolvere le masse; divenire infine una immagine senza peso, quasi senza materia – la quale immagine assumendo su di sè l'intera responsabilità dell'espressione, fu resa sempre più ricca e più preziosa. E così è avvenuto, che tutta la forma di Venezia è colore, vale a dire, superficie. È per questo che i palazzi veneziani a qualunque epoca appartengano, dal punto di vista formale, non sono che facciate: le quali determinano, su tutta la loro estensione sottilmente traforata e docile ai riflessi, un sistema non di volumi e di piani, ma d'ombre e di luci, di incisioni e di rilievi tenuissimi, che non chiede quasi nulla alle evidenze volumetriche.«

[24] Luigi Scarpa, in a November 1995 conversation with the author about his work designing the 1956 Klee exhibition in Rome, says that he tried to recreate Mondrian's compositions with paper strips and studied the different effects of transformed fields or grids of color before he began work on the exhibition.

### Chapter 3.1

[1] For an exact description of the Castelvecchio's history, see: Richard Murphy, *Carlo Scarpa & Castelvecchio*, Venice, 1990, pp. 4–9.

[2] Licisco Magagnato, »Storia e genesis dell'intervento nel museo del Castelvecchio«, *Quaderns*, 158, 1983, p. 26. Original text: »In particolare Carlo Scarpa, in modi che non vanno assolutamente confusi con l'ecletticismo del cosidetto postmoderno, rifuggendo ogni approcio teorizzante, indagava il singolo caso concreto, nella particolare situazione storica obiettivamente esplorata, e ripulendo il brano fino allo strato autentico, ma senza distruggere gli interventi più validi, lavorava intorno a queste preesistenze con accostamenti di elementi modulati e graduati, secondo una sintassi neoplastica che è sempre la base fondamentale della sua formazione culturale.«

[3] Jörg Stabenow and Jozé Plecnik, *Städtebau im Schatten der Moderne*, Braunschweig and Wiesbaden, 1996, p. 123.

[4] Maria Antonietta Crippa, *Carlo Scarpa, Il pensiero il disegno i progetti*, Milan, 1984, p. 40: »Sopratutto nel ripristino di antichi edifici, in particolare come si vedrà – a Castelvecchio in Verona, Scarpa utilizzò possibilità figurative neoplastiche, trasformando la compattezza e chiusura degli antichi volumi in continuità spaziali tra esterno ed interno tramite assi visivi, aperture di finestre e più sottili e complesse strutturazioni geometriche dell'insieme spesso non immediatamente percepibili.«

[5] Richard Murphy, *Carlo Scarpa & Castelvecchio*, Venice, 1991, p. 14. Original text: »L'amore di Scarpa per l'acqua durò tutta la vita e si manifesta in quasi tutti i suoi progetti ... A Castelvecchio quest'idea è ripresa un'altra volta: letteralmente, da una grande vasca per i pesci da cui l'acqua quasi trascina e a cui Scarpa accosta un vialetto leggermente in salita, e metaforicamente all'interno del museo, a pianterreno, dove Scarpa si servì della stessa fonte di ispirazione per la pavimentazione. Qui però l'acqua è sostituita dal calcestruzzo frattazzato o dallo stucco lucido omogeneo e riflettente delle basi delle sculture figurative.«

[6] Ibid., p. 111, see also the essay of Licisco Magagnato at the end of the book *Cangrande della Scala a Castelvecchio di Verona*. Cangrande was one of the most important Signori of the Scaligeri; the statue in the Castelvecchio is one of three that originally stood on the Piazza Signoria.

[7] Ibid., p. 14.

[8] Martin Dominguez, »Entrevista a Carlo Scarpa«, *Quaderns*, 158, 1983.

[9] Carabottini: Venetian wood grille structures.

### Chapter 3.2

[1] Ennio Concina, *Storia dell'architettura di Venezia del VII–XX Secolo*, Milan, 1995, p. 336: »... l'intervento alla Fondazione Querini s'incarna sul duplice rapporto stabilito con la città e la sua equorea natura ideale: accogliendo le acque quite del canale sul quale guarda il palazzo.«

[2] Giuseppe Mazzariol, »Esperienze di etica dell'architettura«, in: *Per Giuseppe Mazzariol – In occasione della giornata di studio*, Venice, 11 May 1990, p. 10. Original text: »usò un'linguaggio attuale, adoperando lemmi, strutture e un lessico di oggi, del 1968, quando fece l'intervento; ma lo spirito era quello di ricomporre una realtà precedente, e di tramandarla, di raccomandarla e affidarla a domani.«

[3] Giuseppe Mazzariol, »Un'opera di Carlo Scarpa: il riordino di un antico palazzo veneziano«, *Zodiac*, 13, 1964, p. 40: »Alla Querini, l'acqua entra, si snoda lungi i cunicoli di contentimento, costituisce un medium tra esterno e interno, diventa spechio luminoso. L'acqua è assunta come un diaframma orizzontale che gradua le altezze objettivamente mutate degli spazi.«

[4] Giorgio Busetto, »Mazzariol alla Querini«, in: *Giuseppe Mazzariol. 50 artisti a Venezia*, Milan, 1993, p. 17: »Penetrante è l'acribia metodologica che tutto vuole per addizioni rilevate e separate dalle preesistenze sempre recuperabili: per muri perimetrali fodere aeree in marmorino su forati sorretti da telai staffati alle pareti lasciate libere di respirare ...«

[5] Richard Murphy, »Querini Stampalia«. Original text: »Un microcosmo veneziano«, in: Marta Mazza, *Carlo Scarpa alla Querini Stampalia*, Venice, 1996, p. 45: »A mio parere, la stratificazione di materiali pregiati disposti in pannelli stessi pericolosamente sopra l'acqua è come un riferimento simbolico alla precarità stessa della preziosa città di Venezia di fronta al pericolo maree.«

[6] The organization of the overall complex was considerably changed in recent years. These descriptions document the traffic flow of the intervention in the time of Carlo Scarpa.

[7] Kenneth Frampton, *Studies in Tectonic Culture*, Cambridge, MA, 1995, pp. 301 f.

[8] The strip of paint on the ceiling was removed during the last modifications.

### Chapter 3.3

[1] There were several conversations with a collaborator in the project, Walter Rossetto, who worked on the Banca Popolare as a young architect.

[2] Marco Frascari, »Das Wahre und die Erscheinung«, *Daidalos*, 6, 1982, p. 37.

[3] Ibid.

[4] Roland Günter, »Balance: De Stijl und die Tradition der niederländischen Stadtkultur«, *Daidalos*, 15, 1985, p. 82.

[5] Luigi Meneghelli, *Arte Triveneta*, 1980, vol. 10, p. 38: »L'elemento singolo ha una sua forza solo quando si prospettivamente si aggrega ad altri.«

[6] Marco Frascari, »Das Wahre und die Erscheinung«, *Daidalos*, 6, 1982, p. 41.

### Final remarks

[1] Heinz Tesar, »Denken in Schichten«, in: *Architektur der Gegenwart*, Stuttgart, Berlin and Cologne, 1993, p. 206.

[2] Licisco Magagnato, »History and Genesis of Scarpa's work on the Museum of Castelvecchio«, *Quaderns*, 158 (July, August, September), 1983.

[3] This is documented by numerous conversations between the author and craftspeople who worked together with Scarpa (Eugenio de Luigi, the Anfodillo brothers, et al.).

[4] Rai, *Un'Ora con Carlo Scarpa*, TV documentary film on video cassette, 1970: Scarpa speaks about the arrangement of the sculptures in the Castelvecchio, and about the opportunity to draw visitors' attention to details by the way the sculptures were positioned, something they might have otherwise overlooked.

## Bibliography

### Stratification


Abel, Adolf, *Vom Wesen des Raumes in der Baukunst*, Munich, 1952.

Alfonsin, Anthony, »Grundformen: Eine Einführung in die ›Versenkte Fläche‹«, *Archithese*, 6, 1990.

Antoniades, Anthony C., *Poetics of Architecture. Theory of Design*, New York, 1990.

Arnheim, Rudolf, *Kunst und Sehen. Eine Psychologie des schöpferischen Auges*, Berlin, 1965.

Arnheim, Rudolf, *Die Dynamik der architektonischen Form*, Cologne, 1980.

Auer, Gerhard, »Begehrlicher Blick und List des Schleiers«, *Daidalos*, 33, 1989.

Bachelard, Gaston, *Poetik des Raumes*, Frankfurt/Main, 1994.

Barbieri, S. Umberto, »Architecture and Colour«, *Dutch Architecture Today*, 19, 1986.

Battisti, Eugeneo, »Concetti dell'ornato e dell'arte decorativa«, *Rassegna*, 3, 1990.

Baumgart, Fritz, *Stilgeschichte der Architektur*, Cologne, 1969.

Blaser, Werner, *Struktur und Textur*, Krefeld, 1976.

Bollnow, Otto Friedrich, *Mensch und Raum*, Stuttgart, Berlin and Cologne, 1994.

Boudon, Philippe, *Der architektonische Raum*, Basel, Berlin and Boston, 1991.

Breukelmann, Alfred, »Architektur der variablen Häute«, *Arch+*, 104, 1990.

Broadbent, Geoffrey, Richard Blunt and Charles Jencks, *Signs, Symbols, and Architecture*, Chichester, New York, Brisbane and Toronto, 1980.

Brommer, Gerald F., *The Art of Collage*, Worcester, Mass., 1978.

Compagno, Andrea, *Intelligente Glasfassaden. Material, Anwendung, Gestaltung*, Basel, Boston and Berlin, 1996.

Conrads, Ulrich, and Peter Neitzke (eds.), *Mensch und Raum – Das Darmstädter Gespräch 1951*, Braunschweig, 1991.

Czech, Hermann, *Zur Abwechslung. Ausgewählte Schriften zur Architektur*, Vienna, 1978.

Daniels, Klaus, »Skin Technology: Lösen polyvalente Wände technische Probleme?«, *Archithese*, 3, 1992.

Davies, Mike, »Eine Wand für alle Jahreszeiten: die intelligente Umwelt erschaffen«, *Arch+*,104, 1990.

Davis, William Morris, and Gustav Braun, *Grundzüge der Physiogeographie,* vol. 1*, Grundlagen und Methodik*, Stuttgart, 1977.

Durant, Stuart, »Grammatiche Ornamentali«, *Rassegna*, 3, 1990.

Eisenman, Peter, »Giuseppe Terragni e l'idea di testocritico«, in: *Giuseppe Terragni*, exhibition catalogue, Milan, 1996.

Fanelli, Giovanni, and Roberto Gargiani, *Il principio del rivestimento. Prologomena a una storia dell'architettura contemporanea*, Rome and Bari, 1994.

Feldtkeller, Christoph, *Der architektonische Raum: eine Fiktion*, Braunschweig and Wiesbaden, 1989.

Fischer, Günther, *Architektur und Sprache*, Stuttgart and Zurich, 1991.

Flusser, Vilém, »Über Fassaden«, *Arch+*, 108, 1991.

Flusser, Vilém, »Dach- und mauerlose Architektur«, *Arch+*, 104, 1990.

Franco, Fonatti, *Giuseppe Terragni. Poet des Razionalismo*, Vienna, 1987.

Frampton, Kenneth, Grundlagen der Architektur Studien zur Kultur des Tektonischen, Munich and Stuttgart, 1993.

Frank, Josef, *Architektur als Symbol. Elemente deutschen neuen Bauens*, Vienna, 1931.

Fuhrmann, Ernst, *Der Sinn im Gegenstand*, Munich, 1923.

Geißler, Rainer, *Soziale Schichtung und Lebenschancen in Deutschland*, Stuttgart, 1994.

Gelernter, Mark, *Sources of Architectural Form. Critical History of Architectural Form*, Manchester and New York, 1995.

Giedion, Sigfried, *Architektur und das Phänomen des Wandels*, Tübingen, 1969.

Giedion, Sigfried, *Time, Space, and Architecture*, Cambridge, Mass., 1941.

Giedion, Sigfried, *1888–1968 – Der Entwurf einer modernen Tradition*, Zurich, 1989.

Goethe, Johann Wolfgang von, »Morphologie«, in: *Goethes Werke*, Hamburg, 1966, vol. XIII.

Goulet, Patrice, Paul Virilio, »Ästhetik des Verschwindens: Jean Nouvel im Gespräch mit Patrice Goulet und Paul Virilio«, *Arch+*, 108, 1991.

Grimm, Friedrich, and Clemens Richarz, *Hinterlüftete Fassaden*, Stuttgart and Zurich, 1994.

Habig, Inge, and Kurt Jauslin, *Der Auftritt des Ästhetischen. Zur Theorie der architektonischen Ordnung*, Frankfurt/Main, 1990.

Hall, Edward T, *Die Sprache des Raumes*, Düsseldorf, 1976.

Harather, Karin, *Haus-Kleider, Zum Phänomen der Bekleidung in der Architektur*, Vienna, Cologne and Weimar, 1995.

Hartoonian, Gevork, *Ontology of Construction*, Cambridge, 1994.

Heilmeyer, Wolf-Dieter, and Wolfram Hoepfner, *Licht und Architektur*, Tübingen, 1990.

Heiz, André Vladimir, »Vorwand einer Anatomie. Die Fassade«, *Archithese*, 3, 1992.

Herzog, Jacques, and Pierre de Meuron, Harry Gugger and Christine Binswanger, »Minimalismus und Ornament«, *Arch+*,12, 1995.

Hoffmann-Axthelm, Dieter, »Regionale Schichten der Moderne«, *Umbau*, 12, 1990.

Holgate, Alan, *Aesthetics of Built Form*, Oxford, New York and Melbourne, 1992.

Husserl, Edmund, *Ding und Raum*, Hamburg, 1991.

IRB-Literaturauslese Nr. 639, *Innenraumgestaltung von Wänden*, Stuttgart, 1988.

Janofske, Eckehard, *Architektur-Räume. Idee und Gestalt bei Hans Scharoun*, Braunschweig and Wiesbaden, 1984.

Kadatz, Hans-Joachim, *Wörterbuch der Architektur*, Leipzig, 1988.

Kelp, Zamp, »Die Haut als Botschaft«, *Arch+*, 108, 1991.

Kenyon, Kathleen Mary, *Jerusalem: excavating 3000 years of history*, London, 1967.

*Kepes, Gyorgy*, exhibition catalogue, Cambridge, 1978.

Kepes, Gyorgy, *Language of Vision-painting, Photography, Advertising Design*, Chicago, 1964.

Knapp, Franz, *Das geistige Leben der Person in den persönlichkeitspsychologischen Schichttheorien*, Mannheim, 1967.

Kollhoff, Hans (ed.), *Über Tektonik in der Baukunst*, Braunschweig and Wiesbaden, 1993.

Kotob, Basel, *Spatial Layering: An effect of Cubist Concepts on 20th Century Architecture*, thesis, MIT, Cambridge, Mass., 1991.

Krämer, Hans Leo, *Soziale Schichtung: Einführung in die moderne Theoriediskussion*, Frankfurt/Main, 1983.

Kugler, Hans, and Max Schwab, Konrad Billwitz, *Allgemeine Geologie, Geomorphologie und Bodengeographie*, Gotha and Leipzig, 1980.

Lynn, Greg, »Leicht und Schwer«, *Arch+*, 124, 125, 1994.

Machado, Rodolpho, and Rodolphe El-Khoury, *Monolithic Architecture*, Munich and New York, 1995.

Manzini, Ezio, *La materia dell'invenzione*, Milan, 1989.

Marcianò, Ada Francesca, *Giuseppe Terragni opera completa 1925–1943*, Rome, 1987.

Masiero, Roberto, »Elogio della decorazione contro la superficialità«, Rassegna, 3, 1990.

Meisenheimer, Wolfgang, »Von den Hohlräumen in der Schale des Baukörpers«, *Daidalos*, 13, 1984.

Meiss, Pierre von, *The Elements of Architecture: from Form to Place*, London, 1990.

Meiss, Pierre von, *Vom Objekt zum Raum zum Ort-Dimensionen der Architektur*, Basel, Boston and Berlin, 1994.

Mitchell, William J. *The Logic of Architecture*, London, 1990.

Müller, K.O., *Handbuch der Archäologie*, Breslau, 1830.

Murphy, Jan, »Intelligent Buildings«, *Arch+*, 104, 1990.

Oechslin, Werner, *Stilhülse und Kern*, Zurich and Berlin, Ernst & Sohn, 1994.

Oechslin, Werner, »Vom Umgang mit Fragmenten – die Unzulänglichkeit der Collage«, *Daidalos*, 15, 1985.

Oechslin, Werner, »Zwischen Außen und Innen: Die Wand und ihre Schauseite, die Fassade«, *Archithese*, 3, 1992.

Oswald, Philipp, »Gebäudehüllen – Massimiliano Fuksas im Gespräche mit Philipp Oswald«, *Arch+*, 108, 1991.

Plummer, Henry, »Poetics of Light«, *A+U Architecture and Urbanism*, Tokyo, 1987.

Raff, Thomas, *Die Sprache der Materialien. Anleitung zu einer Ikonologie der Werkstoffe*, Munich, 1994.

Reuther, Romain, »Von der Tiefgründigkeit der Oberflächlichkeit«, *Archithese*, 3, 1992.

Richards, Jonathan, *Facadism*, London and New York, 1987.

Riley, Terence, *Light Construction*, New York, 1995.

Rothacker, Erich, *Die Schichten der Persönlichkeit*, Bonn, 1948.

Rowe, Colin, and Fred Koetter, *Collage City*, Basel, Boston and Berlin, 1984.

Rowe, Colin, *The Mathematics of the ideal Villa and other Essays*, Cambridge, London, 1976.

Rowe, Colin, *As I was saying. Recollection and Miscellaneous Essays*, vol. 1, Cambridge, 1996.

Rowe, Colin, and Robert Slutzky, *Transparenz. Le Corbusier Studien 1*, Basel and Stuttgart, 1968.
Ruttkowski, Wolfgang Victor, *Typen und Schichten. Zur Einteilung des Menschen und seiner Produkte*, Bern and Munich, 1978.
Schwarz, Rudolf, *Die Bebauung der Erde*, Heidelberg, 1949.
Scruton, Roger, *The Aesthetics of Architecture*, Princeton, New Jersey, 1979.
Seitz, William Chapin, *The Art of Assemblage*, New York, 1961.
Shepheard, Paul, *What is architecture? An essay on landscapes, buildings, and machines*, Cambridge, MA, 1994.
Slutzky, Robert, »›Transparenz‹ – Wiedergelesen«, *Daidalos*, 33, 1989.
Smith, Peter F., *Architektur und Ästhetik: Wahrnehmung und Wertung der heutigen Baukunst*, Stuttgart, 1981.
Tegethoff, Wolf, »Zur Entwicklung der Raumauffassung im Werk Mies van der Rohes«, *Daidalos*, 13, 1984.
Thiele, Klaus-Jacob, *Über Hans Scharoun – Hinweise auf Ideen und Weg*, Berlin 1996.
Tschumi, Bernard, *Questions of Space*, London, 1990.
Ule, Willi, *Grundriß der allgemeinen Erdkunde*, Stuttgart, 1931.
van de Ven, Cornelius, *Space in Architecture*, Assen, 1977.
Wigley, Mark, *White Walls, Designer Dresses: The Fashioning of Modern Architecture*, Cambridge, MA, 1995.
Wines, James, *De-architecture*, Rizzoli, 1987.
Wittgenstein, Ludwig, *Bemerkungen über die Farben*, Oxford, 1978.
Zardini, Mirko, »Pelle, muro, facciata«, *Lotus*, 82, 1994.
Zevi, Bruno, *Saper vedere l´architettura*, Turin, 1993 (first edition 1948).
Zevi, Bruno, *Giuseppe Terragni*, Zurich, 1989 (first edition 1980).
Zumthor, Peter, *Drei Konzepte*, Luzern, 1997.

### Carlo Scarpa

Accademia nazionale di San Luca, *Carlo Scarpa – Disegni, exhibition catalogue*, Rome, 1979.
Albertini, Bianca, and Sandro Bagnoli, *Scarpa – Museen und Ausstellungen*, Tübingen, 1992.
Alofsin, Anthony, »Grundformen – Eine Einführung in die ›Versenkte Fläche‹«, *Archithese*, 6, 1990.
Ambasz, Emilio, »Farewell ›Caro Maestro‹«, *Progressive Architecture*, May, 1981.
Bächer, Max, »Sanfte Ruhe in Venetien«, *Der Architekt*, 4, 1981.
Baillon, Jean-Pierre, »Nell'Entroterra del lago di Garda: Un gigante disteso tra le vigne«, *Casa Vogue*, 116, 1981.
Baillon, Jean-Pierre, »La Maison de Monsieur Ottolenghi«, *Architecture, Mouvement, Continuité*, 116, 1979.
Barovier, Marina, *I vetri di Murano*, Venice, 1991.
Benezra, Neal David, *The murals and sculpture of Josef Albers*, New York and London, 1985.
Bettini, Sergio, »L´architettura di Carlo Scarpa«, *Zodiac*, 6, 1960.
Boissière, Olivier, »Ein Wohn-Denkmal. Die Villa Veritti«, *Der Aufbau*, 5, 1986.
Boskamp, Jochen, »Was alles zwischen den Zeilen steht«, *Baumeister*, 1, 1987.
Bottero, Maria, »The Scarpa Phenomen«, *Abitare*, 229, 1984.
Bottero, Mario, »Carlo Scarpa: Lo Spazio Poetico del Cimitero Brion«, *Abitare*, 278, 1989.
Brawne, Michael, »Object on View«, *Architectural Review*, 753, 1959.
Brusatin, Manlio, »Carlo Scarpa Architetto Veneziano«, *Controspazio*, 3/4, 1972.
Brusatin, Manlio, »Considerazioni attorno ai problemi di rilievo«, *Zibaldone*, 1, 1979.
Buchanan, Peter, »Garden of death and dreams«, *Architectural Review*, 1063, 1985.
Buzas, Stefan, »John Soane e Carlo Scarpa«, *L'umana aventura*, 2, 1989.
Buzas, Stefan, and Judith Carmel-Arthur, *Carlo Scarpa – Museo Canoviano, Possagno*, Stuttgart, 2002.
Canella, G., »Figura e Funzione nell´architettura italiana dal Dopoguerra agli anni sessanta«, *Hinterland*, 1980.
*Carlo Scarpa, A+U Architecture and Urbanism*, *10*, extra edition, Tokyo, 1985.
»Carlo Scarpa, 1906–1978«, *A+U Architecture and Urbanism*, 229, 1989.
»Carlo Scarpa & Castelvecchio, una mostra a Verona«, *Domus*, 732, 1991.
»Casa Veritti a Udine 1960«, *Casabella*, 254, 1961.
Ceccarelli, Paolo, Sergio Los, Giuseppe Mazzariol, Italo Zannier, *Verum Ipsum Factum*, Venice, 1985.
Codello, Renata, *Il restauro dell'architettura contemporanea: Carlo Scarpa, aula Manlio Capitolo*, Milan, 2000.
Compagno, Andrea, »Das Gesetz des Details«, *Archithese*, 4, 1983.
Cortese, Matteo, »Un Ingresso firmato da Carlo Scarpa«, *Marco Polo*, 4, 1984.
Crippa, Maria Antonietta, *Carlo Scarpa*, London, 1986.
Crippa, Maria Antonietta, »Musées et expositions«, *Le Cahiers de la recherche architecturale*, 19, 1986.
Crippa, Maria Antonietta, »Continuità di rapporto e autonomia di intervenzione fra Carlo Scarpa e Frank Lloyd Wright nell´architettura per abitazioni«, *Quaderns d´arquitectura e urbanisme*, 184, 1983.
Dal Co, Francesco, »Venezia Galleria dell´Accademia: Carlo Scarpa« (exhibition), *Gran Bazaar*, Giugno–luglio, 1984.
Dal Co, Francesco, »Die Reifezeit Carlo Scarpas«, *DBZ Deutsche Bauzeitschrift*, 8, 1995.
Dal Co, Francesco, »Carlo Scarpa«, *Quaderns d'arquitectura e urbanisme*, 158, 1983.
Dal Co, Francesco, and Giuseppe Mazzariol, *Carlo Scarpa 1906–1978. Opera Completa*, Milan, 1984.
Dal Co, Francesco, and others, »Arredare secondo Carlo Scarpa«, *Casa Vogue*, 166, 1985.
Damisch, Hubert, »Dans l'épaisseur du plan«, *Les Cahiers de la recherche architecturale*, 19, 1986.
»Das Konstruktionsdetail als Entwurfsthema«, *Werk, Bauen und Wohnen*, 10, 1983.
Detti, Edoardo, »Scarpa et la ville«, *Architecture, Mouvement, Continuité*, 50, 1979.
Doordan, Dennis P., *Building Modern Italy: Italian Architecture 1914–1936*, New York, 1988.
Duboy, Philippe, »Chronique d'un amour«, *Les Cahiers de la recherche architecturale*, 19, 1986.
Duboy, Philippe, *Dilemma del futuro di Firenze*, Milan, 1993.
Duboy, Philippe, »›Dieses ist lange her‹ – Die Grabanlage von Carlo Scarpa«, *Daidalos*, 38, 1990.
Duboy, Philippe, »L'Oevre des années 70«, *Architecture, Mouvement, Continuité*, 50, 1979.
Eccher, Andrea de, and Giulia del Zotto, »Carlo Scarpa: Venezia e il Veneto«, *Clup Guide di Città Studi Edizioni s.r.l.*, Venice, 1994.
»Elenco cronologico dell'attività«, *Architetti Verona*, 4/5, 1980.
Esposit, Anselmo, and Luciano Polifrone, »Scarpa a Venezia«, *Domus*, 678, 1986.
Esposito, Silvia, »Ineffabilità e correlazione«, *Casabella*, 483, 1982.
Fischer, Holger, »Totenstädte«, *db Deutsche Bauzeitung*, 10, 1991.
Fonatti, Franco, *Elemente des Bauens bei Carlo Scarpa*, Schriftenreihe der Akademie der Bildenden Künste 15, Vienna, 1984.
Fortin, Jean-Patrick, »Le Musée Municipal de Trévise«, *Architecture, Mouvement, Continuité*, 50, 1979.
Franzoia, Ferruccio, »Feltre, progetto per il museo archaelogico sotterraneo«, *Rassegna*, 7, 1981.
Frascari, Marco, »Das Wahre und die Erscheinung: Der italienische ›Fassadiasmus‹ und Carlo Scarpa«, *Daidalos*, 6, 1982.
Frascari, Marco, »Carlo Scarpa in Magna Graecia – The Abatellis Palace in Palermo«, AA Files, 14, 1985.
Frascari, Marco, »Some ›mostri sacri‹ of Italian architecture«, AA Files, 14, 1987.
Frascari, Marco, »The body and architecture in the drawings of Carlo Scarpa«, *Res*, 14, 1987.
Fumagalli, Paolo, »Museumsarchitektur«, *Werk, Bauen und Wohnen*, 1/2, 1994.
Fumagalli, Paolo, »Scarpa kehrt nach Venedig zurück«, *Werk, Bauen + Wohnen*, Oktober, 1984.
Galli, A., »Inedito di Carlo Scarpa: Tomba Galli a Nervi, Genova«, *L'Architettura Chronache e Storia*, 7, 1983.
Gardella, Ignazio, »From History to imagination«, *Lotus international*, 42, 1984.
Gatti, Ilaria, and Piero Ostilio Rossi, »Allusione e illusione«, *Rassegna*, 10, 1982.
Gazzola, Pietro, »Ricordo di Carlo Scarpa«, *Bollettino del Centro Internazionale di Studi di Architettura Andrea Palladio*, 21, 1979.
Gemin, Luciano, *Banca Popolare di Gemona*, Ponzano, 1986.
Giordano, Sandro, *Il mestiere di Carlo Scarpa; Collaboratori, Artigiani, Commitenti*, tesi di laurea, Venezia: sessione estiva, 1983/84.
De Giorgi, Manolo, »Lo Scarpa che lo vedremo«, *Domus*, 713, 1990.
Givord, Jean-Pierre, »Impressions de San Vito«, *Le Cahiers de la recherche architecturale*, 19, 1986.
Grassi, Marco, and Vittorio Savi, »Nuovo Teatro Carlo Felice«, *Domus*, 719, 1991.
Guizzardi, Luigi, »A San Sebastiano a Venezia: un progetto inedito di Carlo Scarpa«, *Casabella*, 527, 1986.

Hoh-Slodczyk, Christine, *Carlo Scarpa und das Museum*, Berlin, 1987.

Huet, Bernard, »Entretien sur les amours«, *Architecture, Mouvement, Continuité*, 50, 1979.

»Il gusto veneto«, *Abitare*, 272, 1979.

»Il nuovo orientamento della Galleria«, *Casabella*, 214, 1957.

»Il padiglione di Venezuela«, *Domus*, 323, 1956.

»International a Firenze«, *Domus*, 545, 1975.

IRB-Literaturauslese 1350, *Architekten – Carlo Scarpa*, Stuttgart, 1992.

Istituto Universitario Statale di Architettura di Reggio Calabria, *Carlo Scarpa – Disegni*, Rome, 1981.

Itoh, Tetsuo, »Scenes in sequences«, *A+U Architecture and Urbanism*, 184, 1986.

König, Giovanni Klaus, »Dialogando con l'acqua«, *Ottagono*, Giugno, 1984.

»La Ca' d'Oro de nouveau«, *Connaissance-des-Arts*, 404, 1985.

»L'altra citta di Carlo Scarpa«, *Casabella*, 53, 1989 (Nov.).

Lange, Bente, »Carlo Scarpa«, *Arkitekten*, 11, 1986.

Laudani, Marta, »Questioni di dettagli«, *Rassegna*, 58, 1994.

Laudani, Marta, and Gloria Tammeo, »Un'Opera inedita di Carlo Scarpa Casa-Studio Scatturin a Venezia«, *L'Architettura Chronache e Storia*, 318, 1982.

Lazarini, Orietta, *Carlo Scarpa L'architetto e le arti – Gli anni della Biennale di Venezia 1948–1972*, Venice, 2003.

»Libreria 1935«, *Ottagono*, 58, 1980 (Sept.).

Lombardo, Franco, »Le Travail de Scarpa«, *Architecture, Mouvement, Continuité*, 50, 1979.

Lootsma, Bart, »Architecture and poetry of Carlo Scarpa«, *De Architect*, 4, 1990.

Los, Sergio, *Carlo Scarpa*, Cologne, 1993.

Los, Sergio, »Zwei Restaurierungen von Carlo Scarpa«, *Werk*, 7, 1969.

Luporini, Eugenio, »Un'Albergo a Firenze«, *Zodiac*, 7, 1960.

Magagnato, Licisco, »Il museo di Carlo Scarpa«, *Lotus International*, 35, 1982.

Magagnato, Licisco, »Storia e genesis dell'intervento nel museo de Castelvecchio«, *Quaderns d'arquitectura e urbanisme*, 184, 1983.

Magnago Lampugnani, Vittorio, *Carlo Scarpa Architektur*, Stuttgart, 1986.

Manzelle, Maura, *Carlo Scarpa – L'opera e la sua conservazione*, Venice, 2002.

Marcianò, Ada Francesca, *Carlo Scarpa*, Zurich and Munich, 1986.

Mariacher, G., »L'allestimento della Quadreria Correr«, *Bollettino dei Musei Civici Veneziani*, 1, 1960.

Marinelli, Sergio, *Castelvecchio a Verona*, Milan, 1991.

Masiero, Roberto, »Un'architettura differita: il museo Revoltella di Carlo Scarpa«, *Casabella*, 588, 1992.

Massa, Renata, »Gli allestimenti di Carlo Scarpa alla Biennale di Venezia«, *Architetti Verona*, 1980.

Mateo, Josep Lluis, »Sistema e frammento«, *Quaderns d'arquitectura e urbanisme*, 184, 1983.

Mazzariol, Giuseppe, *Un'architettura di Le Corbusier per Venezia*, Venice, 1965.

Mazzariol, Giuseppe, »Opere di Carlo Scarpa«, *L'Architettura Chronache e Storia*, 3, 1955.

Mazzariol, Giuseppe, »Scarpas Vermächtnis. Die Banca Popolare in Gemona«, *Bauwelt*, 25, 1993.

Mazzariol, Giuseppe, »Segno iconico e segno del logos«, *Per Giuseppe Mazzariol in occasione della giornata di studio*, 11, Maggio 1990.

Mazzariol, Giuseppe, »Esperienze di etica dell'architettura«, *Per Giuseppe Mazzariol in occasione della giornata di studio*, 11. Maggio 1990.

Mazzariol, Giuseppe, »Von der Tradition zur Moderne«, *Topos*, 2, 1993.

Mazzariol, Giuseppe, »Storia e genesis dell'intervento nella fondazione Querini«, *Quaderns d'arquitectura e urbanisme*, 184, 1983.

Mazzariol, Katarina, »Il mosaico di De Luigi nel giardino di Scarpa alla Querini Stampalia«, Manuscript owned by Eugenio di Luigi.

Meisenheimer, Wolfgang, »Die funktionale und die poetische Zeichnung«, *Daidalos*, 25, 1987.

Mendini, Alessandro, »Lettera a Rina Brion«, *Domus* 614, 1981.

Meneghelli, Luigi, »La Banca Popolare di Verona, il testamento spirituale di Carlo Scarpa«, *Arte Triveneta*, 10, 1980.

Michai Tonelli, M. Christina, »Carlo Scarpa fra lavoro e progetto«, *Ottagono*, 72, 1984.

Miller, Nory, »Banca Popolare in Verona«, *Bauwelt*, 13, 1983.

Miotto, Luciana, *Carlo Scarpa et le Musée de Verone*, Paris, 1984.

Monti, Paolo, »Carlo Scarpa and Castelvecchio, una mostra a Verona«, *Domus*, 732, 1991.

Morello, Paolo, *Palazzo Abatellis*, Treviso, 1989.

Morello, Paolo, »Carlo Scarpa. L'allestimento della Galleria di Palazzo Abatellis 1953–1954«, *Domus*, 708, 1989.

Morton, David, »On the Grand Canal«, *Progressive Architecture*, 11, 1984.

Moschini, Vittorio, »La nuova sistemazione delle Gallerie di Venezia«, *Bollettino d'arte del ministero della P.I.*, 4, 1949.

Moschini, Vittorio, »Nuovi Allestimenti e Restauri alle Gallerie di Venezia«, *Bollettino d'arte del ministero della P.I.*, 1, 1957.

Mulazzani, Marco, *I padiglioni della Biennale*, Milan, 1995.

Mulazzani, Marco, »Storia del Padiglione Italia«, *Casabella*, 551, 1988.

Nasi, Franco, »La mostra delle regioni«, *Casabella*, 252, 1961.

Nepi-Scirè, Giovanna, *Die Accademia in Venedig – Meisterwerke venezianischer Malerei*, Venice, 1991.

Nestler, Paolo, *Neues Bauen in Italien*, Munich, 1954.

Nicolin, Pierluigi, »La sua opera più importante«, *Lotus International*, 38, 1983.

Nicolin, Pierluigi, »L'incompiuta: La Banca di Carlo Scarpa«, *Lotus International*, 28, 1980.

Noever, Peter, and Philippe Duboy, *The other City – Carlo Scarpa*, Vienna, 1989.

Noever, Peter, *Carlo Scarpa. Das Handwerk der Architektur*, Ostfildern-Ruit, 2003.

Norri, Marji-Riitta, »Six Journeys into architectural reality«, *The Architectural Review*, 1190 (April), 1996 volume CXCIX.

Noviant, Patrice, »Carlo Scarpa Architecte«, *Architecture, Mouvement, Continuité*, 50, 1979.

»Olivetti-Geschäft in Venedig«, *Baumeister*, 3, 1961.

Oneto, Gilberto, »Oasi in Laguna«, *Ville Giardini*, 222, 1987.

Pallucchini, R., »La Presentazione della Mostra del Bellini«, *Bollettino d'arte del ministero della P. I.*, 4, 1949.

Pastor, Valeriano, »L'Architettura e la storia«, *Anfione Zeto-Quaderni di Architettura*, 1994.

Pavan, Vicenzo, *Architetture di pietra*, Venice, 1987.

»Per ricordare Carlo Scarpa: i giardini della Fondazione Querini Stampalia a Venezia«, *Abitare*, 172, 1979.

Persico, Edoardo »Décoration intérieure à Venise«, *Le Cahiers de la recherche architecturale*, 19, 1986.

Pietropoli, Guido, »L'invitation au voyage«, *Spazio e Società*, 50, 1990.

Pietropoli, Guido, and C. Maschietto, »Carlo Scarpa. Friedhof in San Vito di Altivole, Italien«, *Bauen in Beton*, 1, 1986.

Pietropoli, Guido, and others, »La Faculté des lettres San Sebastiano«, *Architecture, Mouvement, Continuité*, 50, 1979.

Pirrone, Gianni, »Une interview inutile«, *Le Cahiers de la recherche architecturale*, 19, 1986.

Podrecca, Boris, »Carlo Scarpa – Eine Ausstellung«, *Bauforum*, 106, 1984.

Polano, Mulazzani, »Forgotten works of Carlo Scarpa«, *A+U Architecture and Urbanism*, 204, 1987.

Polano, Sergio, *Carlo Scarpa. Palazzo Abatellis*, Milan, 1989.

Polano, Sergio, »Carlo Scarpa nell'isola«, *Abitare*, 320, 1993.

Polano, Sergio, »Sicilian Fragments«, *Lotus International*, 53, 1987.

Polano, Sergio, Francesco Dal Co and Manfredo Tafuri, *Carlo Scarpa*, exhibition, New York Chapter American Institute of Architects, New York, 1986.

»Polemica sull' architetto a fettine«, *L'Architettura Chronache e Storia*, 12, 1983.

Polin, Giacomo, »Il deserto arredato di Carlo Scarpa«, *Quaderns d'arquitectura e urbanisme*, 58, 1983.

Portoghesi, Paolo, »In Ricordo di Carlo Scarpa«, *Controspazio*, 3, 1979.

»Posate in Oro e Argento«, *Domus*, 588, 1978.

Radice, Barbara, »Colloqui di Modo. Carlo Scarpa: un' architetto a regola d'arte«, *Modo*, 16, 1979.

Radice, Barbara, »Dernier entretien avec Carlo Scarpa«, *Le Cahiers de la recherche architecturale*, 19, 1986.

Ragghianti, Carlo Ludovico, »La Crosera di Carlo Scarpa«, *Zodiac*, 4, 1960.

Ranalli, George, and Ross Miller, »His own monument«, *Progressive Architecture*, May, 1981.

Rayon, Jean-Paul, »Scarpa à la salle Cortot: L'Amour et la Discorde«, *Le Cahiers de la recherche architecturale*, 19, 1986.

Rinaldi, Rosa Maria, »L'utopia dell'unità«, *Domus*, 644, 1983.

Rizzi, Paolo, and Enzo di Martino, *Storia della Biennale 1895–1982*, Milan, 1982.

Romanelli, Giandomenico, »Per mettersi in mostra«, *Rassegna*, 10, 1982.

Rudi, Arrigo, »A Udine, un Opera di Carlo Scarpa: I Vent'Anni di casa Veritti«, *Casa Vogue*, 139, 1983.
Rudi, Arrigo, »Brescia, progetto per il Monumento ai Caduti in Piazza della Loggia«, *Rassegna*, 7, 1981 (July).
Rudi, Arrigo, »Parigi, progetto per il museo Picasso«, Rassegna, 7, 1981 (luglio).
Rudi, Arrigo, »A posthumous work«, *Progressive Architecture*, May, 1981.
Rudi, Arrigo, »Conclusion: Scarpa as educator«, *Progressive Architecture*, May 1981.
Rudi, Arrigo, »Nota bibliografica, curriculum dell'attività didattica e scientifica«, *Architetti Verona*, 4/5, 1980.
Rudi, Arrigo, »Il riordino e l'ampliamento della banca Popolare di Verona«, *Architetti Verona*, 4/5, 1980.
Rudi, Arrigo, »›Designer‹ per l'arredamento«, *Architetti Verona*, 4/5, 1980.
Sammartini, Tudy, »The Masieri Story«, *Architectural Review*, 1038, 1983 (August).
Samonà, Giuseppe, *L'urbanistica e l'avvenire della città negli Stati europei*, Bari, 1959.
Sandri, Domenico »Il momento dell'invenzione«, *Zibaldone*, 1, 1979.
Santini, Pier Carlo, »Ricordando Carlo Scarpa«, *Ottagono*, Dec., 1979.
Santini, Pier Carlo: »Scarpiana«, *Casabella*, 374, 1973.
Santini, Pier Carlo, »Un'opera distrutta di Carlo Scarpa«, *Zodiac*, 9, 1962.
Santini, Pier Carlo »Three model operations in ancient contexts«, *GA Global Architecture*, 51, 1979.
Santini, Pier Carlo, »La mostra delle regioni«, *L'Architettura Chronache e Storia*, 4 1961.
Santini, Pier Carlo, »Progetto per una casa a Ronco di Carimate«, *Ottagono*, 2, 1966 (July).
Santini, Pier Carlo, »Costruire‹ con l'acqua«, *Ottagono*, June, 1984.
Santini, Pier Carlo, »L'ultima opera di Carlo Scarpa«, *Ottagono*, 59, 1980.
Santini, Pier Carlo, »Tre progetti per il teatro di Vicenza«, *Ottagono*, 15, 1969.
Santini, Pier Carlo, and Giuseppe Mazzariol, »Un'opera di Carlo Scarpa: Il restauro di un antico Palazzo Veneziano«, *Zodiac*, 13, 1964.
Scalvini, Maria Luisa, »God is also in the details«, *Domus*, 662, 1985.
Scarpa, Carlo, »Monumenti in memoriam Iosephi Brion, ab Honorina uxore filiisque facti, his chartis continentur imagines«, *Memoriae Causa*, Verona, 1977.
Scarpa, Carlo, »L'architecture peut-elle être poésie?«, *Les Cahiers de la recherche architecturale*, 19, 1986.
Scarpa, Carlo, »Inscription à l'ordre des architectes de la province de Venise« (documents, 1926), *Les Cahiers de la recherche architecturale*, 19, 1986.
Scarpa, Carlo, »Leçon sur le Liberty« (notes, 1947), *Les Cahiers de la recherche architecturale*, 19, 1986.
Scarpa, Carlo, »Leçon sur la gypsothèque« (transcription de Franca Semi), *Les Cahiers de la recherche architecturale*, 19, 1986.
Scarpa, Carlo, »Volevo ritagliare l'azzurro del cielo«, *Quaderns d'arquitectura e urbanisme*, 158, 1983.
Scarpa, Carlo, and Bruno Morassutti, »Casa Romanelli, Udine«, *Architectural Review*, 1038, 1983.
Scarpa, Gigi, »Un negozio in Piazza San Marco a Venezia«, *L'Architettura Chronache e Storia*, 43, 1959.
Scarpa, Gigi, »Mostra commemorativa di Frank Lloyd Wright« (L'anti-catalogo della dodicesima Triennale di Milano), *L'Architettura Chronache e Storia*, 61, 1960.
»Scarpa visto da Warhol«, *Domus*, 603, 1980.
Schattner, Karljosef, »C. Scarpa 1906–1978«, *Baumeister*, 10, 1981.
Semerani, Luciano, »Vitalità nell'arte a Palazzo Grassi«, *Casabella-Continuitá*, 45, 1959.
Semi, Franca, »Casa Romanelli-Udine«, *Architectural Review*, 1038, 1983.
Semi, Franca, »Carlo Scarpa, Une façon d'enseigner«, *Architecture, Mouvement, Continuité*, 50, 1979.
Semi, Franca, »Le dessin dans l'œuvre de Carlo Scarpa«, *Les Cahiers de la recherche architecturale*, 19, 1986.
Semi, Francesca, »La storia di un progetto, Masieri Memorial a Venezia«, *Gran Bazaar*, Settembre, Ottobre, 1983.
Semmio, Mario, »L'oro della Ca' d'oro torna a splendere«, *AD Venezia*, 36, 1984.
Smetana, Donatella, »Carlo Scarpa revisited«, *Architectural Review*, July, 1984.
Soroka, Ellen, *Carlo Scarpa-Connections in Design, A Generic Attitude*, thesis, Master of Architecture, MIT, Cambridge, MA, 1979.
Soulier, Nicolas, »Rudi, Arrigo, Le siège central de la banque mutuelle populaire de Vérone«, *Architecture, Mouvement, Continuité*, 50, 1979.
Steward, David, »Carlo Scarpa, Casa Ottolenghi, Bardolino, Italy 1975«, *GA-Houses*, 10, 1982.
»Sull'opera di Carlo Scarpa. Il dubbio metodico«, *Casabella*, 508, 1984.
Tafuri, Manfredo, *History of Italian Architecture 1944–1985*, Cambridge, MA, 1989 (original Turin, 1982).
Tafuri, Manfredo, *Theories and History of Architecture*, London, New York and Granada, 1980.
»Telefoni publici«, *Metron*, 45, 1952.
Tentori, Francesco, »Progetti di Scarpa«, *Casabella-Continuitá*, 222, 1958.
Tentori, Francesco, »Un Padiglione di Carlo Scarpa alla Biennale di Venezia«, *Casabella-Continuitá*, 212, 1956.
Tentori, Francesco, »Verso uno nuovo interazionalismo«, *Casabella-Continuitá*, 474/475, 1981.
Teyssot, G., »Frammenti per un Discorso Funebre«, *Lotus international*, 38, 1983.
Tolmein, Gabriele, »Ein schlichtes Palazzetto wurde zur Passion«, *Häuser*, 4, 1990.
Tommasi, Giuseppe, »Un'opera di Carlo Scarpa«, *Quaderns d'arquitectura e urbanisme*, 158, 1983.
Tommasi, Giuseppe, and others, »Carlo Scarpa. Villa Ottolenghi«, *Piranesi*, 3, vol. 2, 1993.
»Un Tavolo di Carlo Scarpa«, *Domus*, 493, 1970.
Various authors, »Expo Universale '67 Il padiglione italiano«, *L'Architettura Chronache e Storia*, 141, 1967.
Various authors, »La XXXI. Biennale«, *L'Architettura Chronache e Storia*, 6, 1962.
Various authors, »Carlo Scarpa Frammenti 1926, 1978«, *Rassegna*, 7 luglio, 1981.
Various authors, »Scarpa monographisch«, *Quaderns d'Arquitetura i Urbanisme*, 158, 1983.
Vercelloni, I., »Sul lago di Zurigo. Una villa ricostruita da un architetto poeta«, *Casa Vogue*, 27, 1973.
Vercelloni, I., »Un restauro vissuto come felice storia familiare«, *Casa Vogue*, 62, 1976.
Véry, Françoise, »Kann Architektur Poesie sein«, *Architecture, Mouvement, Continuité*, 50, 1979.
Watari, Koichi, *Carlo Scarpa-Villa ›Palazzetto‹*, Tokyo, 1993.
Weisner, Ulrich, *Ich will Architektur zeigen wie sie ist – Klaus Kinold Fotograf*, Bielefeld, 1993.
Yokoyama, T., »Carlo Scarpa Savina Zentner House in Zurich«, *GA-Houses*, 1, 1975.
Zambonini, Giuseppe, »Process and theme in the work of Carlo Scarpa«, *Perspecta*, 20, 1983.
Zambonini, Giuseppe, »Notes for a theory of making in a time of necessity«, *Perspecta*, 24, 1987.
Zardini, Mirko, »Gli eccessi di Scarpa«, *Casabella-Continuitá*, 502, 1984.
Zevi, Bruno, »I premi nazionali di architettura e urbanistica a Carlo Scarpa e Ludovico Quaroni«, *L'Architettura Chronache e Storia*, 15, 1957.
Zevi, Bruno, »Padiglione dei libri d'arte«, *Metron*, 38, 1950.

### History of architecture

Adam, Robert, *Classical Architecture? A complete Handbook*, Harmondsworth, Middlesex, 1990.
Barry, Michael, *Color and Symbolism in Islamic Architecture*, London, 1995.
Blaser, Werner, *Orient/Okzident. Einfluß auf Design und Architektur*, Düsseldorf, 1991.
Bodonyi, J., *Entstehung und Bedeutung des Goldes in der Spätantike*, diss., Vienna, 1932.
Burckhardt, Jakob, *Die Kultur der Renaissance in Italien*, Stuttgart (first edition 1960), 1987.
Chang, Chao-Kang, and Werner Blaser, *China-Tao in der Architektur*, Basel, Berlin and Boston, 1987.
Deichmann, Friedrich Wilhelm, *Die Spolien in der spätantiken Architektur*, Munich, 1975.
Deichmann, Friedrich Wilhelm, »Studien zur Architektur Konstantinopels«, *Deutsche Beiträge zur Altertumswissenschaft*, 4, 1956.
Deichmann, Friedrich Wilhelm, *Rom, Ravenna, Konstantinopel, Naher Osten. Gesammelte Studien zur spätantiken Architektur und Geschichte*, Wiesbaden, 1982.
Dummer, Jürgen (ed.), *Griechische Tempel. Wesen und Wirkung*, *Beiträge der Winckelmanngesellschaft*, 8, Stendal, 1977.
Finke, Werner, »Islamische Architektur, eine Bekleidungsarchitektur«, *Bauwelt*, 26, 1986.
Gombrich, Ernst H., *Die Kunst der Renaissance*, Stuttgart, 1985.
Graefe, Rainer (ed.), *Zur Geschichte des Konstruierens*, Stuttgart, 1989.
Grécy, Jules, *Die Alhambra zu Granada*, Worms, 1990.
Gruben, Gottfried, *Die Tempel der Griechen*, Munich, 1968.
James, Liz, *Light and Colour in Byzantine Art*, Oxford, 1996.
Kähler, Heinz, *Wandlungen der antiken Form*, Munich, 1949.
Kähler, Heinz, *Der römische Tempel*, Berlin, 1970.
Kähler, Heinz (Dt. Archäologisches Institut), *Hadrian und seine Villa bei Tivoli*, Berlin, 1950.

Knell, Heiner, *Grundzüge der griechischen Architektur*, Darmstadt, 1980.

Krautheimer, Richard, *Early Christian and Byzantine Architecture*, Harmondsworth, Middlesex, 1965.

Lauter, Hans, *Die Architektur des Hellenismus*, Darmstadt, 1986.

Mango, Cyril, *Byzanz*, Stuttgart, 1986.

Martin, Roland, *Griechenland*, Stuttgart, 1987.

Mertens, Dieter, *Der Tempel von Segesta*, Mainz, 1984.

Mislin, Miron, *Geschichte der Baukonstruktion und Bautechnik*, Düsseldorf, 1988.

Müller-Wiener, Wolfgang, *Griechisches Bauwesen der Antike*, Munich, 1988.

Norberg-Schulz, Christian, *Vom Sinn des Bauens. Die Architektur des Abendlandes v. d. Antike bis zur Gegenwart*, Stuttgart, 1979.

Oakeshott, Walter, *Die Mosaiken von Rom, vom dritten bis zum vierzehnten Jahrhundert*, Vienna and Munich, 1967.

Palladio, Andrea, *I Quattro Libri di Architettura. Die vier Bücher zur Architektur*, Munich and Zurich, 1993 (original edition: 1570).

Puppi, Lionello, *Andrea Palladio, Das Gesamtwerk*, Stuttgart, 1994.

Quatremère de Quincy, Antoine Chrysostome, *De l'Architecture Egyptienne*, Paris, 1803.

Riegl, Alois, *Spätrömische Kunstindustrie*, Vienna, 1901.

Thilo, Thomas, *Klassische chinesische Baukunst*, Zurich, 1977.

Ward-Perkins, John B., *Rom*, Stuttgart, 1988.

Wurster, Wolfgang W., »Die Architektur des griechischen Theaters«, *Antike Welt*, 1, 1994.

**Theoretical foundations**

Alberti, Leon Battista (translation: Max Theuer), *Zehn Bücher über die Baukunst*, Darmstadt, 1975 (original edition: 1485).

Berlage, Hendrik Petrus, *Über Architektur und Stil – Aufsätze und Vorträge*, Basel, Berlin and Boston, 1991.

Brinckmann, A. E., *Plastik und Raum*, Munich, 1924.

Burckhardt, Jakob, *Aesthetik der bildenden Kunst*, Darmstadt, 1992.

Cataneo, Pietro, *I Quattro Primi Libri di Architettura*, Ridgewood, New Jersey, 1964 (reprint).

Choisy, Auguste, *L'Art de bâtir chez les Byzantins*, Paris, 1883.

Choisy, Auguste, *Histoire de l'Architecture*, Paris, 1899 (original edition), reprint 1996.

Conrads, Ulrich (ed.), *Programme und Manifeste zur Architektur des 20. Jahrhunderts*, Frankfurt/Main and Vienna, 1964.

Croce, Benedetto, *Nuovi Saggi di Estetica*, Bari, 1948.

Croce, Benedetto, *Gesammelte philosophische Schriften – Die Philsosophie Giambattista Vicos*, Tübingen, 1927.

Durand, Jean-Nicolas-Louis, *Précis de lecons d'architecture*, donnés à l'ecole Royale polytechnique, Paris 1817–1821.

Durand, Jean-Nicolas-Louis, *Racueil et Parallèle des Edifices en tout Genre, anciens et modernes*, Paris, 1799.

Düttmann, Martina (ed.), *Eugène Viollet-le-Duc. Definitionen, Sieben Stichworte aus dem »Dictionnaire raisonné de l'architecture française du XIe au XVI siècle«*, Basel, Berlin and Boston, 1993.

Fiedler, Konrad, and Gottfried Böhm (eds.), *Über das Wesen der Baukunst, Schriften zur Kunst II*, Munich, 1991.

Gantner, Josef, *Revision der Kunstgeschichte. Semper und Le Corbusier*, Vienna, 1932.

Gau, Franz C., *Neu entdeckte Denkmäler von Nubien an den Ufern des Nils*, Stuttgart, 1975.

Giedion, Sigfried, *Architektur und das Phänomen des Wandels*, Tübingen, 1969.

Giedion, Sigfried, *Raum, Zeit und Architektur*, Zurich, Munich and London, 1992.

Hammer, Karl, *Jakob Ignaz Hittorff. Ein Pariser Baumeister 1792–1867*, Stuttgart, 1968.

Herrmann, Wolfgang, *Gottfried Semper, Theoretischer Nachlass an der ETH Zurich*, Basel, Boston and Stuttgart, 1981.

Herrmann, Wolfgang, *Gottfried Semper im Exil, Paris, London 1849–1855, Zur Entstehung des »Stil« 1840–1877*, Basel and Stuttgart, 1978.

Hitchcock, Henry-Russell, *Der internationale Stil*, Braunschweig, 1985 (first edition: New York, 1932).

Hübsch, Heinrich, *Die Architektur und ihr Verhältnis zur heutigen Malerei und Skulptur*, Tübingen, 1985 (original edition: 1847).

König, Giovanni Klaus, *Architettura e communicazione*, Florence, 1974.

Kruft, Hanno Walter, *Geschichte der Architekturtheorie*, Munich, 1991.

Kugler, Franz, *Über die Polychromie der griechischen Architektur und Skulptur*, Berlin, 1835.

Kultermann, Udo, *Geschichte der Kunstgeschichte. Der Weg einer Wissenschaft*, Munich, 1990.

Laudel, Heidrun, *Gottfried Semper, Architektur und Stil*, Dresden, 1991.

Laugier, Marc-Antoine, *Das Manifest des Klassizismus*, Zurich and Munich, 1989.

Laugier, Marc-Antoine, *An essay on architecture*, Los Angeles, 1977.

Lönne, Karl-Egon, *Benedetto Croce als Kritiker seiner Zeit*, Tübingen, 1967.

Mallgrave, Harry Francis, *Gottfried Semper, Architect of the Nineteenth Century*, New Haven and London, 1996.

Mallgrave, Harry Francis, *The idea of style, Gottfried Semper in London*, diss., Pennsylvania, 1933.

Middleton, Robin, *The Beaux-Arts and nineteenth-century French architecture*, Cambridge, 1982.

Middleton, Robin, and David Watkin, *Klassizismus und Historismus*, Stuttgart, 1987.

Middleton, Robin, »Perfezione e colore, la policromia nell'architettura francese del XVIII e XIX secolo«, *Rassegna*, 23, 1985.

Palladio, Andrea (translation: Andreas Beyer and Ulrich Schütte), *Die vier Bücher zur Architektur, nach der Ausgabe Venedig 1570*, Zurich and Munich, 1993.

Prinzhorn, Hans, *Gottfried Sempers Aesthetische Grundanschauungen*, Stuttgart, 1909.

Quatremère de Quincy, Antoine Chrysostome, *Canova et ses Ouvrages de memoires*, Paris, 1834.

Quatremère de Quincy, Antoine Chrysostome, *Dictionnaire Historique d'Architecture, vol. 1/2*, Paris, 1832.

Quatremère de Quincy, Antoine Chrysostome, *Histoire de la vie et des ouvrages des plus célèbres architectes du XIe siècle jusqu'à la fin du XVIIIe.*, Paris, 1830.

Quatremère de Quincy, Antoine Chrysostome, *Le Jupiter Olympien ou l'art de la sculpture antique*, Paris, 1815.

Quatremère de Quincy, Antoine Chyrsostome, *Recueil de dissertaions sur differents sujets d'antiquité*, Paris, 1819.

Quitsch, Heinz, *Die ästhetischen Anschauungen G. Sempers*, Berlin, 1962.

Quitsch, Heinz, *Gottfried Semper, praktische Ästhetik und politischer Kampf*, Braunschweig, 1981.

Riegl, Alois, *Historische Grammatik der Bildenden Künste*, Graz and Cologne, 1966.

Ruskin, John, *Die sieben Leuchter der Baukunst*, Duisburg, 1994.

Rykwert, Joseph, *Adolf Loos, Das neue Sehen, Ornament ist kein Verbrechen*, Architektur als Kunst, Cologne, 1983.

Saddy, Pierre, *Henry Labrouste architecte 1801 à 1875*, Paris, 1977.

Schmarsow, August, *Unser Verhältnis zu den bildenden Künsten*, Leipzig, 1903.

Schneider, Donald David, *The works and doctrine of Jaques Ignace Hittorff*, New York and London, 1977.

Schriftenreihe Sektion Architektur TU Dresden 1980, Heft 13, *Gottfried Semper 1803–1879, Sein Wirken als Architekt und revolutionärer Demokrat*, Dresden, 1979.

Schuster, Franz, *Der Stil unserer Zeit*, Vienna, 1948.

Sedlmayr, Hans, *Verlust der Mitte*, Salzburg, 1948.

Sedlmayr, Hans, *Spätantike Wandsysteme*, Munich, 1958.

Semper, Gottfried, *Der Stil in den technischen und tektonischen Künsten oder praktische Ästhetik*, vol. 1 and 2, Mittenwald, reprint 1977.

Semper, Manfred and Hans (eds.), *Kleine Schriften von Gottfried Semper*, Berlin and Stuttgart, 1884.

Sörgel, Herman, *Theorie der Baukunst*, vol. 1, *Architektur-Ästhetik*, Munich, 1918.

Stockmeyer, Ernst, *Gottfried Sempers Kunsttheorie*, Zurich and Leipzig, 1939.

Viollet-le-Duc, Eugène, *Dictionnaire raisonné de l'architecture française du XIe au XVIe siècle*, Paris, 1968 (original edition: 1854–68).

Viollet-le-Duc, Eugène, *Description et histoire du château de Pierrefonds*, Paris, 1881.

Vitruvius, Marcus, (translation: August Rode), *Baukunst*, Zurich and Munich, 1987.

Wingler, Hans M. (ed.), *Wissenschaft, Industrie und Kunst und andere Schriften über Architektur, Kunsthandwerk und Kunstunterricht*, Mainz and Berlin, 1966.

Wittgenstein, Ludwig, *Schriften, Tractatus logico-philosophicus, Tagebücher 1914–1916*, Frankfurt/Main, 1960.

Wölfflin, Heinrich, *Kleine Schriften*, Basel, 1946.

Wölfflin, Heinrich, *Italien und das deutsche Formgefühl*, Munich, 1931.

Zoege von Manteuffel, Claus, *Die Baukunst Gottfried Sempers (1803–1879)*, diss., Freiburg, 1952.

### Vienna School

*Adolf Loos zum 60. Geburtstag am 10. Dezember 1930*, exhibition catalogue, Vienna, 1930.
Amanshauser, Hildegund, *Untersuchungen zu den Schriften von Adolf Loos*, diss., Vienna, 1985.
Baroni, Daniele, and Antonio D'Auria, *Josef Hoffmann und die Wiener Werkstätte*, Stuttgart, 1984.
Bernabei, Giancarlo, *Otto Wagner*, Zurich, 1986.
Czech, Hermann, *Zur Abwechslung. Ausgewählte Schriften zur Architektur Wien*, Vienna, 1978.
Czech, Hermann, and Wolfgang Mistelbauer, *Das Looshaus*, Vienna, 1976.
Forsthuber, Sabine, *Moderne Raumkunst. Wiener Ausstellungsbauten von 1898 bis 1914*, Vienna, 1991.
Fröhlich, Martin, »Über Gottfried Sempers Verhältnis zu Eisen und Glas«, *Archithese* 4, 1980.
Geretsegger, Heinz, and Max Peintner, *Otto Wagner 1841–1918, Unbegrenzte Groszstadt. Beginn der modernen Architektur*, Salzburg and Vienna, 1983.
Graf, Otto Maria, *Otto Wagner. Die Einheit der Kunst. Weltgeschichte der Grundformen*, vol. 3, Vienna and Cologne, 1990.
Gravagnuolo, Benedetto, *Adolf Loos – Theory and Works*, New York, 1982.
Hofmann, Werner, »Il dibattito sullo stile nella Scuola di Vienna«, *Rassegna*, 3, 1990.
Hvattum, Mari, »Gottfried Semper. Towards a comparative science of architecture«, *arq*, 1, 1995.
Kolb, Günther, *Otto Wagner und die Wiener Stadtbahn*, vol. I + II, diss., Munich, 1989.
Kühn, Christian, *Das Schöne, das Wahre und das Richtige. Adolf Loos und das Haus Müller in Prag*, Braunschweig and Wiesbaden, 1989.
Kurrent, Friedrich, and Alice Strobl, *Das Palais Stoclet in Brüssel von Josef Hoffmann*, Salzburg, 1991.
Lerup, Lars, »Maki und Semper«, *Werk, Bauen+ Wohnen*, 5, 1988.
Loos, Adolf, *Ins Leere gesprochen*, Vienna, 1981.
Loos, Adolf, *Die Potemkinsche Stadt*, Vienna, 1983.
Moravánszky, Ákos, *Die Architektur der Donaumonarchie*, Berlin, 1988.
Moravánszky, Ákos, *Die Architektur der Jahrhundertwende in Ungarn und ihre Beziehungen zu der Wiener Architektur der Zeit*, Vienna, 1983.
Moravánszky, Ákos, *Die Erneuerung der Baukunst. Wege zur Moderne in Mitteleuropa 1900–1940*, Salzburg and Vienna, 1983.
Moravánszky, Ákos, »Byzantinismus in der Baukunst Otto Wagners als Motiv seiner Wirkung östlich von Wien«, in: Gustav Peichl, *Die Kunst des Otto Wagner*, Vienna, 1984.
Münz, Ludwig, and Gustav Künstler, *Der Architekt Adolf Loos*, Vienna and Munich, 1964.
Opel, Adolf (ed.), *Kontroversen. Adolf Loos im Spiegel der Zeitgenossen*, Vienna, 1985.
Peichl, Gustav (ed.), *Die Kunst des Otto Wagner*, *Wiener Akademie Reihe*, vol. 16, Vienna, 1984.
Rukschcio, Burkhard, and Roland Schachel, *Adolf Loos. Leben und Werk*, Salzburg and Vienna, 1987 (2nd edition).
Rykwert, Joseph, »Morfologia di Semper«, *Rassegna*, 3, 1990.
Rykwert, Joseph, »Semper et la construction du style«, *Macula*, 5/6, 1986.
Rykwert, Joseph, *Ornament ist kein Verbrechen*, Cologne, 1983.
Sekler, Eduard F., *Josef Hoffmann*, Salzburg and Vienna, 1982.
Semper, Gottfried, (translation: John W. Root), »Development of Architectural Style«, *Inland Architect and News Record*, 7 (Dec.), XIV, 1989.
Semper, Gottfried (translation: John W. Root), »Development of Architectural Style«, *Inland Architect and News Record*, 8 (Jan.), XIV, 1990.
Semper, Gottfried (translation: John W. Root), »Development of Architectural Style«, *Inland Architect and News Record*, 1 (Feb.), XV, 1990.
Semper, Gottfried, (translation: John W. Root), »Development of Architectural Style«, *Inland Architect and News Record*, 2 (Mar.), XV 1990.
Stadt Karlsruhe (ed.), *Gründerzeit – Adolf Loos*, Karlsruhe, 1987.
Wagner, Otto, *Die Baukunst unserer Zeit*, Vienna, 1977 (first edition 1914).
Wagner, Otto, *Einige Skizzen. Projekte und ausgeführte Bauwerke von Otto Wagner*, Tübingen 1987.
Wirth, Hermann, »›Kunstform‹ und ›Kernform‹«, *Gottfried Sempers Architekturtheorie*, *Wissenschaftliche Zeitschrift der Hochschule Weimar*, 1, 1982.
Worbs, Dietrich, *Der Raumplan – Entwicklung der Raumbildung bei Villen- und Massenwohnbauten von Adolf Loos.* diss., Stuttgart, 1982.

### Frank Lloyd Wright

Benevolo, Leonardo, *Geschichte der Architektur des 19. und 20. Jahrhunderts*, vol. 2, Munich, 1984.
Bolon, Carlol R., Robert S. Nelson and Linda Seidel, *The Nature of Frank Lloyd Wright*, Chicago and London, 1984.
Ford, Edward R., *Das Detail in der Architektur der Moderne*, Basel, Berlin and Boston, 1994.
Gebhard, David, *›Romanza‹ The California Architecture of Frank Lloyd Wright*, London, 1988.
Graf, Otto Antonia, *Die Kunst des Quadrats – Zum Werk von Frank Lloyd Wright I*, Vienna, 1983.
Heinz, Thomas A., *Frank Lloyd Wright*, London, 1992.
Hildebrand, Grant, *The Wright Space*, Seattle, 1991.
Kaufmann, Edgar (ed.), *An American Architect, Frank Lloyd Wright*, New York, 1955.
Kaufmann, Edgar, and Ben Raeburn (eds.), *Frank Lloyd Wright. Schriften und Bauten*, Munich and Vienna, 1963.
Larkin, David, and Bruce Brooks Pfeiffer, *Frank Lloyd Wright. Die Meisterwerke*, New York, 1993.
Laseau, Paul, and James Tice, *Frank Lloyd Wright, Between Principle and Form*, New York, 1992.
Levine, Neil, *Frank Lloyd Wright*, Princeton, NJ, 1996.
Lind, Carla, *The Wright Style*, *London*, 1992.
Nute, Kevin, *Frank Lloyd Wright and Japan*, London, 2000.
Sergeant, John, *Frank Lloyd Wright's Usonian Houses*, New York, 1976.
Storrer, William Allin, *The Architecture of Frank Lloyd Wright. A complete catalog*, Cambridge, MA, 1979 (first edition: 1974).
Treiber, Daniel, *Frank Lloyd Wright*, Basel, Boston and Berlin, 1988.
Wright, Frank Lloyd, *Genius and the Mobocracy*, London, 1972.
Wright, Frank Lloyd, *The Story of the Tower*, New York, 1956.
Wright, Frank Lloyd, *Humane Architektur*, 1972.
Wright, Frank Lloyd, *Die Zukunft der Architektur*, Munich and Vienna, 1953.
Wright, Frank Lloyd, *Das natürliche Haus*, Munich, 1961.
Wright, Frank Lloyd, *Frank Lloyd Wright. Schriften und Bauten*, Munich and Vienna, 1960.
Wright, Frank Lloyd, *Usonien*, Berlin, 1950.
Wright, Frank Lloyd, *An Organic Architecture. The Architecture of Democracy*, London, 1970.
Wright, Frank Lloyd, *An Autotobiography*, London, 1977 (first edition: 1932).
Wright, Frank Lloyd, *Ein Testament*, Munich, 1959.
Wright, Frank Lloyd, *Ausgeführte Entwürfe und Bauten von FLW*, Berlin, 1910 (reprint 1986).
Wright, O. L., *The Work of Frank Lloyd Wright*, New York, 1965.
Zevi, Bruno, *Frank Lloyd Wright*, Zurich, 1979.

### Japan

Adler, Bernhard, *Japan-Beiträge zur Architekturexkursion April 1990*, Lehrstuhl für Entwerfen von Bauten und industrielle Formgebung TU München, Munich, 1990.
Alex, William, *Architektur der Japaner*, Ravensburg, 1965.
Ashihara, Yoshinobu, *The Hidden Order*, Tokyo and New York, 1989.
Blaser, Werner, *Tempel und Teehaus in Japan*, Lausanne, 1955.
Blaser, Werner, *Wohnen und Bauen in Japan*, Teufen AR, 1958.
Blaser, Werner, *Struktur und Gestalt in Japan*, Zurich, 1963.
Blaser, Werner, *Orient/Occident. Einfluß auf Design und Architektur*, Düsseldorf, 1991.
Boyd, Robin, *New Directions in Japanese Architecture*, New York, 1968.
Chang, Ching-Yu, »Japanese Spacial Conception 1«, *The Japan Architect*, 8404, 1984.
Chang, Ching-Yu, »Japanese Spacial Conception 2, Introduction«, *The Japan Architect*, 8405, 1984.
Chang, Ching-Yu, »Japanese Spacial Conception 3, The general notion of beauty 2«, *The Japan Architect*, 8406, 1984.
Chang, Ching-Yu, »Japanese Spacial Conception 4, Religious and philosophical influences on Japanese space«, *The Japan Architect*, 8407, 1984.
Chang, Ching-Yu, »Japanese Spacial Conception 5, Duality of spacial expression«, *The Japan Architect*, 8408, 1984.
Chang Ching-Yu, »Japanese Spacial Conception 6, Synthesis of architectural space«, *The Japan Architect*, 8409, 1984.
Chang, Ching-Yu, »Japanese Spacial Conception 7, Fencing the space«, *The Japan Architect*, 8410, 1984.

Edberg-Consten, Eleanor von, *Grundsätze des Wohnens im westlichen und östlichen Raum, Baustil und Bautechnik in Amerika und Japan*, Cologne and Opladen, 1964.
Greenbie, Barrie B., *Space and Spirit in Modern Japan*, New Haven and London, 1988.
Gropius, Walter, Kenzo Tange, Yasuhiro Shimoto and Herbert Bayer, *Katsura. Tradition and Creation in Japanese Architecture*, New Haven, 1960.
Gutschow, Nils, *Die japanische Burgstadt*, Paderborn, 1976.
Harada, Jiro, *The Lessons of Japanese Architecture*, New York, 1986 (original edition: London, 1936).
Inoue, Mitsou, *Space in Japanese Architecture*, New York and Tokyo, 1985.
Isozaki, Arata, *Katsura. Raum und Form*, Stuttgart and Zurich, 1967.
Isozaki, Arata, and Osamu Sato, *Katsura. Der Kaiserpalast in Kyoto*, Stuttgart and Zurich, 1993 (first edition: 1983).
Itoh, Teiji, *Alte Häuser in Japan*, Stuttgart, 1984.
Izutsu, Toshihiko and Toyo, *Die Theorie des Schönen in Japan*, Cologne, 1988.
Kultermann, Udo, *Neues Bauen in Japan*, Tübingen, 1967.
Morse, Edward S., *Das Haus im alten Japan*, Hamburg, 1983 (first edition: 1886).
Schaarschmidt-Richter, Irmtraut, *Japanische Gärten*, Baden-Baden, 1976.
Schneider, Roland, Hans Stumpefeld, Klaus Wenk, and Wolfgang Muntschick (eds.), *Das traditionelle japanische Bauernhaus. Eine kulturhistorische Studie*, Hamburg, 1985.
Seike, Kiyoshi, Kudo Masannobo and Walter Schmidt, *Japanische Gärten und Gartenteile*, Stuttgart, 1983.
Takeshi, Nishikawa, and Naito Akira, *Katsura. Ein Ort der Besinnung*, Stuttgart, 1978.
Tetsuro, Yoshida, *Japanische Architektur*, Tübingen, 1952.

### De Stijl

Bock, Manfred, *De Stijl, 1917–1931 – Visions of Utopia*, Minneapolis, Walker Art Center, New York, 1982.
Bois, Yve-Alain, »Metamorphosen der Axonometrie«, *Daidalos*, 1, 1981.
Bois, Yves-Alain, »Zur Definition des ›De Stijl‹«, *Werk, Bauen + Wohnen*, 7/8, 1983.
Bollerey, Franziska, and Kristiana Hartmann, »Das kleine Land und die großen Monumente«, *Baumeister*, 4, 1987.
Bucarelli, Palma, »La mostra di Piet Mondrian a Roma«, *L'Architettura Chronache e Storia*, 17, 1957.
*De Stijl – Cercle et Carré*, exhibition catalogue, Cologne, 1917.
Doesburg, Theo van, *De Stijl – Schriften und Manifeste zu einem theoretischen Konzept ästhetischer Umweltgestaltung*, Leipzig and Weimar, 1984.
Doesburg, Theo van, *Theo van Doesburg. Das andere Gesicht*, Munich, 1983.
Doesburg, Theo van, *Grundbegriffe der neuen gestaltenden Kunst*, Munich, 1983.
Doesburg, Theo van, *Über europäische Architektur*, Basel, Berlin and Boston, 1990.
Ehrmann, Walter Eugen, *Moderne Architektur und konstruktivistisches Bild, unter besonderer Berücksichtigung der ›De Stijl-Bewegung‹*, diss., Karlsruhe, 1972.
Fanelli, Giovanni, *Stijl-Architektur. Der niederländische Beitrag. zur frühen Moderne*, Stuttgart, 1985.
Fosso, Mario, »Robert van't Hoff. L'enigma dell'architettura moderna«, *Casabella*, 456, 1980.
Günter, Roland, »Balance, De Stijl und die Tradition niederländischer Stadt-Kultur«, *Daidalos*, 15, 1985.
Hedrik, Hannah Lucille, *Theo van Doesburg, propagandist and practitioner of the avant-garde 1909 to 1923*, Ann Arbor, Mich., 1980.
Jaffe, H. L. C., *De Stijl, 1917–1931*, Amsterdam, 1986 (first edition: 1956).
Kotob, Basel, *Spatial Layering. An Effect of Cubist Concepts on 20th Century Architecture*, thesis MIT 1991, Cambridge, MA, 1991.
Lemoine, Serge, *Mondrian und De Stijl*, Geneva, 1988.
Locatelli, Vittorio, »Mondrian e De Stijl, fra ›astrazione‹ e architettura«, *Abitare*, 290, 1990.
Padovan, Richard, »The Pavillon and the Court – cultural and spacial problems of De Stijl architecture«, *Architectural Review*, 1018, 1981.
Posener, Julius, »De Stijl-Gruppe«, *Arch+*, 12, 1979.
Posener, Julius, »Die Architektur und das Eisen, Labrouste, Semper, Gurlitt, Gropius«, *Arch+*, 69/70, 1983.
Reichlin, Bruno, »Le Corbusier e De Stijl«, *Casabella-Continuita*, 520/521, 1986.
Warncke, Carsten-Peter, *Das Ideal als Kunst. De Stijl, 1917–1931*, Cologne, 1990.

### Venice

Arslan, Edoardo, *Gothic Architecture in Venice*, Milan, 1970
Banca Cattolica del Veneto (ed.), *Venezia e la Germania*, Milan, 1986.
Bettini, Sergio, *Venezia – nascita di una città*, Milan, 1988.
Corbineau-Hoffmann, Angelika, *Paradoxie der Fiktion. Literarische Venedig-Bilder 1797–1984*, Berlin and New York, 1993.
Cristinelli, Giuseppe, *Restauro e tecniche. Saggi e ricerche sulla costruzione dell'architettura a Venezia*, Venice, 1992.
Ennio, Concina, *Storia dell'architettura di Venezia*, Milan, 1995.
Franzoi, Umberto, *Le chiese di Venezia*, Venice, 1976.
Furlan, Italo, and others, *Venezia e Bisanzio*, Venice, 1974.
Gage, John, *Colour and Culture. Practice and Meaning form Antiquity to Abstract*, London, 1993.
Lanciotti, Lionello, *Venezia e l'Oriente*, Florence, 1987.
Lauritzen, Peter, and Alexander Zielcke, *Venezianische Paläste*, Munich, 1980.
Lebe, Reinhard, *Kleine Geschichten aus Venedig*, Stuttgart, 1991.
Lieberman, Ralph, *The Church of Santa Maria dei Miracoli in Venice*, New York, 1986.
Romanelli, Giandomenico, *Venezia Ottocento, materiali per una storia architettonica e urbanistica della citta nel secolo XIX*, Rome, 1977.
Romanelli, Giandomenico (ed.), *Venezia – Vienna*, Milan, 1983.
Tafuri, Manfredo, *Venice and the Renaissance*, Cambridge, MA, 1989.
Wiener, Samuel Gross, *Venetian Houses and Details*, New York, 1929.
Zorzi, Alvise, *Österreichs Venedig*, Düsseldorf, 1990 (original edition: Rome and Bari, 1985).

**Index**

**Illustration credits**

Accademia Nazionale di San Lucca, Rome 279
Akademie der Künste, Berlin 186, 187, 188, 206, 213, 215, 311
Albertina, Vienna 210
Bianca Albertini and Sandro Bagnoli, *Scarpa – Museen und Ausstellungen*, Tübingen, 1992 50, 51, 54–56, 59, 60, 61, 62, 178
Andreae 1972 281
*Androgyn*, 1986 30
Archäologischer Park Carnuntum 29
Architekturmuseum der TU München 273
Arkitektur Museet Stockholm 233
*art*, 6, 1993 106, 115, 116
Archive of Tadao Ando 5, 6, 7
Archive of Maria Auböck 120
Archive of Dieter Bogner 1, 170, 288
Archive of Peter Cook 172
Archive of Coop Himmelb(l)au 246, 248, 250
Archive of Günther Domenig 153, 154
Archive of Günther Feuerstein 8, 9, 10, 11, 12, 13, 14, 15, 17, 19, 20, 22, 33, 46, 50, 58, 76, 80, 81, 86, 87, 88, 94, 107, 114, 117, 118, 131, 140, 143, 145, 148, 159, 160, 167, 168, 175, 181, 183, 185, 189, 195, 199, 204, 209, 214, 218, 231, 232, 239, 243, 253, 258, 262, 266, 282, 286, 287, 289, 290, 292, 293, 296, 298, 300, 302, 308
Archive of Haus-Rucker Co. 122, 155, 158, 249, 275
Archive of Hans Hollein 119, 137, 236, 237, 305, 306, 307
Archive of Wolfgang Hutter 92
Archive of Helmut Kleine-Kraneburg 277
Archive of Edelbert Köb 108
Archive of Engelbert Kremser 156
Archive of Adolf Krischanitz 194, 280
Archive of Helmut Lander 285
Archive of Peter Noever 138
Archive of Wolfgang Pehnt 211
Archive of Gustav Peichl 4, 240
Archive of Walter Pichler 99, 100, 101, 102, 139, 177, 264, 265
Archive of Jan Pieper 257, 270, 271, 272, 294, 295
Archive of Guido Pietropoli 2, 39, 121, 140, 157, 259, 248, 276
Archive of Christiane Pressel 141
Archive of Walter Michael Pühringer 197, 252
Archive of Hans Dieter Schaal 135
Archive of Manfred Scharpf 89
Archive of Karl Schwanzer 193
Archive of Edda Seidl-Reiter 97, 98
Archive of Peter Skubic 111
Archive of Paolo Soleri 144, 278
Archive of Heinz Tesar 3, 165, 176, 179
Archive of Stanley Tigerman 128, 178
Archive of Hans Turba 96
Rudolf Arnheim, *Kunst und Sehen*, Berlin, 1965 23
ASAC Archivio della Biennale Venezia 27
Ashmolean Museum of Art and Archeology, Oxford 260
*Atalanta fugiens*, 1618 34
Augustinermuseum Rattenberg, Tirol 43
Aurnhammer 1986 23, 39
Avery Architectural and Fine Art Library, Columbia University, New York 190, 191
Banca Popolare di Lecco, Como 310
Baumann 1986 18, 21
*Bauwelt*, 5, 1996 234
*Aubrey Beardsley*, 1967 82, 83
Bibliothèque Nationale, Paris 55, 79, 200, 201, 228, 242, 245
Biedermann 1987 284, 291
Marina Barovier, *I vetri di Murano*, Venice, 1991 41
Guido Beltrami, Kurt W. Forster and Paola Marini, *Carlo Scarpa, Mostre e Musei, Case e Paesaggi*, Milan, 2000 347
Stefan Buzas, Judith Carmel-Arthur, *Carlo Scarpa – Museo Canoviano, Possagno*, Stuttgart, 2002 136, 175, 194
Francesco Dal Co and Giuseppe Mazzariol, *Carlo Scarpa 1906–1978. Opera completa*, Milan, 1984, 36, 42, 43, 44, 45, 46, 47, 48, 52, 58, 105, 112, 137, 139, 145, 155
Francesco Dal Co, *Villa Ottolenghi*, New York, 1998 103
Renata Codello, *Il restauro dell'architettura contemporanea*, Milan, 2000 49
Andrea Compagno, *Intelligente Glasfassaden*, Basel, Boston and Berlin, 1996 20
Klaus Daniels, *The Technology of Ecological Building*, Basel, Boston and Berlin, 1995 19
Clifford Eitel, »Study of Transparency«, in Gyorgy Kepes, *Language of Vision*, Chicago 1964 25
Franco Fonatti, *Giuseppe Terragni-Poet des Razionalismo*, Wien, 1987 10–16
Mildred Friedman, *Carlo Scarpa Architect – Intervening with History*, Canadian Center for Architecture, Montreal, 1999 26
Heinz Geretsegger and Max Peintner, *Otto Wagner 1841–1918: Unbegrenzte Groszstadt – Beginn der modernen Architektur*, Salzburg and Vienna, 1983 86, 98
Manfred P. Gwinner, *Geologie der Alpen*, Stuttgart, 1978 6
Thomas A. Heinz, *Frank Lloyd Wright*, London, 1992 109
Arata Isozaki and Osamu Sato, *Der Kaiserpalast in Kyoto*, Stuttgart and Zürich, 1993 (original edition: 1967) 130, 134, 141
Eckehard Janowske, *Architektur-Räume. Idee und Gestalt bei Hans Scharoun*, Braunschweig and Wiesbaden, 1984 7, 8, 9
Friedrich Kurrent and Alice Strobl, *Der Palais Stoclet in Brüssel von Josef Hoffmann*, Salzburg, 1991 91
Orietta Lanzarini, *Carlo Scarpa – L'architetto e le arti*, Regione del Veneto, Venice, 2003 53
David Larkin and Bruce Brooks Pfeiffer, *Frank Lloyd Wright – Die Meisterwerke*, New York, 1992 118
Martha Laudani, »Questioni di dettaglio«, *Rassegna* 58, 1994 (analysis by author) 122
Neil Levine, *The Architecture of Frank Lloyd Wright*, Princeton, 1996 104, 111, 115
Sergio Los and Klaus Frahm, *Carlo Scarpa*, Cologne, 2001 38
Vittorio Magnago Lampugnani, *Carlo Scarpa. Architektur*, Stuttgart, 1986 70, 71, 92, 114, 116, 127
Ada Francesca Marcianò, *Carlo Scarpa*, Zurich, 1989 57, 108, 138, 144, 150, 348
Robin Middleton, »Perfezione e colore: La policromia nell'architettura francese del XVIII e XIX secolo«, *Rassegna*, 23, 1985 63, 64
Richard Murphy, *Carlo Scarpa & Castelvecchio*, Venice, 1991 34, 159, 195, 196, 197, 199, 201, 202–204, 259
Richard Murphy, *Stampalia Querini Foundation – Carlo Scarpa*, Architecture in Detail, London, 1993 30, 276, 287, 288
Takeshi Nishikawa and Akira Naito, *Katsura: Ein Ort der Besinnung*, Stuttgart, 1978 126
Paul Overy, *De Stijl*, London, 1991 147, 148, 158
Collin Rowe and Robert Slutzky, *Transparenz*, Basel and Stuttgart, 1968 22, 24
Arrigo Rudi and Valter Rossetto, *La sede Centrale della Banca Popolare di Verona*, Verona, 1983 298–301
Burkhardt Rukschcio and Roland Schachel, *Adolf Loos: Leben und Werk*, Salzburg and Vienna, 1987 95
Anne-Catrin Schultz 1, 3, 4, 5, 17, 18, 21, 28, 29, 31, 32, 33, 35, 40, 66, 67, 68, 69, 72, 73, 74, 75, 76, 78, 79, 80, 81, 82, 83, 85, 87, 89, 93, 94, 96, 97, 99, 100, 106, 110, 117, 123, 124, 128, 129, 131, 133, 135, 142, 143, 145, 146, 149, 151, 152, 161 to 176, 178, 179, 180, 183, 184, 185, 186, 187, 188 189, 190, 191, 192, 193, 198, 200, 205, 206, 207, 208–210, 211–257, 260 –275, 277–287, 289–297, 302–338
Eduard F. Sekler, *Josef Hoffmann*, Salzburg and Vienna, 1982 88, 90
Gottfried Semper, *Der Stil in den tektonischen Künsten*, vol. Munich, 1878 65
John Sergeant, *Frank Lloyd Wright's Usonian Houses*, New York, 1976 112
Yoshida Tetsuro, *Das Japanische Wohnhaus*, Tübingen, 1963 125, 132
Daniel Treiber, *Frank Lloyd Wright*, Basel, Boston and Berlin, 1983 101, 102, 117, 119
Carsten-Peter Warncke, *De Stijl, 1917–1931*, Cologne, 1990 156, 154, 160
Frank Lloyd Wright, *Ausgeführte Entwürfe von Frank Lloyd Wright*, Berlin, 1818 (reprint 1986) 107, 120
Frank Lloyd Wright, *Die Zukunft der Architektur*, Munich and Vienna, 1953 (redrawn by author) 106
Bruno Zevi, *Giuseppe Terragni*, Zürich, 1989 37

All analytical drawings in chapter 3.1 are drawn after Richard Murphy, *Carlo Scarpa & Castelvecchio*, Venice, 1991. All analytical drawings in chapter 3.2 are drawn after Richard Murphy, *Stampalia Querini Foundation – Carlo Scarpa*, London, 1993.